STRENGTH TRAINING
FOR
SOCCER

NSCA®
NATIONAL STRENGTH AND
CONDITIONING ASSOCIATION

Daniel Guzman, MS, CSCS

Megan Young, MS, MSEd, CSCS, FRC, USAW SPC, RSCC*D

EDITORS

T0383312

HUMAN KINETICS

Library of Congress Cataloging-in-Publication Data

Names: Guzman, Daniel, 1990- editor. | Young, Megan, 1984- editor. |
  National Strength & Conditioning Association (U.S.)
Title: Strength training for soccer / Daniel Guzman, Megan Young, editors.
Description: Champaign, IL : Human Kinetics, [2023] | "National Strength
  and Conditioning Association." | Includes bibliographical references and
  index.
Identifiers: LCCN 2022001673 (print) | LCCN 2022001674 (ebook) | ISBN
  9781492598343 (paperback) | ISBN 9781492598350 (epub) | ISBN
  9781492598374 (pdf)
Subjects: LCSH: Soccer--Training. | Weight training. | Muscle strength. |
  BISAC: SPORTS & RECREATION / Soccer | SPORTS & RECREATION / Coaching /
  Soccer
Classification: LCC GV943.9.T7 S76 2023 (print) | LCC GV943.9.T7 (ebook)
  | DDC 796.33407/7--dc23/eng/20220225
LC record available at https://lccn.loc.gov/2022001673
LC ebook record available at https://lccn.loc.gov/2022001674

ISBN: 978-1-4925-9834-3 (print)

Senior Acquisitions Editor: Roger W. Earle; **Managing Editors:** Miranda K. Baur and Kevin Matz; **Copyeditor:** Marissa Wold Uhrina; **Indexer:** Andrea Hepner; **Permissions Manager:** Dalene Reeder; **Senior Graphic Designer:** Joe Buck; **Cover Designer:** Keri Evans; **Cover Design Specialist:** Susan Rothermel Allen; **Photograph (cover):** ANP Sport via Getty Images; **Photographs (interior):** © Human Kinetics, unless otherwise noted; **Photo Asset Manager:** Laura Fitch; **Photo Production Specialist:** Amy M. Rose; **Photo Production Manager:** Jason Allen; **Senior Art Manager:** Kelly Hendren; **Illustrations:** © Human Kinetics, unless otherwise noted; **Printer:** Versa Press

We thank Keith E. Cinea, MA, CSCS,*D, NSCA-CPT,*D, and Mel Herl, MS, CSCS,*D, RSCC, at the National Strength and Conditioning Association in Colorado Springs, Colorado, for overseeing the photo shoot for this book.

Human Kinetics books are available at special discounts for bulk purchase. Special editions or book excerpts can also be created to specification. For details, contact the Special Sales Manager at Human Kinetics.

Printed in the United States of America

10 9 8 7 6 5 4 3 2 1

The paper in this book is certified under a sustainable forestry program.

Human Kinetics
1607 N. Market Street
Champaign, IL 61820
USA

United States and International
Website: **US.HumanKinetics.com**
Email: info@hkusa.com
Phone: 1-800-747-4457

Canada
Website: **Canada.HumanKinetics.com**
Email: info@hkcanada.com

E8078

Tell us what you think!
Human Kinetics would love to hear what we
can do to improve the customer experience.
Use this QR code to take our brief survey.

STRENGTH TRAINING
FOR
SOCCER

CONTENTS

Foreword by Tim Howard   vii

Introduction by Bob Bradley   ix

PART I   PRINCIPLES OF SPORT-SPECIFIC RESISTANCE TRAINING

1   **Importance of Resistance Training**   3
Garga Caserta and William E. Amonette

2   **Analysis of the Sport and Sport Positions**   17
Scott Piri

3   **Testing Protocols and Athlete Assessment**   39
Ernie Rimer and Jo Clubb

4   **Sport-Specific Program Design Guidelines**   67
Megan Young, Garga Caserta, and Matt Howley

PART II   EXERCISE TECHNIQUE

5   **Total Body Exercise Technique**   85
Scott Caulfield and Bryan Mann

6   **Lower Body Exercise Technique**   97
Scott Caulfield and Bryan Mann

7   **Upper Body Exercise Technique**   117
Ian Jeffreys

8   **Anatomical Core Exercise Technique**   145
Cat Wade and Kevin Cronin

PART III PROGRAM DESIGN GUIDELINES AND SAMPLE PROGRAMS

9   **Off-Season Programming**   181
Julia Eyre and Ivi Casagrande

10   **Preseason Programming**   201
Daniel Guzman and Joey Harty

11   **In-Season Programming**   215
Melissa Terry and Matt Howley

12   **Postseason Programming**   229
Ryan Alexander

References   240
Index   249
About the NSCA   255
About the Editors   256
About the Contributors   257

FOREWORD

TIM HOWARD

To answer the question of why resistance training is important—or rather, imperative—for soccer athletes, we must first identify a key point. What demands are being put on athletes to perform at the highest levels of the games today? Women and men, girls and boys of all ages are being asked to play the game with grace and agility, all the while doing it as powerfully as humanly possible at the speed of a race car. Blending all these elements together is the ultimate challenge. This challenge is the reason I became obsessed with resistance training in my own career.

There was a time in my early to mid-20s when genetically I was more physically dominant than most of my competitors. I came to realize that if I did not become more diligent with my work away from the ball, I would soon be surpassed. When competing against athletes of a similar level or skill set, it is important to have any advantage, no matter how minor, whether physical or mental. Once I truly invested time, energy, and thought into my body to make it stronger all around, I felt unstoppable. That belief allowed me the physical and, more importantly, the mental edge I was looking for. Here are a few things I learned that helped me understand its importance.

Resistance training offered major benefits in terms of my longevity. It seems simple enough, but in order to use that training to my advantage on the field, I actually must be on the field every game. When my body is fitter and stronger, it is better equipped to handle the rigors of the modern game. Therefore, it is much more able to avoid potential injuries and heal more quickly from the ones that do creep up.

Recovery is another factor along those same lines. When I ask so much of my body from a performance standpoint, I must also recognize its need to recover fully. Being committed to resistance training will allow my body to be stronger and healthier, making it into a machine that will recover at a much faster rate.

As I have now moved into the other side of the game as a sporting director, I cannot impress upon my athletes enough the importance of sport science and resistance training. I impart so much of the knowledge I have learned from both Daniel and Megan. While working with Daniel during my time with the U.S. Men's National Team (USMNT), I became a sponge, soaking up his energy, passion, and precise training methods. I have known Megan professionally for years. Seeing her work with female and male athletes at various levels has led to the most intriguing and in-depth discussions on the topic of resistance training, something about which we are both incredibly passionate.

The knowledge they have shared with me personally is right here in this book. What I have learned over many years, you will learn in these pages. But the message is simple. Stronger athletes make better soccer athletes. Period!

INTRODUCTION

BOB BRADLEY

Strength and conditioning in soccer has made important strides. For years, many teams borrowed methods from other sports and looked for ways to implement these ideas into training. It was a first step that led to strength and conditioning coaches working closely with technical staffs to put together programs to fit the specific needs of soccer athletes.

Tailoring strength and conditioning ideas to soccer requires a deep understanding of the demands of the game. Preparing athletes for 90 minutes of game actions—accelerating, decelerating, changing direction, turning, jumping, managing physical duels—is a challenge. Players need to be as strong and lean as possible but must also have the capacity to cover distances of 6 to 7 miles (10-11 km) in a game. Additionally injury prevention for a 10-month season that includes stretches with three games in a week is a key part of the best programs.

Many models start with an in-depth look at how an athlete moves on the field. Finding strengths, weaknesses, and imbalances provides starting points for individual programs. Training movement patterns that can build into warm-ups on the field is a feature for many top coaches and strength and conditioning professionals. Increasing loads as athletes adapt is necessary to build speed, strength, resilience, and overall fitness. This work has to be managed properly to fit the different periods of the season.

As strength and conditioning professionals continue to evolve in their work with athletes and teams, this book is a great resource for all those who are working to bring strength and conditioning ideas to the game of soccer.

PART I

PRINCIPLES OF SPORT-SPECIFIC RESISTANCE TRAINING

1

IMPORTANCE OF RESISTANCE TRAINING

GARGA CASERTA AND WILLIAM E. AMONETTE

Resistance training positively affects multiple aspects of health and performance for soccer athletes. Training with weights and other forms of resistance increases strength, power, hypertrophy (i.e., muscular size), and local muscle endurance and improves other skill-related biomotor abilities such as mobility, acceleration, speed, and agility. Recognizing the profound benefits, performing exercises against one's own body weight, external weights (free weights), elastic bands, and other forms of resistance has become a regular practice in the physical preparation of soccer athletes. Although the basic principles of resistance training have existed for years, the science and specificity for soccer and other sports have evolved. The first controlled trial, studying the concept of performing exercise against resistance and progressively increasing the weight to increase strength (i.e., progressive overload) was conducted in the 1940s by Dr. Thomas DeLorme. DeLorme, a physician in the Army Medical Corps, theorized that overloading muscles using weights could result in an improvement in strength and reduce recovery time after injury (39). After piloting this concept in an injured soldier with positive results, he published his seminal article in 1946 on the use of heavy resistance training using progressive overload to induce improvements in strength. DeLorme used 10RM loads to significantly improve rehabilitation outcomes in 300 injured soldiers (11). This unconventional approach led to a paradigm shift in physical preparation for combat and sports, and it began seven decades of advancements in how to best apply loading to induce neuromuscular adaptations. It is now known how, from a systemic physiologic and molecular level, the load, volume of exercise, rest periods, velocity of an exercise, the order of exercise, and all of the acute programming variables affect performance outcomes (30, 36). The primary focus of this chapter is to introduce the foundational benefits of resistance training in the context of soccer athletes; however, before discussing such information it is important for strength and conditioning professionals to understand some mechanisms that underpin adaptations from exercise.

MECHANISMS OF ADAPTATION

Fundamentally, resistance training increases stress on the neuromuscular and skeletal tissues. When the athlete is provided with sufficient recovery, these stresses result in tissue remodeling and adaptation. This theory is based on the work of Hans Selye, an Austrian physician and scientist, who coined the term *general adaptation syndrome* (33, 34). His theory and DeLorme's study provide the two core principles upon which training theory is based: in order for adaptation to occur, a system must be stressed beyond its current capabilities, and recovery is profoundly important to prevent maladaptation or, in the case of training, nonfunctional overreaching or overtraining (figure 1.1). Selye's theory was first integrated into resistance training theory, at least in written format, by Stone and colleagues in the early 1980s and was expanded on and applied to sport by many others (37). Resistance training improves performance in part by stressing metabolic, hormonal, and neurologic pathways.

Metabolic Stress and Adaptation

Energy is needed for life and to fuel the grueling demands of soccer. In cells, adenosine triphosphate (ATP) is the metabolic energy source needed to survive and thrive. ATP can be derived from metabolism through one of three pathways: from creatine phosphate (CP) that is stored within skeletal muscle (immediate energy system), from blood glucose from food or glucone-

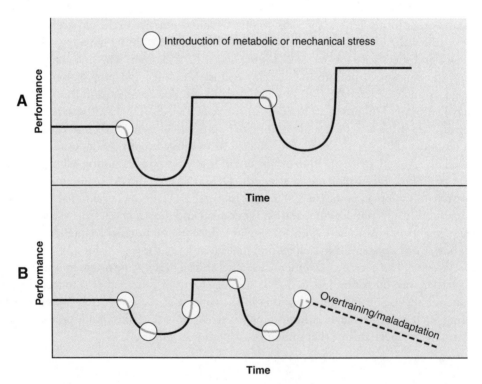

Figure 1.1 Theoretical stress and recovery response to metabolic or physical stress. A indicates the expected response with adequate recovery; B shows the expected response when errors are made in training and too much stress is applied without adequate recovery.

Adapted from Stone et al. (1982).

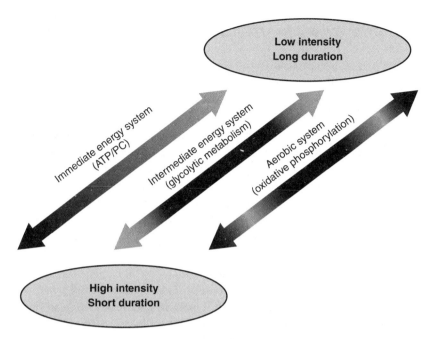

Figure 1.2 Predominant energy system contribution is dependent on the intensity and duration of activity.

ogenesis or glycogen stored within the liver or skeletal muscle (i.e., glycolytic metabolism, an intermediate system), or through oxidative phosphorylation (i.e., aerobic metabolism). Each system is critical during soccer performance, and the dependence on them varies by position (see chapter 2). Resistance training can stress each of these systems by altering the intensity (i.e., load or effort) and duration (i.e., repetitions or time) of a resistance training set, as well as the rest permitted between sets. These variables—most notably intensity and duration—dictate the predominant energy system used for an activity (figure 1.2). When resistance training is performed with heavier resistances, with high effort, and for relatively short periods of time, most of the adaptations that occur are to the ATP-PC and glycolytic systems.

When metabolic work occurs, the intracellular pH of the muscle changes, decreasing in key enzymes and increasing in oxidative stress that triggers adaptations to allow for increased training capacities in subsequent exercise sessions or competition. Some of the key metabolic adaptations include increases in the genetic expression of the genes associated with oxidative metabolism, in metabolic enzyme concentrations, in glycogen content, and an increase in muscle protein synthesis (7), as well as improvement in insulin sensitivity and glucose control (1, 5 , 6, 13, 20, 35, 40). Varying the sets, repetitions, load, and effort within a set and the rest period between sets can stress the enzymatic and biochemical pathways that result in improved work capacity and physical structure of a muscle (35, 40). When these pathways are repetitively stressed and allowed to recover, adaptations occur that allow for greater work capacity within the specific system that is stressed in training.

Hormonal Stress and Adaptation

The metabolic and mechanical stress from resistance training also results in hormonal releases that can create an environment conducive to neuromuscular and skeletal remodeling (for a review of exercise responses see 21, 22). Testosterone, a steroid hormone that increases muscle protein synthesis, is released from its secretory glands in response to the stimulus from resistance training (29). It is well known that the amount of testosterone released is related to sex, the intensity of exercise (i.e., weight lifted), and the amount of muscle tissue stressed. For example, exercises such as the deadlift, back squat, and power clean result in a greater testosterone release than the biceps curl or triceps extension exercises. Likewise, resistance training can trigger the anterior pituitary in the brain to release growth hormone, which is actually a superfamily of growth hormone isoforms that can directly increase muscle protein synthesis by binding to receptors on the muscle tissue or indirectly by facilitating the release of insulin such as growth factor-1 (IGF-1) from the liver, another hormone that is anabolic in skeletal muscle. Growth hormone and IGF-1 are both released in an intensity-dependent manner; their release may also be related to exercises using more muscle mass and shorter rest periods between sets, resulting in a decrease in muscle pH. Combined, these anabolic hormones create an environment whereby athletes can recover and thrive from exercise stimulus.

Exercise also increases cortisol release from the adrenal gland (26). Acutely, cortisol increases glucose availability, which is important for exercise metabolism in soccer. It also facilitates the anti-inflammatory responses resulting from exercise. However, if cortisol remains elevated for extended periods, it can be detrimental in that it exhibits catabolic effects on skeletal muscle. Cortisol also competes for androgen receptors, which can decrease the effectiveness of testosterone, among the many negative effects (26). Therefore, when cortisol remains high and testosterone is suppressed for long periods of time, performance might be affected and the athlete risks overtraining (3). Overtraining syndrome is a complex physiological phenomenon resulting in poorer mood, depression, reduced sleep quality, and performance decrements (24). Thus, it is important when prescribing exercise in athletes, especially soccer athletes who undergo high metabolic loads in practice and competition, to consider the overall stress resulting from training sessions and the sport load.

Neurologic Stress and Adaptation

Perhaps the most important effect resistance training has on performance arises from stressing the central and peripheral neurologic systems, resulting in improvements in coordination, strength, and motor performance. Training against any type of resistance activates motor units, exciting skeletal muscle to overcome the load. This occurs first through activation of areas within the motor cortex and cerebellum that coordinate functional, smooth, and precise movements. Neurochemical signals travel from the brain to the spinal cord; at the appropriate nerve root, this signal is transmitted to the correct motor neuron, and when this signal, or action potential, reaches the motor endplate, the skeletal muscle is excited and contracts. This complex activation pathway occurs thousands of times to elicit the movements required to overcome or accelerate the load of the body or an external weight in perfect order and synchrony to coordinate the skills required in soccer. These pathways of communication become more complex, flexible, and faster with repetition and result in myelination of skill-related pathways and ultimately precision of movement.

Resistance training activates the motor cortex, resulting in neuromuscular recruitment and motor pattern development (for a review of motor adaptations see 6). In fact, strength is in part the result of coordination, or the learned efficiency of neuromuscular recruitment. With resistance, agility, and sprint training, the central nervous system codifies patterns of movement and learns to activate more motor units and to inhibit the inhibitory mechanisms within the musculotendon unit such as the Golgi tendon organs. The result is the ability to generate more force; that is, the acquisition of strength.

An evolving and fascinating benefit of resistance training involves the expression of a powerful protein-based molecule within the nervous system, brain-derived neurotrophic factors (BDNF). BDNF is expressed predominantly in the hippocampus of the brain but also to some extent in the peripheral nervous system; it is a protein important for neuroplasticity, neuroprotection, and cognition (15). Church and colleagues demonstrated an acute increase in the expression of BDNF subsequent to resistance training (9). Their research indicates BDNF is elevated with both low- and high-intensity exercise. Although much of the research is in animal models or older adults, an evolving body of research suggests that BDNF expression following resistance training improves memory, especially visual spatial memory. These findings highlight yet another important adaptation that can occur in response to resistance training, and future studies likely will demonstrate its importance in competitive soccer athletes.

All of these adaptive mechanisms are crucial to programming, regardless of the sport. Strength and conditioning professionals must understand how to best apply physiologic stress, while avoiding overstress, to prescribe most precisely the resistance training loads, volumes, exercises, and velocities of movements to result in improved soccer performance and reduced injuries.

RESISTANCE TRAINING IMPROVES PHYSICAL CAPABILITIES IN SOCCER ATHLETES

Resistance training is integral in improving the physical capabilities of soccer athletes. Though only practice can increase the skill-related aspects of soccer, training with weights, resistance bands, and other implements can make a skillful soccer athlete stronger, more powerful, and agile and can help prevent injuries. The degree to which a soccer athlete expresses these physical capabilities varies by playing level, age, and position (31). Interestingly, several studies indicate no differences in general between the physiologic characteristics of starters and reserve athletes (32). Nonetheless, soccer athletes must exhibit an array of motor abilities and maintain these capabilities throughout match play while covering 5 to 6 miles (8-10 km) in a game (12). Additionally, female soccer athletes have unique needs. Because female soccer athletes are at increased risk for knee injury during landing and cutting maneuvers, special strength and movement training might be needed to prevent non-contact knee injuries.

Improves Strength

Strength is the ability of the neuromuscular system to generate force; **force** is defined in Newtonian physics as the product of mass and acceleration (Newton's second law). Depending on the mass of the object being accelerated, force is expressed at higher or lower accelerations and velocities. The inverse relationship between force and velocity in skeletal muscle was first described by Hill (18). In athletics, this relationship is discussed and applied with resistance training and sport as a concept called the *force–velocity curve*. This concept suggests that force is expressed across a continuum at an array of velocities. On one end of the continuum, tasks requiring acceleration of large masses or the generation of high forces occur over relatively longer durations and at low velocities. On the other end of the continuum, smaller masses or tasks requiring lower forces when performed at high intentional efforts occur at high velocities.

Different sports, or tasks within sports, require athletes to express force at higher or lower velocities depending on the mass of the object that is being accelerated and inertia of the movement (figure 1.3). For example, more force is generated at a slower rate when throwing a

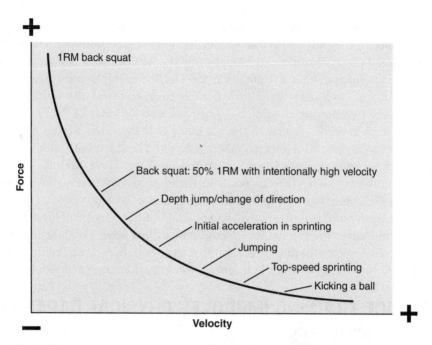

Figure 1.3   Different movements require the production of force at different velocities.

16-pound (7.3 kg) shot in track than a 0.4-pound (0.2 kg) baseball. However, the arm velocity in throwing a baseball is higher than the arm velocity in putting the shot. Thus baseball, or at least the task of throwing the ball, occurs toward the velocity end of the curve and putting a shot more toward the force end. Likewise, it requires more force to decelerate and change directions when running at top speed because of inertia (Newton's first law) than to initiate the acceleration phase of sprinting when beginning from the stopped position. However, the force demands of a 1RM back squat are greater than sprinting but occur at a much lower velocity.

Because of the nature of sport and tasks within the sport, soccer athletes most commonly express force on the velocity end of the curve. While systematically and progressively overloading the weight used during lower body exercises, resistance training is an effective way to address the development of low velocity force. If the exercise selected is similar in movement patterns to those involved in the acceleration phase of sprinting, athletes would benefit from increasing the amount of force they can produce relative to their body weight, as well as the neuromuscular pathway development that can lead to more consistent and eventually faster movement over time.

It is also important to consider the variety of velocity demands in muscle contraction during sport skills, including passing, shooting, and sprinting movements that occur on the high velocity end of the curve. To improve force at high velocities, one can lift lighter weights or even one's own body weight at intentionally high velocities (19). Resistance training allows for a controlled environment where these different types, ranges, and speed of contractions can be used to elicit development specific to the demands of the game.

When considering the strength demands of a sport, it is also important to consider the muscular contraction types. The majority of actions in soccer stress muscles and tendons through cycles of isometric, eccentric, and concentric muscle actions. **Isometric contractions** occur when the muscle contracts with no change in length, while **eccentric actions** occur when the muscle lengthens under tension. **Concentric contractions** occur when the muscle contracts and

Alex Menendez/Getty Images

Jumping involves an eccentric muscle action, a brief amortization period, then a concentric contraction.

shortens. For example, during the loading or downward phase of jumping, the eccentric load is high as muscle groups involved are lengthening. This is followed by a brief isometric moment, referred to as *coupling time* or *amortization period*. This brief, undetectable pause is followed by a concentric drive to launch the body upwards. It is essential to identify these differences as they play important roles in the development of power. Improving strength during each phase of the stretch-shortening cycle, which will be discussed in more detail next, is highly effective in supporting improvements in power and speed.

Improves Power

Before discussing the role of resistance training in developing power for soccer athletes, it is important to understand and define power within the context of physics. **Power** is the rate of performing work. **Work** is the product of the force applied to an object and the distance the force is applied. Power is therefore computed as work divided by time. Alternatively, this equation can be rearranged and expressed as the product of force and velocity. Therefore, if discussing the development of power for athletes, the variables of force, direction, time, and velocity should be considered. Because of this relationship between force and velocity, peak power occurs at 30% of peak isometric force production, or between 40-80% of the 1RM depending on the nature of the exercise (figure 1.4 [8]).

The goal of power development is to increase athletes' speed and quickness with which they perform sport actions. The expression of power and the variables associated with the computation of power can be identified across sport actions and in the context of the force–velocity

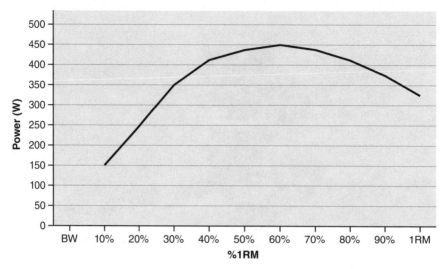

Figure 1.4   Theoretical relationship between power and percent of 1RM for a traditional resistance training exercise (not an explosive/power exercise or Olympic lift) performed at a high velocity.

curve. When a forward (athlete) sprints to position him- or herself behind a defender, a relatively large force is exerted into the ground to maximize acceleration as each leg pushes against the ground (Newton's third law). In contrast, when the forward strikes the ball with the foot, a relatively low amount of force is necessary to move the ball but very high leg velocity is needed to generate pace on the shot. Both of these situations require power, but the expression of power is different in each. Once the strength and conditioning professional understands the variables associated with power and how to practically apply these constructs to soccer, he or she can train each variable or focus on deficiencies to optimize performance abilities.

Similar to improving strength, using compound movements that are relatively similar in pattern and direction to the movements in soccer will lead to an increase in soccer-specific power. This can be done by progressively increasing the load in exercises such as the single-leg deadlift, which is similar in pattern to the initial steps in acceleration. On the velocity side of the curve, plyometric exercises such as linear bounds, split squat jumps, and cycle jumps can train the athlete to generate force at a high rate, optimizing leg swing velocity and improving the power required to strike a ball with speed.

The **stretch-shortening cycle** (SSC) is key to power development. The SSC describes the elasticity of muscles and tendons creating potential energy when rapidly stretched. Additionally, the SSC uses the neurologic stretch-reflex response of the muscle spindles to aid in force production. When an athlete learns to coordinate the elastic energy from a stretch, an involuntary reflex force production, and the subsequent purposeful concentric contraction, the result is greater instantaneous power production and potential to express these qualities in soccer.

Improves Speed

Running velocity (i.e., speed) is an essential athletic quality needed for the sport of soccer and is more important for some positions than others. **Speed**, or the capacity to run at high velocities, can be improved by enhancing strength and power (2, 28). Due to the nonlinearity of soccer, it is important to understand the different aspects of speed. Sprinting speed can be categorized into the following components: acceleration, maximum velocity, deceleration, and transitions (i.e., changing directions). Each component stresses the athlete differently, and understanding the demands of each component is important to understand what type of actions should be trained with resistance training. (For more detail, see pages 28-37 in chapter 2.)

Acceleration

Acceleration, or an increase in velocity, begins when the athlete initiates a sprint to perform a sport action. It can be initiated from a static position, walking, or slow running. Velocity increases rapidly at the beginning of the movement, and acceleration decreases as an athlete approaches top speed (figure 1.5). Creating a positive shin angle and pushing back against the ground (propulsive force), the leg actions during acceleration patterns are piston-like, driving up and down in a linear pattern to generate force against the ground with both vertical and horizontal force production (27). A relatively large amount of force is required to initiate a sprint, and the more force an athlete can generate relative to his or her body weight the greater potential for acceleration. Ground reaction forces during accelerations have been shown to reach 1,500 to 3,500 newtons, which applied to a 165-pound (75 kg) athlete equals 2 to 4.5 times an athlete's body weight per leg drive (41). The forces are exerted over a relatively long ground contact time (approximately 0.18 s) during initial steps and increase over the subsequent steps until the acceleration rate reaches zero at the maximum-velocity phase (i.e., top speed). These high-force, piston-like patterns are similar to the movements performed in unilateral triple extension exercises like the split squat. The movements are also supported by hinging movements such as the Romanian deadlift. Improving performance in these exercises after developing a foundation in bilateral squatting and hinging movements can complement the development of sprinting mechanics and force generation when sprinting, potentially increasing speed outcomes.

Maximum Velocity

As the athlete transitions into maximum velocity and acceleration diminishes with each step, the mechanical purpose of the arm and leg actions is to maintain speed as opposed to continuing to increase velocity (23). When transitioning from acceleration to top speed, the athlete's body

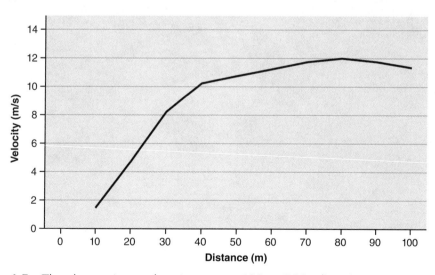

Figure 1.5   The change in acceleration over a 100-m (109 yd) sprint.

position is progressively taller and perpendicular to the ground. The mechanical patterns during maximum velocity phase are more cyclical in nature, facilitating the generation of high vertical ground reaction forces to maintain sprinting velocity. At this point, stride frequency is faster, and high eccentric forces in the SSC occur throughout the hips and shoulder joints. Thus, peak velocity is determined by the frequency of strides and the **stride length** (i.e., the distance the center of mass moves with propulsion step). Research indicates that maximum velocity is mostly related to the stride length created by the magnitude of the ground reaction force, the ultimate biomechanical determinant of peak running velocity (42, 44, 45). Thus, strength and power are profoundly important for speed. No athlete who is weak relative to body weight is also fast. Resistance training exercises with fast eccentric and short coupling time, and that permit the development of high ground reaction forces (e.g., kettlebell swing, power clean, jump squat) provide similar stimuli that could lead to improvements in maximum velocity running. Note, however, that only a small proportion of a soccer match involves running at maximum velocity.

Deceleration

The **deceleration** phase is usually initiated or triggered by the completion of a task, such as crossing the finish line after a 100-meter (109 yd) sprint. In soccer, for example, a deceleration might be triggered by a defender's recognition that an opponent is about to initiate their first touch, in preparation to react to the ball. Recognizing triggers is a key component of agility. Decelerations are a known mechanism of non-contact injuries that often occur when exerting breaking forces on the ground with poor mechanics. Deceleration mechanics occur mostly in

Juan Manuel Serrano Arce/Getty Images

Deceleration often occurs in the sagittal plane when exerting breaking forces on the ground.

the sagittal plane but can occur in the frontal plane in reactive environments. Resistance and plyometric training can improve deceleration capabilities (1). The patterns demonstrated in decelerations are similar to and can be reinforced by exercises such as the depth jump, reverse lunge, and front squat.

Transitions

Once the body is sufficiently decelerated, a transitional movement is used to initiate the next acceleration. Unless the athlete is simply reaccelerating linearly in the same direction, a movement strategy is used to change direction for the next acceleration phase. Many transitional strategies exist, but shuffling, cutting, crossing over, and drop stepping are the most common and effective skills (see chapter 2). These movements are rotational in nature and demand appropriate rotational mobility, stability, and propulsive power at the trunk, hips, knees, and ankles.

Various resistance training exercises and strategies can improve transitions in soccer athletes (25). Training for strength and power with free weights can develop the force production required to maximize acceleration mechanics. Ballistic movements with fast SSC demands like the kettlebell swing, power clean, jump squat, and reactive plyometrics can support the development of force and power to execute the transition properly. In addition, resistance training gives the athlete the opportunity to work on each segment of all functioning parts of these movements to remove limitations and optimize mobility, coordination, and the capacity to perform each task.

When combined, deceleration, transitions, and accelerations constitute the construct of **agility**, which is essential in soccer and more important than top speed. Resistance and plyometric exercise can enhance the athlete's capabilities to perform agility movements (4, 46), but it is important to note that the sport itself is the best way to develop task-specific agility in athletes. In other words, it is the role of the strength and conditioning professional to develop the engine and capacity for acceleration, but these skills must be applied in practice to optimize transfer of skill to the competition.

Improves Body Composition

Among the numerous benefits of resistance training for soccer, an improvement in body composition occurs with appropriate resistance training. Muscular **hypertrophy** (i.e., growth in size) that results from resistance training is well known. Although soccer athletes do not need to possess as much muscle mass as linebackers in American football, they do need enough muscle to improve the efficiency of strength, power, speed, and agility. Moreover, soccer athletes in certain positions typically possess more muscle to support the physical aspects of the game such as shielding (i.e., by the defenders) (38). Another important aspect to consider is the maintenance of skeletal muscle in season. Soccer games and practice require large amounts of jogging, sprinting, and walking. The resulting energy demand can be catabolic to skeletal muscle and could result in the loss of muscle gained in off-season training. Both nutrition and resistance training play an important role in stimulating muscle anabolism and preventing the loss of muscle that could result from the energetics of the sport.

Prevents Non-Contact Injuries

Injury risk can be assessed globally for soccer athletes by identifying mobility demands of movement tasks involved in the sport. Then, the strength and conditioning professional can determine if the athlete possesses the mobility to achieve the end-point range of motions (**position**), can efficiently move through the range of motion between positions (**patterns**), and can do so against resistance or at high velocities (power). This concept is described as *building a movement foundation before performance.*

If an athlete cannot achieve a position (e.g., insufficient internal rotation of the hip), he or she will be at an increased risk of knee ligament injury when required to do a movement involving hip internal rotation. Since hip rotation is limited, medial or lateral collateral ligaments of the knee might be put under undue stress. This can occur throughout the body when a specific joint function is limited, affecting adjacent joints (10). Mobility needs can be addressed within a resistance training program, especially if specific joints' functional range is established and trained progressively with similar strength or power development required within the sport tasks.

Similarly, achieving certain positions is key to reducing injury risks; the ability to move through patterns from one position to another with rhythm and coordination is essential. Because soccer athletes are required to sprint, the ability to move through synchronized patterns between opposing segments smoothly can greatly reduce the risk of injuries arising from movement compensations. An inability to achieve positions within a pattern will affect the global outcome of the pattern. Resistance training provides the strength and conditioning professional a controlled environment in which to assist an athlete to achieve positions A and B, as well as establishing a foundation of movement between A and B. For example, a single-leg deadlift requires the athlete to stand on one leg (position A), load into a hinge on the stance leg (position B), then return to standing on one leg (position A). A similar hip flexion pattern (position A to B) and hip extension pattern (position B to A) occurs during running, with the stance and flight legs moving in a synchronous pattern and repeating. If the athlete compensates when performing these patterns in a controlled environment such as with resistance training, he or she likely will experience issues in a more complex, intense, and less controlled environment such as in sprinting.

Considering the importance of enhancing patterns via resistance training, the strength and conditioning professional should use compound exercises against one's own body weight or free weight resistance versus using machines that segmentalize and isolate (see chapter 4). These exercises allow for the development of power and the capacity to tolerate the power production demanded during the sport's action. Injury risk is greatest when athletes have not been exposed to the demands of the sport; thus the tissue has not adapted and become more resilient to those stresses. This concept is defined in part by the **SAID principle** (specific adaptation to imposed demands); that is, the body should be exposed in training to the specific demands of the sport and its kinematic (movement) and kinetic (force) requirements. For soccer athletes, resistance training can reduce the risk of muscle strains by progressively increasing the volume and intensity of training on the musculoskeletal tissues used in soccer. Sprinting, jumping, kicking, stopping, and cutting can demand high levels of tissue tolerance; therefore, the strength and conditioning professional should impose similar demands on the athlete in the controlled environment of training to prepare the tissue for competition.

Sex Differences

Resistance training might be particularly important for female soccer athletes. Evidence suggests that women have an increased risk of non-contact knee injuries, especially injuries to the anterior cruciate ligament (ACL) (14, 43). Although several reasons for this increased risk are intrinsic and inherent to the uniqueness of female anatomy such as a wider Q-angle, smaller ACL relative to body weight, and smaller femoral notch, others can be affected by training.

It is thought that the predominant injury mechanism to the knee occurs when jumping, landing, or changing directions (16). When the foot is in contact with the ground, or in a closed chain, the quadriceps, when contracted, pull the tibia forward relative to the femur, acting as an antagonist to or placing strain on the ACL. Conversely, in a closed chain, the hamstring muscles pull the tibia backward on the femur, acting as an agonist and reducing strain on the ACL. Thus, if the quadriceps contract sooner or with more force in landing or cutting, an anterior pull is placed on the knee and hyperextension might occur, which can result in failure of the fibers of the ACL. Likewise, with muscular imbalances or poor neuromuscular control, the hip might internally rotate and adduct upon landing, creating a torsional load and valgus knee movement (figure 1.6); all can lead to damage or rupture of the ACL.

Some studies indicate that, in general, women tend to have weaker hamstrings relative to quadriceps (14). Moreover, they might exhibit gluteus medius and minimus weakness, resulting in more internal rotation and knee abduction in jumping, landing, and cutting. Thus, some have proposed that specific strengthening of the hamstrings and hip external rotators could be an important aspect of training female athletes (17). Though this hypothesis may be valid, the injury mechanisms are more likely related to coordination in cutting and landing. Evidence strongly supports progressive plyometric exercise that instruct proper force reduction and hip and knee control during jumping, as well as agility exercises to prevent knee injuries (17). Some have shown such specific instruction in jumping, landing, and cutting alone might correct strength imbalances irrespective of specific resistance training exercises. Gilchrist and colleagues introduced a warm-up routine incorporating these exercises and demonstrated a marked reduction in the risk of ACL injuries (14). Therefore, strength and conditioning professionals working with females should screen for knee injury mechanisms and introduce specific exercises into the warm-up and training sessions to prevent non-contact knee injuries.

Figure 1.6   Internal rotation of the hip and valgus knee movements are associated with increased risk of injury to the knee.

CONCLUSION

Strength and power are foundational physical qualities for nearly all sport-specific movements in soccer. Strength, power, and soccer-specific athletic improvements are developed through stressing the muscular, metabolic, hormonal, and neurologic pathways associated with adaptation. When these mechanisms are stressed to an appropriate extent with specificity and when adequate rest is provided, a soccer athlete becomes stronger and more powerful. Strength and power form a foundation for the development of sprinting, acceleration, deceleration, agility, and injury prevention. After strength and power are acquired, they must be applied and translated to soccer through practice. In order to reduce injury potential, athletes must be stressed in sport-specific ways by gradually introducing and controlling mechanisms of injury. The challenge for a strength and conditioning professional working with soccer athletes is that these attributes must be stressed while competing and practicing a sport that requires high metabolic and physical workloads. The amount depends on the position, which will be discussed in the next chapter.

2

ANALYSIS OF THE SPORT AND SPORT POSITIONS

SCOTT PIRI

The beautiful game of soccer creates numerous memories for the fans. During a match, moments when athletes are creative with the ball (in their control) is what many enthusiasts remember the most. Even though the ball is the centerpiece of the sport and it dictates the flow, action, and score of a match, soccer has many performance aspects that need to be examined more closely. By nature, soccer is an intermittent sport with long durations of low-intensity activity and short periods of high-intensity activity that usually require several physical actions. In this chapter the general movement and physiological demands will be highlighted while presenting position-specific factors for the soccer athlete.

BIOMECHANICAL ANALYSIS

When athletes are introduced to the game of soccer, they must learn numerous aspects of the sport. Technique with the ball is crucial and why athletes spend so much time building those specific skills (e.g., receiving, passing, shooting, heading, tackling). Equally as important, technique without the ball affects the capability of a team to maintain or regain possession of the ball. How much time or space directly relates to these concepts and the athlete's ability to get open from an opponent or close distance, apply pressure, and mark an opponent are fundamental to how the match is played.

Tactical concepts can have a considerable influence on the style of play. Offensive and defensive strategies come from the coach's principles of play and game model. For example, the playing formation (e.g., 4-5-1, 4-4-2, 4-3-3, 3-5-2, 3-4-3) usually prioritizes the coach's offense or defense philosophies. Analyzing further, soccer is like many team (e.g., field) sports in that athletes have to understand the important tactical principles of the game, which consist of offense, defense, and transition. As athletes evolve within the sport, they must understand offense, defense, and transitional play with and without the ball. How quickly athletes and teams can transition from offense to defense and defense to offense is key to the modern game. At these vital moments within the match, speed, powerful actions, and quick decision-making are required to gain an advantage against the opposition.

Match Play

Creating a physical performance activity profile for soccer teams and athletes is another way to showcase how essential **high-intensity actions** (i.e., speed and power) are to the game. One of the ideal ways to do this is through advanced technology. The ability to monitor the physical performance data within a game or practice has progressed over the years. Many high-tech match analysis companies provide these services for professional soccer teams, and wearable devices offer a simple and realistic solution for athletes at all levels. Looking at match analyses establishes trends, tendencies, and baselines on physical performance for groups and individuals. But most of all, it confirms the relationship of the major physical performance variables within the match to generate standards for athletes. Evaluating different kinds of performance data markers can be simple or complex. Looking at the total time during a match that an athlete expresses certain athletic actions by percentage is a good starting reference: "During a typical English Premier League match, players stand still for 6% of the total time. Low-intensity activity represents 85% of the total time, which comprises 59% walking and 26% jogging. High-intensity actions represent 9% of the total time, which is broken down further into 6% running, 2% high-speed running, and 1% sprinting" (5). Despite high-intensity actions only taking up a small percentage of the total time during a match, it is important to illustrate how high-intensity actions take up a very high percentage of the total distance covered during the match.

When looking at the different levels of soccer athletes (novice to expert) around the world, standing still, walking, and jogging all occur in games. Mohr and colleagues point out that "the majority of the distance (in the match) is covered by walking and low-intensity running and it is mainly the high-intensity exercise periods which are important. The amount of high-speed running is what distinguishes top-class players from those at a low level. Computerized time motion analysis has demonstrated that international top-class players perform 28% more high-intensity running (2.42 vs. 1.90 km) and 58% more sprinting (650 vs. 410 m) than professional players at a lower level" (10). Athletes can do a great deal of walking and jogging and still cover plenty of distance for the entire game. However, the importance of high-intensity actions performed by the athlete during a game needs to be studied: "Although high-intensity actions make up a relatively low percentage of the match, these actions cannot be underestimated because they can change the outcome of the match" (7).

These high-intensity actions vary among players at different levels: "Match analyses have revealed that there are only minor differences between players at different standards of competition regarding total distance covered in a game. However, there are large differences within the intense movement categories. For example, top-class players from the Italian Serie A engaged in around 30% more high speed running and about 60% more sprinting in a game than did male Scandinavian elite players" (1). Many times, these high-intensity actions create opportunities while in transition, defending, or attacking phases of play. Most notably, the ability to create these actions in sequence can become deciding moments for a team. At the most intense periods of the match, it is common to see an increased number of sprints, high-speed runs, and runs.

Studies have demonstrated how high-intensity actions are a game changer within soccer. Evaluating the characteristics of explosive actions in detail brings better understanding of these activities. For example, "in a football [soccer] game, the high intensity running bouts range from 5-70 meters, but the majority of these runs are less than 20 meters. In addition, the player should be able to accelerate, decelerate, and change direction, which are essential variables in intense football [soccer] runs and need to be included in a football-specific test" (2).

Many short-duration powerful actions are done in various directions. Soccer, like many team sports, functions in an environment where athletes must move well in all directions: "Most of

Stu Forster/Getty Images

A soccer athlete's ability to make explosive turns is critical to effective movement in all directions.

the sprints in a game are curved runs that are often initiated after explosive turns. The angle of turns in a match have been determined and a player performs around 800 turns in a game, with the majority being within angles of 0-90°" (4).

In the end, soccer requires many more actions than standing still, walking, jogging, running, high-speed running, and sprinting. For context, a majority of technical skills (e.g., receiving, passing, dribbling, shooting, tackles, challenges) call for touch or contact with the ball, which can be powerful and explosive in nature. Due to the scope of this chapter, the technical skills of the game will be highlighted but not in detail. But it is equally important to recognize the fundamentals of technical skills and the association with high-intensity actions within soccer.

Acceleration, deceleration, and change of direction are key components of high-intensity actions. Taking these actions and showcasing the movement qualities in more detail can be beneficial to the sport.

Action and Movement

When examining a soccer athlete's performance, it is common to refer to the actions that take place within the game, but that can be short-sighted because the analysis and any associated research about the performance typically only focuses on certain characteristics of the action. For example, research regarding sprinting usually focuses on its cardiovascular and metabolic effects (see the General Physiological Analysis section), not the biomechanical aspects of sprinting.

A direct relationship exists between action and movement for human performance (see figure 2.1). Even though action and movement are similar in many ways, it is important to understand the small differences. **Action** is usually the intent to achieve a specific goal with the body. **Movement** emphasizes the position or change of the body.

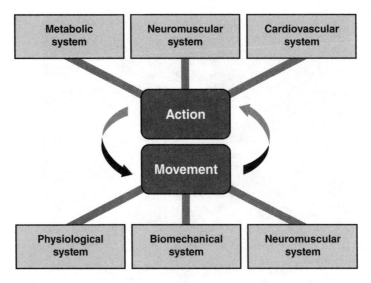

Figure 2.1   Action and movement relationship.

In this chapter, the fundamental connection between biomechanical analysis and movement quality for soccer athletes will be explained. When athletes focus on movement quality, their efficiency and durability improve and their overall performance improves. In short, this allows athletes to do more with less effort, which is a game changer in soccer. Since acceleration, deceleration, and change of direction are significant movements to the sport, it is necessary to describe the notable movement qualities for each.

Before talking about the technique for acceleration, however, it is important to establish that all athletes need to maintain or enhance fundamental movement characteristics for soccer. Fundamental movement is a foundation to general movement characteristics (e.g., walking, jogging, running, high-speed running, sprinting). Simply, an individual must display a certain level of mobility, stability, efficiency, and coordination (e.g., body control) to express the appropriate technique for acceleration.

Acceleration

Throughout a soccer game, there are many moments when being fast or having speed is beneficial to the athlete and team. All athletes strive to increase speed in relation to the position and the sport. **Acceleration** is a component of speed and can be developed through quality training. Nevertheless, an athlete's genetics (e.g., strength and power) dictate how much improvement can be made, but all athletes can increase acceleration through proper technique (e.g., sprint form), which lets athletes achieve a higher level of speed.

Soccer athletes are not just standing in place before accelerating during a match. Many times, athletes accelerate from a walk, jog, or run position. The direction of the acceleration is linear to the position or the way the body is facing. Also, the movement of acceleration will not always be exactly straight ahead. Accelerating at angles of 10, 15, and 20 degrees of the linear movement (i.e., going forward) is common in the sport. For context, the characteristics of acceleration technique differ slightly from certain positions (e.g., walking and running), but the principles remain the same. Many decisions are made right before the time when acceleration is needed during the game, but the direction and intent (e.g., how fast and how far) of the movement is usually determined by the individual at that instant. Moreover, the laws and concepts of inertia, force, magnitude, and velocity come into play for the athlete.

The term *acceleration cycle* refers to a continuum that includes the different phases a leg and foot moves through from start to finish (e.g., examining the movements of the right leg and foot from the side view and analyzing them through all the phases to complete the sprinting movement). The acceleration cycle includes the stance phase, which has subcomponents of the contact phase and push phase, and the swing phase, which has subcomponents of the recovery phase and drive phase. The priority is placed on the lower body because of the majority of force production properties through the acceleration cycle. However, the influence of the upper body movement is provided to complete the sequence.

Stance Phase   During the first movement action of acceleration, the **stance phase** recognizes the gravity of the lead leg making initial contact and full contact with the ground. The stance leg (i.e., lead leg) absorbs the force of the body into the ground during the **contact phase**. The hip is in a flexed position while the ankle, knee, and hip transfer and then eventually generate horizontal force to produce horizontal velocity in a linear direction. Establishing a low vertical position of the pelvis (i.e., hip flexion) through the contact phase is favorable for transitional force production and to overcome gravity. When the stance leg continues under the body's center of mass through foot contact, the hip goes from flexion to extension through muscular application of eccentric, isometric, and then concentric forces on the hip, knee, and ankle. This applies to the stance leg if momentum (e.g., walking or jogging) has been established before acceleration. In contrast, if the athlete is starting from a stationary position, the concentric forces of the stance leg are prominent during the muscular application of movement since there is little to no contact between the stance leg and the ground. This allows the push phase to be applied directly from this position. Following the contact phase is the push phase with the stance leg. The **push phase** uses coordination of the body going forward and completes extension at the hip, knee, and ankle (i.e., triple extension) for horizontal velocity. As the forefoot (e.g., ball of the foot) remains touching the ground, the overall body position is angled forward. The torso should stay straight (i.e., maintain posture) while leaning forward over the center of mass. A straight torso will allow the hips and shoulders to be efficient in applying the velocity necessary for acceleration.

As acceleration continues through the push phase, the stance leg travels further behind the body's base of support. Eventually, after the focus on hip extension and supporting knee extension to create horizontal force production, the foot will transition from heel off to toe off the ground to complete the push phase and horizontal velocity. Think of an airplane taking off. As the plane develops speed, it ultimately produces enough propulsion so the wheels come off the ground with a horizontal projection. Likewise, athletes are usually moving before going into acceleration. The athlete's momentum from the previous movement (e.g., walk or jog) makes it easier for the athlete to create force, break inertia, and overcome gravity, which is more present when standing still. Therefore, a bigger torso lean is needed when starting from a standing still position, and a smaller torso lean is demanded when starting from a walking, jogging, or running position for acceleration. During the stance phase, the ankle is key in developing the power demands for acceleration. First, the ankle of the stance leg needs to absorb the body weight and overcome force load during the contact phase. The forefoot (e.g., ball of foot) should support the main contact (i.e., stance leg) with the surface. Second, the ankle must maintain tension (i.e., dorsiflexion), which allows force transfer through the push phase. Finally, the ankle needs to stay rigid during ground contact time to set up ankle extension (i.e., plantarflexion) and favorable push mechanics.

The pelvis being in a lower vertical position, compared to higher vertical position, during the stance phase (i.e., contact phase and push phase) depends on the individual's genetics (e.g., strength, height, and weight) and training adaptation. Additionally, the overall big or small torso lean for acceleration in the stance phase are dictated by the previous limitations.

Swing Phase   During the first movement action of acceleration, the **swing phase** focuses on the lead leg going from exchange to return during flight. As the swing leg (i.e., lead leg) adjusts from being behind the body to the front of the body during the **recovery phase**, it must adapt quickly due to the horizontal focus and limited vertical displacement through acceleration. Furthermore, the swing leg must transition rapidly because of the aggressive forward trunk lean at the beginning of the recovery phase. The swing leg works in synergy with the stance leg as the swing leg crosses the middle line of the body during exchange. This movement reveals the pelvis adjusting from less hip extension to more hip flexion through the recovery phase. The **drive phase** takes place from the appropriate hip flexion to initial contact with the ground and finishes with the swing leg being driven down into the ground behind the body's center of mass. All of this accentuates the advantageous positions to apply ground reaction forces with the lower body.

The ankle movement is critical during the swing phase for acceleration. Maintaining ankle dorsiflexion is essential for proper timing of the swing leg hip and knee. During the recovery phase, the swing leg ankle crosses with the stance leg ankle in more of a sweeping motion. This technique also facilitates a better overall body lean forward. Once the hip flexion is established with the swing leg, the drive phase quickly transitions the ankle into a diagonal push step underneath and behind the body's base of support.

The acceleration cycle requires the torso and pelvis to synchronize to create more velocity. The shoulders and hips counterrotate at the same time to create tension through the center of the body. The arm movement is a transfer of what happens at the shoulders. This tension through the trunk helps absorb and then deliver force directly from the lower body to upper body during acceleration.

In short, here is a summary of some of the main traits observed during the acceleration cycle:

- *Stride length:* Progresses from a short movement to long movement over time
- *Stride frequency:* Transfers from a slow movement to fast movement through the sequence
- *Forward torso lean:* Transitions from a bigger angle to smaller angle step by step
- *Arm swing:* Begins with a big movement and merges into a smaller movement in relationship with stride length and stride frequency
- *Velocity:* Starts from slow and progressively gets faster through the cycle

Deceleration

Soccer athletes are asked to slow down, stop, and prepare for the next movement on a regular basis during a game. These changes are used frequently during the sport and set up the subsequent movement or movements. **Deceleration** is a linking movement between acceleration and change of direction. Moreover, athletes will accelerate, decelerate, and reaccelerate many times while playing. Due to the sheer volume of deceleration by an athlete in a match and how it contributes to the following movements, it is beneficial to discuss the major aspects of deceleration in detail.

At those moments when deceleration is needed by an athlete, reaction is crucial at that instant, so the distance and time (e.g., how far and how quickly) to slow down or stop is processed by the individual at that second. The muscular application of concentric, isometric, and eccentric forces is pivotal to lowering the center of mass from a higher position during deceleration. As the pelvis drops closer to the ground, it emphasizes muscular eccentric action through hip flexion to hip extension. Said in another way, concentric actions are prioritized at the start of acceleration and eccentric actions are the focus at the beginning of deceleration. Notably, the opposing muscle actions for acceleration (i.e., isometric and eccentric) or deceleration (i.e., isometric and concentric) contribute to the movement, but the attention shifts. Genetics and training adaptation increase deceleration quality through the ability to tap into higher levels of strength and maintain proper technique. Absorbing and redistributing vertical and horizontal forces during deceleration are fundamental to improving performance and decreasing the potential for injury.

The movement of deceleration has two phases: the lowering phase and the base phase.

Lowering Phase   As the individual completes the **lowering phase** (of the center of mass) of deceleration, the ankle and foot position are out in front of the body's base of support to facilitate the technique. The stance phase and the stride phase gradually decrease with quality technique in relation to the distance and time demands to decelerate. Depending on the type of deceleration needed, soccer requires the athlete to be versatile and regain a balanced position to support movement.

Base Phase   As the athlete continues through the lowering phase, the **base phase** is when the individual finds an adequate base of support while finalizing the slowing down or stopping position. At this instant, time and distance within the game dictate how rapid the linking movement is used because of little to no momentum. The base phase consists of many variables happening simultaneously. The athlete has to anticipate what will happen next to establish mechanics. Distance, time, space, direction, opponent, offense, defense, and transition play are some of the variables to consider within the game.

Improving the base phase within deceleration is central due to all the starting and stopping in the sport. Establishing different types of **stances** (i.e., bases of support) offers versatility that is needed in the game. For reference, the stances discussed here are described as if the athlete is facing straight ahead to the playing situation.

Here are a few of the main stances:

- *Base stance:* Having two feet side by side (e.g., squat position) is the most common and easiest for athletes to improve. The ability to use both legs equally to absorb force permits athletes to move well in all directions from this position.
- *Split stance:* One foot is directly out in front of the other (i.e., a narrow-base split stance). Many times, soccer dictates a lead leg during a stance. This stance is used primarily to move through linear or lateral planes of motion.
- *Staggered stance:* One foot is placed out in front of the other (i.e., a wide-base split stance). The game is unpredictable, so athletes position the lead leg in a diagonal orientation and the back leg off center to meet the demands of the sport. This stance allows the athlete to be ready for motion in linear, lateral, and rotational planes.

- *Single-leg stance:* Only one leg contacts the ground (e.g., a single-leg squat) at a time. This stance is the most difficult due to absorbing force and distributing force relative to strength demands of the athlete. In addition, this stance is difficult since proficiency is demanded in all three planes of motion. The athlete must prepare to move throughout a sequence of movements to put together a movement skill to be used for any direction while reacting to the continuous demands of the game.

Here are some of the major characteristics observed during deceleration technique:

- *Stride length:* Transfers from a long movement to short movement through distance
- *Stride frequency:* Gradually decreases from a faster movement to slower movement in correlation to the technique, time, and distance of the movement
- *Torso lean:* Transition from a smaller forward angle to a more vertical or upright position during the process of slowing down
- *Arm swing:* Goes from a small movement to a relatively still movement to match stride length
- *Velocity:* Progresses from faster to slower during the time of the movement

Change of Direction

Like many team sports, an athlete's quality of fundamental movement is foundational to their general movement qualities, such as acceleration, deceleration, and change of direction. Change of direction is a small part in all the physical qualities that an athlete owns, but it is linked to almost all other movement skills required for soccer. As discussed in the deceleration section, soccer demands that an athlete quickly decelerate, transition, and then reaccelerate in the same or another direction. The ability to adjust rapidly to the various movements and different situations is necessary within the game. Hence, **change of direction** is a component of agility that is influenced by many factors including strength, power, speed, mobility, stability, coordination, biomechanics, and decision-making.

Soccer is a sport in which athletes are constantly moving during the game. This means that reaction and understanding of the environment is critical to change of direction. The previous sections on acceleration and deceleration discussed the prioritization of the linear plane of motion while facing the action of play. Nonetheless, soccer athletes must react to the ball, contact, opponent, and teammates around them all the time. Therefore, change of direction emphasizes lateral and rotational planes of motion within movement skills. The position of the foot initiates how the entire body adapts to change of direction. First, before the foot contacts the ground, the ankle should maintain dorsiflexion to best absorb and transfer force. Next, the **foot position** works better when the main contact with the ground is through the forefoot (e.g., balls of the feet). Establishing an inside or outside edge (of the shoe with the ground) during foot contact is essential in dictating the degree of lateral or rotational movement required.

As the foot transitions through the surface, the ankle, knee, and hip go from absorbing force to generating force. This follow-through by the ankle, knee, and hip is the basis of power development for change of direction. Two major factors affect change of direction in relation to **foot location**: how far the foot is placed outside the body's base of support and where the foot is placed outside the body's base of support. When looking at both factors together, the location and distance the foot is placed (in relation to the body's base of support) guides change of direction. Where the foot is placed directly affects the angle of the lower leg (i.e., ankle, knee, and hip). The athlete's angle of attack during movement can be small or large in relation to the center of mass. This angle of attack dictates how aggressive the athlete can be with the movement in the lateral and rotational planes. At the same time, the upper body lean (e.g., trunk or torso) is coupled with the lower body angle to maintain synergy and the ability to overcome gravity quickly. The total body angle creates an optimal position for reactive force production.

Athletes must respond and always change direction during the game. The proper coordination of foot position, foot location, and angles of attack support movement skill qualities. Change of direction is a base movement to more established movement skills like shuffle, cut, crossover, drop step, open step, and more. Hip control through flexion and extension is necessary for athletes during linear, lateral, and rotational movement skills. As the physical demands of the match increase for an athlete, so will the velocity and ground reaction forces elevate during change of direction within the game. These game requirements put a spotlight on an individual's genetics and training adaptation during this linking movement. Improved strength, power, and elasticity will allow change of direction to be better expressed by the individual. During high-velocity change of direction movements, dynamic hip control integrates more abduction, adduction, external rotation, and internal rotation into this base movement.

During a match, an athlete needs an extensive number of physical attributes. Agility is a major physical attribute and a catalyst within movement skills. How well athletes move and respond to situations throughout the game is pivotal to the team's success. Understanding the general biomechanics of movement and the relationship to basic aspects of agility is the foundation to improving movement skill qualities. Change of direction is a powerful linking movement within movement skill. It is connected to all movements throughout the game and influences an athlete's efficiency, performance, and durability.

In summary, here are a few characteristics outlined during change of direction technique:

- *Foot position:* Has a small to large degree of emphasis on the inside or outside edge of the foot
- *Foot location:* Is determined by distance and where the foot is placed from the center of the body
- *Angle of attack:* Is guided by how aggressive the lean and angle is produced by the overall body position

GENERAL PHYSIOLOGICAL ANALYSIS

Soccer involves a range of energy systems to drive physical performance, potentially more than any team sport. Some sports might require a greater demand of aerobic endurance (e.g., running a marathon), and other sports might place a higher importance on power (e.g., sprinting 100 m [109 yd]). But few sports test the human body's full ability to perform within multiple energy systems across the conditioning spectrum as soccer does.

Soccer is challenging because it uses a blend of intensity (e.g., high power) and effort (e.g., high aerobic endurance) relatively at the same time for an extended duration. Some sports have a specific need for power or aerobic endurance, while soccer has a unique mix of random actions, which makes it difficult for athletes. When considering the physiological characteristics for soccer, it requires a special balance of both explosive power and aerobic endurance that is specific to the game.

Each position within the sport requires a different integration of power, aerobic endurance, and types of movement skills. Some athletes display a high level of power, and other athletes show a low level. At the same time, athletes can display a high level of aerobic endurance, and other athletes show a low level. Each position within soccer requires specific demands of power and aerobic endurance. Many times, it can be beneficial for forwards to have a higher level of power to create space from the opposition and chances to score. Midfielders usually benefit from a higher level of aerobic endurance in repeated sprints or runs during transitional aspects of play. Defenders often profit from a higher level of power while marking an opponent during set pieces (e.g., corner kicks and free kicks) at goal and a higher level of aerobic endurance while supporting defensive high-pressure team tactics with the midfielders and forwards. Finding the proper balance of energy systems between high levels of power and aerobic endurance specific to each position is pivotal for soccer.

Like many team sports, work capacity (e.g., sprint capacity) in soccer is necessary for athletes and teams to be successful. An individual's ability to produce a high-intensity action—or high-intensity actions in quick succession with brief bouts of recovery over a relatively short amount of time (e.g., power)—is fundamental. Research shows that "the most extreme play during a match can see players perform up to five high-intensity actions within a 1-minute period (one high-intensity action every 12 seconds) and seven within 111 seconds (one every 15 seconds)" (6). In addition, moderate to low intensity action or actions over a long period of time is foundational to physical preparation. That said, "players may also experience temporary fatigue during a game. Male elite football players have on a number of occasions been shown to engage in reduced high-intensity exercise, below game average, in the five-minute period following the most intense period of the match" (9). The better teams and players resist fatigue (e.g., capacity) while maintaining a consistent quality of action or actions improves game play. The synergy of power, aerobic endurance, and capacity training should be highlighted in soccer conditioning.

Incorporating all of these primary principles and different elements into a structure is essential in providing comprehensive conditioning for soccer athletes. All physical actions or combination of actions within the game require a physiological response that needs some further explanation to better understand and implement.

Aerobic System

The aerobic energy system uses oxygen to facilitate energy and is the main system responsible for long-term performance. When the oxygen supply is adequate to provide the energy needed to working muscles, the aerobic system is capable of providing the majority of fuel needed for aerobic endurance. Executing low-intensity activity over long periods of time uses the oxidative (aerobic) system, which consists of either glucose or fat oxidation. This system is the slowest but has the largest range in producing adequate energy supply as long as the intensity matches demand.

Assessing activities of long duration and low intensity, the aerobic system increases during prolonged activities lasting longer than three minutes. The aerobic system works in coordination with the anaerobic system during maximal output (e.g., high-intensity actions). This foundational and well-developed aerobic system is necessary for soccer athletes to elevate the anaerobic system (i.e., phosphagen and glycolysis) to maintain high power output during a match.

Performance activities of long, continuous duration relate to a soccer athlete's aerobic capacity, which is determined by two valuable components: oxygen usage and substrate availability. When the human body is productive these two components, along with physiological factors like $\dot{V}O_2$ max, anaerobic threshold, and relative work intensity, will improve an athlete's aerobic endurance capacity.

Another variable that is significant to the equation of aerobic capacity is **$\dot{V}O_2$ kinetics**. An athlete's ability to shift from using the aerobic system to the anaerobic system and then back again while maintaining low-intensity activity (e.g., walking or jogging) is a basic demand for the game. For instance, sprinting to jogging to sprinting to jogging happens repeatedly throughout soccer. During these periods, if the energy systems involved are agile in transition, athletes will be efficient in the transitional energy supply needed. At the end of the day, an athlete with a faster transition of the aerobic system decreases the anaerobic system involvement, which can be a deciding factor in enhancing physical performance for soccer (11). According to Dupont and McCall, "All this implies that the aerobic energy system is highly taxed during a soccer match. The ability to recover between repetitions of activities and maintain (overall) high intensity during the match is crucial for a soccer player" (8).

Aerobic and Anaerobic Systems

Medium-intensity activity uses both the aerobic and anaerobic energy systems. Producing medium-intensity (e.g., running) actions over a moderate duration of time displays an athlete's ability to maintain power and aerobic endurance. Transition actions are needed between low-intensity and high-intensity activity to reach higher levels of performance. The aerobic system uses aerobic glycolysis, and the anaerobic system uses anaerobic glycolysis simultaneously for energy production.

Aerobic glycolysis (i.e., aerobic system) and anaerobic glycolysis (i.e., anaerobic system) support moderate-intensity actions generally between 60 and 180 seconds. This interconnection of energy systems and energy supply will always happen in some way, large or small, during a game. This merging of both systems is pivotal to performance and dictated by time and intensity of the activity.

Developing conditioning for soccer requires awareness and insight of the comprehensive actions in the game. From a physiological point of view the sport is about how well athletes produce energy. It requires a multitude of energy-generating systems for human performance to be versatile and efficient.

Anaerobic System

The anaerobic energy system uses no oxygen to generate energy and is the primary system responsible for short-term maximal performance. Performing high-intensity actions over a relatively short duration of time is related to an athlete's potential to rapidly develop power and use the anaerobic system. The anaerobic system consists of the phosphagen system and anaerobic glycolysis. The phosphagen system replenishes adenosine triphosphate (ATP) with the use of the substrate phosphocreatine (PCr), whereas anaerobic glycolysis metabolizes glucose and does not require the presence of oxygen.

When examining activities of short duration and high intensity, the phosphagen system is emphasized during physical bursts of up to 10 seconds. To complement these brief maximal efforts, the body uses predominantly anaerobic glycolysis during high-intensity actions lasting between 10 and approximately 60 seconds. These energy systems coordinate together; they do not automatically change from one system to the other. Rather, the energy systems overlap and integrate together while the energy supply of emphasis (i.e., energy production) transitions through each system. All of this is directly related to the variables of time and intensity of the powerful work performed.

Increasing physical performance in soccer requires anaerobic capacity (e.g., sprint capacity). High-intensity activities lasting from a few seconds to around one minute are normally the most decisive periods of time during a match. The ability to maximize a powerful action or a series of explosive actions in succession is usually the differentiating factor of an individual's

POSSESSION GAMES

One way to address these issues of conditioning is through the game itself. Team practice and drills allow athletes to work on different technical and tactical parts of the sport. As such, possession games (i.e., small-sided, medium-sided, and large-sided) can be an important strategy for enhancing athletes' technical and tactical development. In particular, when done with an understanding of the physical side of performance, these possession games can be used as a method for improving athletes' power and aerobic endurance characteristics.

Possession games feature a collaboration of offense, defense, and transition play needed for teams to improve. However, sometimes possession games (e.g., rondo drills) might not deliver the conditioning results that athletes and teams need from practice. This might happen with athletes who participate only in a portion of matches, do not start in matches on a regular basis, or do not take part in matches at all. Because these athletes do not participate in continuous match competition, coaches must consider how to return them to match-level intensities. Additionally, athletes returning to practice from a short-term or long-term injury might need supplementary conditioning to bridge the gap with personal energy system deficiencies.

physical capability. Naturally, genetics can play a role in determining an athlete's performance potential with regards to physical development. Still, all soccer athletes can enhance overall performance through anaerobic capacity conditioning.

Anaerobic capacity measures an athlete's ability to resist fatigue. In soccer, athletes must overcome fatigue in the body to work at a high intensity for long durations. Anaerobic capacity is important for defenders and attackers because these athletes produce high-intensity efforts during critical moments of a match, and midfielders face repeated long periods of high-intensity actions within a game, which requires higher anaerobic capacity. Additionally, some tactical formations can place a special demand on anaerobic capacity for certain positions. Studying the positions within the sport allows for a better understanding of the specific anaerobic capacity demands for each athlete. Upgrading training methods will improve the proficiency to withstand fatigue during high-intensity match play.

POSITION-SPECIFIC ANALYSIS

Soccer is a unique sport in many ways. It is a game that is played with the feet and seldom with the hands (unless the athlete is the goalkeeper). For several reasons, developing and maintaining foot-eye coordination with and without the ball is more difficult than hand-eye coordination. The environment of soccer places a responsibility on the athlete to be able to respond to situations in all directions; that is, the athlete must be able to move well in 360 degrees at any time during the match. Quality of movement is essential in soccer, but the capacity to express it efficiently and quickly with power on a continuous basis is ideal. As mentioned before, agility is a major movement attribute integrated into movement skills and is a partnership between coordination and skill (13).

Increased agility directly affects movement skills that allow athletes to take advantage of certain moments within the sport. The game is not executed one movement at a time in isolation and with programmed responses. It is free-flowing series of movement qualities to create a complete movement skill. A movement skill can range from simple to complex depending on the traits of the athlete, the position, and the game. In addition, a movement skill transitions from one to a series of movement skills combined rapidly and explosively during a match.

The primary movement skills in soccer are change of direction; multidirectional speed; acceleration; deceleration; shuffle and cut; and the rotational movement skills of the crossover, open step, and drop step.

Change of Direction

The development of the movement attributes is a pillar in the foundation of movement skills for soccer. Change of direction, which is a part of agility, in general is influenced by the combination of the athlete and the task (i.e., movement for soccer) within the game. This makes change of direction meaningful as a movement that can be combined with agility, but change of direction has more of a singular, controlled focus to support the athlete during a match. When analyzing the task characteristics of the movement, this isolated perspective of change of direction and movement qualities are the platform for agility to be expressed by the athlete. These movements in the singular dimension have no influence from the genuine soccer environment. Sometimes the ability to change direction is called *basic agility* when it refers to how an athlete executes the task in isolation with no effect from teammates or opponents. This is represented in many types of drills that prepare soccer athletes in practice or buildup to team play. These kinds of drills are done all the time with or without the ball as fundamentals for soccer training. Change of direction is the entire body moving quickly with speed and direction to a situation that is already programmed and controlled. For instance, the athlete knows the structure before starting the drill; the velocity, route, positioning, and layout of the exercise have been decided by the athlete before the process begins. Drills like this develop the physical movement qualities but not in combination with the soccer environment and involve no decision-making or reaction. This means that the athlete has no response to the soccer environment, which consists of the team aspects of tactical skills, technical skills, psychology, and more.

These kinds of drills in soccer develop the individual movement attributes for athletes. The evolution of movement qualities progresses with the inclusion of the athlete, task, and soccer environment. Understanding the environment and the relationship to the athlete and task within soccer is beneficial. The environment within soccer can range from easy to difficult. The addition of a simple stimulus (i.e., visual, auditory, or tactile) into the environment elicits a different response from the athlete, an ability that is sometimes referred to as *reactive agility* because of the reaction to a stimulus that has been added to the environment. This promotes an environment in which the drill is not predetermined for the athlete at the beginning. More importantly, the athlete does not know the exact moment the drill will start, which requires reactive decision-making and strategy usage versus a programmed response. The athlete's ability to process the single stimulus with the correct result is challenged. For example, the athlete is waiting for the coach to give a signal to begin the drill. The athlete knows that the coach will cue right or left to signal the start and direction in which the athlete will proceed. The coach has also added another reaction element to the process of the drill. The coach has informed the athlete that the direction pointed (i.e., right or left) by the coach is not the same direction that the athlete will go. The athlete actually will go in the opposite direction from what the coach has signaled. Of course, this places an emphasis on the athlete to be quick in movement but even quicker in response to the exercise stimulus in the correct direction. Reactive agility drills develop the physical and reactive attributes of movement qualities that support the soccer environment.

Multidirectional Speed

Agility is an important movement attribute and central to all types of movement skills. The traditional perspective on agility references a collection of exercises and drills instead of a modern perspective on movement types. The wide range of movement qualities and movement types needs to be developed in soccer for a better transition from practice to games. This understanding of the relationship with biomechanics, to movement, to movement types, to movement skills allows drills to better integrate into the match environment. **Multidirectional speed** is a collection of movement skills that consists of all movement attributes from closed-skill (i.e., nonreactive) to open-skill (i.e., reactive) situations that happen throughout the game. This is why multidirectional speed best represents the movement quality demands placed on soccer athletes other than just agility or change of direction. **Closed skills** consist of single movement patterns or movement pattern sequences during nonreactive drills or game situations. The athlete understands the drill or situation before starting and begins when ready. **Open skills** include single movement patterns or movement pattern sequences during reactive drills or game situations. The athlete might or might not understand the drill or situation expectations while moving through the moment and reacting to visual, auditory, or tactile stimuli or a combination of these.

The soccer environment is complex, and the relationship with multidirectional speed is comprehensive. Creating a framework to organize the soccer environment allows physical attributes within the game to be prioritized into movement types, which transfers into dynamic multidirectional speed. Understanding the technical and tactical skills within the game establishes a baseline reference about the soccer environment and multidirectional speed. For context, the environment for soccer can be segmented into three general sections. (These segments can have more detail and levels, but this can be used as a guideline.) The basic environment for the athlete is the position (i.e., goalkeepers, defenders, midfielders, and forwards) or role within soccer. The basic environment of soccer includes the general technical skills such as receiving, passing, dribbling, shooting, volleying, heading, tackling, and challenging. The basic environment of technical skills is the athletes' understanding of the fundamental strategies of the game. The intermediate environment for the athlete is his or her position in relation to the individual strategies and the team's formation and style of play. The intermediate environment of soccer consists of progressed tactical skills of the game such as receiving at speed, passing with pace, dribbling with power, shooting with placement, volleying with accuracy, heading with force, tackling with technique, and challenging with timing. Additionally, the intermediate environment of technical skills is the understanding of different formations (e.g., 5-4-1, 4-5-1, 4-2-3-1, 4-1-4-1, 4-4-2, 3-5-2, 3-4-3) used by the team and what style of play (e.g., possession style, long-ball style, direct style, counterattack style) is beneficial to the team. The advanced environment for the soccer athlete is the position in combination with the phases of play and team strategies. The rate of decision-making is faster within the game. The advanced environment of soccer requires a higher level of technical features of the game like combining receiving, dribbling, and passing or tackling, dribbling, and shooting in quick succession. Also, the advanced environment showcases tactical details of the game like offense, defense, transition, and set pieces. In this advanced tactical environment, athletes develop a better understanding of how defenders connect with midfielders, midfielders connect with forwards, defenders connect with forwards, and the culmination of connecting all athletes, positions, and blocks of positions as one within the ultimate team framework.

The soccer environment places a lot on the athlete to process at once and continuously navigate throughout the complexities of the game; thus, multidirectional speed is a necessity.

The capacity for the athlete to change direction well within the game relates to the athlete's understanding of information and stimulus to react accordingly. If done properly, the movement is quick, efficient, repeatable, and minimizes unnecessary steps with the ground by the athlete during change-of-direction situations. Reactive agility is a key attribute to movement, but reactive agility by itself does not provide the full arsenal of movement types required for the game. This is why multidirectional speed is a better representation of all of soccer's movement qualities. How the athlete relates to the task—but more importantly to the task *and* environment—is crucial. This is why developing and maintaining basic agility through physical training is good as a foundation for the game. Furthermore, progressing physical training to involve reactive agility is better for the soccer athlete. Finally, advancing the physical training to integrate with technical and tactical skills is best for transitioning multidirectional speed into the complete soccer environment.

Multidirectional speed repeatably uses closed skills and open skills in the environment of soccer. Multidirectional speed uses many variables and factors to create the overall multidirectional speed qualities. These factors emphasize attributes such as change of direction, anthropometrics, biomechanics, visual scanning, pattern recognition, reaction time, strength, power, speed, and more for both nonreactive and reactive drills and situations within the game (12). The collection of all these multidirectional speed qualities must also be studied in the relationship between movement skills and sport skills together. The different aspects of closed skills and open skills displayed within movement skills and sport skills provide progressions of a single pattern and a pattern sequence. The patterns can advance further with generic and specific stimuli for both movement skills and sport skills. Soccer athletes recognize the variables of stimuli that are encountered while playing the game. Sometimes the specific stimulus can be subtle and not easy to understand. This ability to process a specific stimulus quickly and efficiently with movement skills or sport skills is usually found in more skilled soccer athletes. The best athletes have the capability to absorb and transfer a specific stimulus rapidly with both movement skills and sport skills combined. The transfer of multidirectional speed and the multidirectional speed qualities into the partnership of movement skills and sport skills is key. This provides the platform for soccer athletes to develop and progress the physical attributes for the game.

The structure of multidirectional speed outlines the main types of movement skills in soccer. The movement skills to follow are not all the movement types within the game but represent the movements with a high physical demand or a critical influence on the game. The development of movement skills should be integrated into the training of technical skills and tactical skills within the soccer environment.

Acceleration

Analyzing the movement skill of acceleration from the movement start to movement finish provides soccer position–specific application. At the moment of acceleration, the athlete responds to the direction and intent in the soccer environment. The soccer athlete decides how fast and how far the movement will be at that instant. The athlete has to decide if the start is mostly linear in direction or at an angle to the orientation the athlete is facing to the soccer environment. The first few steps in the movement represent the start of acceleration. The number of foot contacts during the *start stage of acceleration* is determined mostly by the athlete, who has momentum or no momentum. The momentum coming from the athlete's previous actions (e.g., jogging or running) dictate fewer steps at the start stage of acceleration. In comparison, no momentum (e.g., standing still or walking) involve more steps at the start stage of acceleration to break inertia and overcome gravity. The start stage in acceleration is always influenced by proper acceleration technique.

The quality push technique is applied by the athlete during the movement skill of acceleration. The start stage involves one, two, or three steps (e.g., 1 to 3 yards [0.9-2.7 m]) progressing to the transition stage within acceleration. After the first three foot contacts, the athlete creates power through the start stage of acceleration. The *transition stage of acceleration* continues directly after the start stage. The beginning of the transition stage occurs after two to four steps depending on the previous momentum (e.g., walk or run) generated from the start stage. The distance of the acceleration is dictated by some key factors. The main factor is how far the athlete has to accelerate before transitioning into the actions of walking or jogging. The range of an acceleration distance can differ considerably, but the majority of accelerations are between 10 and 20 yards (9-18 m) during the game. In this instance of an acceleration starting and finishing in a single bout, the end of the transition stage is around eight to eleven steps depending on previous momentum actions such as walking, jogging, or running. Moreover, proper technique in combination with characteristics such as strength and power all contribute to the end distance of the acceleration. The beginning to finish of the transition stage of acceleration is around 4 or 5 yards (3.6-4.6 m) to 18 to 20 yards (16-18 m) in relation to the previous factors mentioned. The relationship between the majority of the accelerations during a match (i.e., 10-20 yards [9-18 m]) and the range of the transition stage of acceleration (i.e., 4-5 yards [3.6-4.6 m] to 18-20 yards [16-18 m]) has some major similarities. Of course, the start stage of acceleration is critical to driving the athlete into a better transition stage of acceleration, but acceleration as a whole is a crucial movement skill for soccer athletes to develop in the sport.

As athletes create more speed during acceleration, several main traits progress with this movement skill. Acceleration is produced by the continuous continuum of the stance phase and swing phase through the acceleration cycle. As the velocity of acceleration increases during the start stage and transition stage, the forward torso lean becomes less aggressive during the movement and distance of the acceleration. This is also the moment when soccer athletes still react to the environment and have to make adjustments to how fast and how far the acceleration continues. Additionally, the athlete has to accelerate through a path that is not straight in direction. Many times, the game demands that an athlete's acceleration be in more of a curved pattern or a modified zigzag pattern, which implements skills such as foot position and foot location discussed in the change of direction movement section (pages 24-25). During the start and transition stages of acceleration, the goal is to minimize deceleration as much as possible until the movement skill is close to finishing or linking into another movement skill. Acceleration is valuable in soccer, but often the athlete must use the action of high-speed running to achieve a longer distance in the sport. Acceleration transitions into absolute speed in these exact situations in the game. **Absolute speed** is demanded when the athlete must go from one penalty box to the other penalty box (e.g., end to end) on the field or from one phase to another phase of play as quickly as possible. The momentum and technique from acceleration requires a progression of traits to assist absolute speed. Traits such as stride length, stride frequency, torso lean, arm swing, and velocity transition gradually to support the movement skill of absolute speed. Several moments during the game require the athlete to use the movement skill of absolute speed for 20 to 80 yards (18-73 m), whether linearly or in more of an arcing pattern. The number of foot contacts with the ground will vary depending on each athlete's physical attributes, distance, and pattern of the absolute speed moment. Understanding the absolute speed qualities allows for proper position-specific training for athletes.

Deceleration

The actions of high-speed running and sprinting typically connect into other movement skills. One of the most common movement skills to follow acceleration or acceleration into absolute speed is deceleration. The speed generated from the movement skill of acceleration or absolute speed during the match also will determine the distance it takes for the soccer athlete to decelerate properly with actions such as stopping, walking, or jogging. Deceleration usually is a linking movement skill to other movement skills. Rarely does an athlete decelerate to a stopping action and then follow by doing nothing. The physical demands of the sport illustrate that athletes regularly decelerate only to reaccelerate again. Backpedaling is another movement skill commonly linked with deceleration. Once adequate positioning is achieved from deceleration, which requires maintaining and creating a proper stance, the soccer athlete can link deceleration into a backpedal in a linear or angled direction. The details highlighted about deceleration and backpedal qualities can be used in training athletes for specific positions in soccer.

Shuffle and Cut

The game of soccer demands athletes to be able to move in 360 degrees. The movement skill of **shuffle and cut** emphasizes movement types that place an importance on nonlinear movements. The structure of the shuffle and cut movement skills focus on the lateral plane of motion. It is typical to perform the movements at 90 degrees, but it is very common to execute the shuffle and cut in more of a diagonal forward (e.g., 45 degrees) or diagonal backward (e.g., 135 degrees) movement to the orientation the body is facing. The phases of play during the match (e.g., offense, defense, and transition) demand that soccer athletes regularly use movement skills in combination, such as acceleration, deceleration, and then shuffle or cut. The priority of the movement during the game can transition quickly from a linear to a lateral priority for the athlete. This movement skill places increased stress onto the body due to the change in direction movement. In examining the shuffle and cut, the movement can be split into two general stages of deceleration and acceleration. First, the deceleration stage requires the athlete to rapidly absorb and stabilize against the force of the foot into the ground efficiently. Second, the acceleration stage of the shuffle and cut necessitates that the athlete quickly produce and propel the foot through the ground powerfully at the angle necessary. The distance of the foot from the ground should be minimal to promote quality during both the deceleration stage and acceleration stage of the shuffle and cut. Recognizing the differences between linear- and lateral-emphasized movement skill qualities assists in training athletes for the demands of specific positions.

Rotational Movement Skills

The structure of multidirectional speed emphasizes linear, lateral, and rotational movement skills. The capability of the soccer athlete to move effectively through movement skills that emphasize the linear or lateral planes of motion are foundational to the game. The more demanding movement skills require the rotational plane of motion.

The rotational movement skills consist of crossover, open step, and drop step. These movements can be completed with the body rotating at various degrees of rotation (e.g., 45, 90, 135, and 180 degrees).

The swing leg of defender Meghan Klingenberg (#25) coming across her stance leg during the crossover rotational movement.

Crossover

The **crossover** is facilitated by the athlete's swing leg (i.e., lead leg) coming across the stance leg (i.e., down leg) with minimal to maximal rotation from the upper body, lower body, and hips. The movement skill is typically used when the athlete is facing side-on to the playing situation. The crossover is efficient during times in the match when the distance needed to be covered by the soccer athlete is large, ranging from 20 to 40 yards (18-37 m) and beyond. The movement allows the athlete to be explosive with quality technique in the first few steps and more. During phases of play in transition, the athlete needs to get from one part of the field to another quickly. This has been predetermined by the soccer athlete in the moments leading up to the situation. Longer distances covered by the athlete during the match usually will start with a movement skills sequence of crossover, acceleration, to absolute speed.

Open Step

The **open step** is executed when the athlete's swing leg opens up in the opposite direction from the stance leg with minimal rotation or angle. The open step is usually used when the soccer athlete is side-on to the playing situation. The movement skill is mainly used within the game when the distance covered by the athlete is undetermined. For instance, the playing situation is evolving while the athlete is moving. The distance could be shorter (e.g., 2-6 yards [1.8-5.5 m]) or longer (e.g., 10-30 yards [9-27 m]) depending on the soccer environment. A typical observed movement skills sequence is open step, acceleration, to deceleration.

Drop Step

The **drop step** is accomplished when the athlete's swing leg opens up in the opposite direction from the stance leg with maximal rotation. The movement skill is displayed when the soccer athlete is facing directly opposite to the playing situation and must turn around rapidly. The drop step allows the athlete to be powerful in one step in a 180-degree movement. Several times during the game, the ball is played over the top and behind the defending athlete (e.g., long ball) while the attacking athlete accelerates through to get to the ball first. The defending athlete must turn around and quickly try to get to the ball before the opponent. Taking one step as opposed to several steps to turn around efficiently can determine the success during this situation in the match. The movement skills sequence might be drop step, acceleration, to absolute speed for the defender. The crossover, open step, and drop step movement skills require the athlete to drop into an appropriate base phase to establish body lean and angles (e.g., feet, knees, and hips) to push through the ground. Depending on the selected movement skill, the athlete will use the foot position (e.g., inside or outside) from the stance leg to produce ground contact force at the proper angles. Training soccer athletes for the physical attributes of a specific position within the game directly relates to multidirectional speed. Each position demands certain multidirectional speed qualities from linear, lateral, and rotational movement skills.

In modern soccer, identifying athletes' physical strength and weaknesses with the physical demands of the game is essential. The sport has progressed to the point where technology can be used to varying degrees to assist in the process. The ability to use match tracking analysis (e.g., Amisco and Prozone) during games is beneficial in examining the differences between athletes, positions, formations, and style of play for the team. Comparing match performance data with athletic performance profiling (i.e., from performance testing) develops an analytics platform for athletes and the position-specific demands for the team. Integrating all of this with GPS tracking systems data from practice on a regular basis develops a performance baseline for each athlete. This allows the analytics to recognize trends and tendencies for the athletes and positions within the team. The culmination of the performance data within a system for the athletes, the positions, and the game establishes a foundation for success. Movement skills and sport skills within soccer are always fused together. The capacity to evaluate, isolate, and integrate allows coaches and strength and conditioning professionals to develop the principles to improve soccer athletes for specific positions in the game.

Forwards, midfielders, defenders, and goalkeepers have different physical demands in the game. All positions require movement skills with and without the ball in possession. The movement skills previously discussed can be adjusted to the appropriate technical skills and tactical skills per position. Figures 2.2 through 2.5 highlight the primary and secondary movement skills for each position. This general summary is a basic review and intended to guide awareness, more than anything, about multidirectional speed qualities. Each soccer athlete uses all the primary movement skills but with a higher or lower priority in context to the specific position.

Forwards		
Phases of play		
Offense	Defense	Transition
Hierarchy of movement skills		
Acceleration	**Acceleration**	**Acceleration**
Deceleration	Deceleration	Absolute speed
Shuffle and cut	Shuffle and cut	Deceleration
Open step	Open step	Crossover

Figure 2.2   Movement skills for forwards (primary and secondary).

Midfielders		
Phases of play		
Offense	Defense	Transition
Hierarchy of movement skills		
Acceleration	**Acceleration**	**Absolute speed**
Deceleration	Deceleration	Acceleration
Shuffle and cut	Shuffle and cut	Open step
Open step	Crossover	Crossover

Figure 2.3   Movement skills for midfielders (primary and secondary).

Defenders		
Phases of play		
Offense	Defense	Transition
Hierarchy of movement skills		
Acceleration	**Acceleration**	**Acceleration**
Deceleration	Deceleration	Absolute speed
Shuffle and cut	Backpedal	Drop step
Open step	Shuffle and cut	Crossover

Figure 2.4   Movement skills for defenders (primary and secondary).

Goalkeepers		
Phases of play		
Offense	Defense	Transition
Hierarchy of movement skills		
Acceleration	**Backpedal**	**Shuffle and cut**
Deceleration	Shuffle and cut	Acceleration
Shuffle and cut	Crossover	Deceleration
Open step	Open step	Open step

Figure 2.5 Movement skills for goalkeepers (primary and secondary).

CONCLUSION

The relationship between action and movement creates a context to better understand performance data from all perspectives in soccer. Developing a synergy with the multitude of systems in the body allows athletes to improve specific and overall physical attributes for the game. Establishing a performance baseline of the physical demands for the athlete, the position, and the sport enhances strength and conditioning solutions for the athlete. A systematic and logical approach to multidirectional speed for soccer builds efficient, effective, and quality athletes.

3

TESTING PROTOCOLS AND ATHLETE ASSESSMENT

ERNIE RIMER AND JO CLUBB

Along with technical, tactical, and psychological determinants, the physical component of soccer is crucial for health and performance. As an intermittent team sport, soccer requires well-developed strength, power, speed, agility, and high-intensity aerobic endurance capacity. Athlete assessments can provide valuable information for supporting the process of developing such capacities. Common reasons for carrying out athlete assessments are

- assessing fitness baselines to inform individualized training strategies,
- monitoring changes in fitness and fatigue to gauge readiness for training and competition,
- evaluating the effectiveness of a training program or specific intervention,
- guiding stratification for injury risk–reduction strategies,
- establishing trained healthy baselines for rehabilitation monitoring and return-to-play progressions, and
- comparing physical capacities during recruiting and selection processes.

To fulfill the objectives, coaches are encouraged to establish effective data collection, storage, analysis, and reporting strategies. Quality visualization and reporting can facilitate meaningful conversations, which can both educate and foster relationships with athletes, coaches, and other key stakeholders. The value of an assessment is not in the athlete's raw data, but as a vehicle to support objective decision-making around an athlete's program.

GENERAL TESTING GUIDELINES

Useful test data must demonstrate the following critical factors (19):

- *Validity:* The test measures the characteristics it is supposed to measure.
- *Reliability:* The test provides a consistent result when repeatedly performed without an intervention in between.
- *Sensitivity:* The test can detect small but meaningful changes in performance.

According to team sport and soccer research, the tests in this chapter meet the above-mentioned criteria. However, it is important to acknowledge that how a test protocol is conducted can influence the validity and reliability of that testing session. For instance, poor athlete motivation or effort can deteriorate reliability of an otherwise good test. Therefore, consistency and attention to detail are essential in minimizing random sources of error. General guidelines to facilitate precise data collection include

- calibrating all equipment according to manufacturer guidelines;
- standardizing testing protocols, including consistent warm-ups and data collection procedures (e.g., using pen and paper forms, devices, or software);
- standardizing the testing environment, including coach instructions; and
- establishing consistent testing schedules in terms of timing (e.g., in relation to a game or time of day) and test order.

Consideration should be given to how assessments will be implemented within the specific environment. Coaches should consider logistical constraints, such as the number of athletes to be tested, time constraints, familiarization protocols, potential fatiguing effects, and staffing requirements. It is our responsibility as coaches to ensure all testing is a worthwhile use of the athletes' time.

Coaches are encouraged to stay up to date with the ongoing advancement of soccer assessment technology and research. In conjunction with the test protocols defined in this chapter, special summaries are provided to allude to the evolving landscape of best practice in soccer preparation while offering ways for coaches to go further with their test data.

TESTING PROTOCOLS

For this chapter, a needs analysis of the physical demands of soccer was conducted, and the following physical qualities were identified: strength, power, speed and agility, and high-intensity aerobic endurance capacity. For each of those qualities, evidence-based tests have been selected for discussion in this chapter.

For each assessment included, the purpose, equipment, setup, testing protocol, and descriptive data have been described. In some cases, a variety of approaches exist to assess a specific quality. It remains the responsibility of the coach to determine the most suitable assessment, given the specific testing purpose and environment, as discussed in the General Testing Guidelines section. Similarly, evidence-based testing protocols are provided, along with coaching tips that can promote validity and reliability in data collection. Where available, descriptive data from the literature are provided. However, caution is urged when interpreting such data given the potential variation across populations (see the Appropriate Data Ranges sidebar below), testing procedures, and environments. Coaches are encouraged to determine normative data for the population(s) they serve.

APPROPRIATE DATA RANGES

While published data might not always match a specific population, crossover often exists in normative data across sports given age, sex, and competition level. Therefore, published data from other sports can provide coaches with a starting point to understand appropriate ranges of performance for a given assessment.

Test Finder

Adductor and Abductor Strength 46

Countermovement Jump 49

Hamstring Strength 45

Isometric Belt-Squat 44

Isometric Mid-Thigh Pull 42

Modified 505 52

6 × 30-Meter (33 Yards) Repeated Sprint Ability Test 55

30-Meter (33 Yards) Sprint 54

30-15 Intermittent Fitness Test 62

Yo-Yo Test 58

STRENGTH TESTS

Strength underpins power and also enhances kicking velocity (82), and therefore can be seen as an important capacity for soccer performance. In addition, higher strength capacities can mitigate injury risk among team-sport athletes (46). Consequently, strength improvements can serve to simultaneously improve both physical performance and reduce the odds of suffering a musculoskeletal injury. Therefore, strength tests can enable objective tracking of these capacities.

Paolo Bruno/Getty Images

Strength fortifies power and directly translates to kicking velocity.

ISOMETRIC MID-THIGH PULL

Purpose

Isometric assessments of strength might be preferred to their dynamic counterparts such as 1RM testing, due to increased safety, practicality, time efficiency, and reliability (10). The isometric mid-thigh pull test (IMTP) is one such example that is widely used to assess maximal strength. It provides measures of peak force, expressed both absolute and relative to body weight, as well as rate of force development indices. Force–time metrics from the IMTP have been associated with jumping and sprinting abilities in collegiate soccer athletes (40).

Equipment

The IMTP requires a force plate, a barbell, and a means of fixing the height of the bar. Certain manufacturers produce racks specifically designed for fixing the barbell for the IMTP. Alternatively, the barbell can be fixed underneath the safety bars in a traditional squat rack or by adding adequate weight to the bar to ensure the athlete cannot move the load. A goniometer can be used to measure joint angles.

Setup

Before testing, calibrate the force platform(s) according to manufacturer guidelines. A sampling frequency of 1,000 hertz has been recommended for reliability (18). The test is performed with the athlete standing on a force platform with the fixed barbell positioned at mid-thigh height. The athlete should stand with the shoulders behind the bar, an upright torso, knees over the toes, and feet shoulder-width apart (23). Joint angles must be kept consistent due to the influence of the length–tension relationship. Research recommends the use of a hip angle at approximately 145 degrees and a knee angle between 130 and 140 degrees (10).

Testing Protocol

1. Ensure the force platform is set to zero after calibration and before the athlete steps on.
2. Conduct a standardized warm-up involving dynamic flexibility exercises.
3. Once on the force plate, the specific software might require a collection period for the athlete's body mass. Ensure he or she remains completely still and does not have any of his or her weight on the bar or rack.
4. Prepare the athlete in the correct IMTP position (see Setup).
5. Allow the athlete to rehearse the test at least twice, at approximately a 50% and a 75% effort (18).
6. On the coach's instruction (see Coaching Tips), the athlete should pull hard and fast for 3 to 5 seconds. Ensure there is no movement, including changes in joint angles, throughout the trial.
7. Perform at least two trials, with 2 to 5 minutes of rest between trials to ensure sufficient recovery.

Coaching Tips

- Decisions around the grip (i.e., overhand versus alternated grip, use of lifting straps, use of chalk) can be made by the coach but should thereafter be kept consistent within the specific environment for all future testing.

SYSTEMATIC BIAS

During a testing session involving multiple trials, it is critical to pay close attention to systematic bias, that is, whether performances progressively improve (e.g., from improper warm-up or learning effect) or worsen (e.g., from inadequate recovery time or reduced effort) (76) across trials. Systematic bias can drastically affect reliability and in turn the typical error in measurement of a test, which consequently decreases confidence in whether a change is likely a real one. Coaches should always monitor test results for systematic bias and troubleshoot their protocols to avoid it.

- Always use standardized instructions to the athlete. Research recommends the instruction to "focus on pushing the ground as hard and as fast as you possibly can" for optimal results (32).
- Perform an additional trial if the athlete loses position or grip (11) or if the difference between the first two trials is greater than 250 newtons (40, 49, 67).
- It might be possible to reduce the number of trials or shorten recovery intervals if doing so does not cause systematic bias (see the Systematic Bias sidebar).
- Keeping a record of each athlete's bar height can facilitate more time-efficient setup in the future, removing the need to establish bar height and joint positions each time.

Descriptive Data

Table 3.1 contains normative data for the IMTP. Data for peak force is provided, but readers are directed to the review by Brady and colleagues (10) to learn more about other IMTP variables and their reliability.

Table 3.1   Normative Values for Isometric Mid-Thigh Pull

Subjects	Sex	Age (years) (Mean ± SD)	Peak force (N) (Mean ± SD)
High school–aged athletes (n=51)[a]	F	14.9 ± 1.1	1,580 ± 250
International athletes (n=10)[b]	F	24.5 ± 3.1	1,624 ± 285
High school–aged soccer athletes (n=145)[c]	M	15.8 ± 1.1	2,060 ± 660
Collegiate-aged athletes (n=54)[d]	M	21.2 ± 2.5	2,516 ± 612
International athletes (n=16)[b]	M	23.0 ± 4.8	2,225 ± 493

F = Female; M = Male

[a] Emmonds et al. (2018); Moeskops et al. (2018).

[b] Brady et al. (2018).

[c] Dos'Santos et al. (2018); Morris et al. (2018).

[d] Kuki et al. (2017); McMahon et al. (2015); Thomas et al. (2015).

GOING FURTHER: DYNAMIC STRENGTH INDEX

By using a force plate for both the IMTP and the countermovement jump (CMJ; see Power Tests), coaches can determine an athlete's dynamic strength index (DSI). By combining peak force from the IMTP and CMJ, coaches are provided a representation of an athlete's maximum force capacity in relation to his or her dynamic force capability (70). This has been explored as a potential measure that helps guide training intervention (i.e., DSI <0.6 = ballistic strength; DSI 0.6-0.8 = concurrent; DSI >0.8 = maximal strength focus).

ISOMETRIC BELT-SQUAT

Purpose

The isometric belt-squat (IBSq) might be a reliable alternative to the IMTP (81). Compared to the isometric back squat, IBSq produces greater peak force with reduced lumbar spine moments. Further, isometric back squat yields greater peak force than IMTP (11). While direct comparisons between IMTP and IBSq have not been published, IBSq might be appropriate for athletes with less resistance training experience or those with a history of low-back dysfunction.

Equipment

IBSq requires a load transducer and scale or dual force platforms. Other equipment includes a lifting belt with a chained attachment, carabiners, a ring anchor, goniometer, and a method to mark foot placement.

Setup

The testing apparatus can be set up by mounting a ring anchor to the floor with a load transducer (81), or between two force platforms (43). Before testing, calibrate the load transducer or force platforms according to manufacturer guidelines. Next, determine proper stance width by having the athlete stand with feet approximately shoulder-width apart so that the floor anchor is directly under the midline of the body (43). Mark the foot position, and then have the athlete squat to determine the proper depth with a goniometer (see Setup for IMTP). From the proper squat depth, pull the chain taut and attach it to the transducer or floor anchor with a carabiner.

Testing Protocol

1. After adequate warm-up, rehearse the test twice, using approximately a 50% and a 70% effort (81).
2. Depending on the equipment, either zero the force platforms without the athlete standing on them or the transducer without the athlete attached to it.
3. Instruct the athlete to attach the chain and then assume the isometric squat position.
4. Activate the data acquisition software, and then command the athlete to attempt to stand as hard and fast as possible for 3 to 5 seconds while giving vigorous verbal encouragement.
5. Perform at least two trials, with 2 to 5 minutes of rest between trials to ensure sufficient recovery. Allow the athlete to detach the chain and sit during recovery.

Coaching Tips

- Similar to IMTP, instructions and encouragement should always be consistent.
- Inconspicuous permanent floor markings can expedite foot placement during testing sessions.
- Documenting foot width and chain length can improve time efficiency during future testing.
- Using neoprene or other padding on the bottom edge of the belt can reduce skin abrasion.

- Record the athlete's body weight while wearing the chain if relative force variables are of interest.

Descriptive Data

Limited data is available for IBSq, but researchers (43) have reported relative peak force for physically active women (21.5 ± 5.3 years; 2.59 ± 0.48 N/N_{BW}) and men (22.6 ± 3.4 years; 3.50 ± 0.80 N/N_{BW}).

HAMSTRING STRENGTH

Purpose

Hamstring strain injuries are the most common injury subtype in professional soccer (25), and hamstring strength has been established as a risk factor relating to injury (3). In addition, between-limb imbalance in hamstring strength might heighten the risk of injury in team-sport athletes (9). From a performance perspective, a relationship exists between sprint performance and hamstring (eccentric) strength (47). The importance of strong hamstrings for soccer, along with the improved accessibility of hamstring strength testing, makes it a worthwhile consideration for a testing battery.

Equipment

Multiple tools exist to assess the strength of the hamstring muscle group. Isokinetic dynamometers can provide a wealth of objective data relating to strength across different limbs, ranges of motion, and muscle contraction types. However, they are not always readily available in the soccer environment, nor practical for testing an entire team. Consequently, several portable devices have been manufactured to enable more practical testing and tracking of hamstring muscle strength.

Setup

As mentioned, numerous options exist for measuring hamstring strength. Given the increased popularity of instruments that measure eccentric hamstring strength during a Nordic hamstring exercise (NHE; also called a *Nordic leg curl*, *Nordic hamstring curl*, or *Russian lean*), the setup and testing protocol for this approach will be outlined as an example.

Testing Protocol

1. The athlete kneels on the instrumented Nordic hamstring device with his or her ankles placed under the hooks.
2. Instruct the athlete to lean forward at the knees (not hips), using maximal effort of the hamstrings to resist the forward-falling motion.
3. At the bottom of the lean, the athlete uses his or her hands on the floor to catch him- or herself and then push him- or herself back up to the beginning position.
4. The quantity of repetitions may be determined by the training program. Elsewhere, one set of three repetitions has been used for a testing protocol (14).

Coaching Tips

- The scheduling of the NHE is important given the potential for delayed onset of muscle soreness in the days following eccentric exercise.

- Using band-assisted NHE progressions in the training program can help athletes lacking strength or familiarity with the NHE for testing and training purposes (15).
- Documenting device setup dimensions (e.g., tibial length) can expedite future testing.
- A large correlation exists between eccentric hamstring strength and body mass (BM). The following predictive equation, established by a study with a professional soccer team from U17 to the senior team, has been proposed to control for this effect:

$$\text{Eccentric strength (N)} = 4 \times \text{BM (kg)} + 26.1 \qquad (14)$$

To convert BM from pounds to kilograms, multiply by 0.454.

Descriptive Data

Normative data for eccentric hamstring strength (peak force) from male soccer or team-sport athletes across a range of ages are shown in table 3.2. At the time of publication, little to no data is publicly available for eccentric hamstring force generation in female athletes, measured using an instrumented Nordic device.

Table 3.2 Normative Values for Eccentric Hamstring Strength Using an Instrumented Nordic Device

Subjects	Age (years) (mean ± SD)	Peak force (N) (mean ± SD)	
		Dominant	Non-dominant
High school–aged soccer athletes (n=121)[a]	U15-U19*	285 ± 69	279 ± 73
Collegiate-aged field sport athletes (n=36)[b]	20.0 ± 1.3	277 ± 56	277 ± 52
Elite soccer athletes (n=231)[c]	24.4 ± 4.7**	358 ± 80	335 ± 74

[a] Buchheit et al. (2016); Markovic et al. (2020).

[b] Lodge et al. (2020); Markovic et al. (2020).

[c] Buchheit et al. (2016); Markovic et al. (2020); Wik et al. (2019).

*Range is provided because age statistics were not indicated by (47). U = Under (represents youth age groups)

**Excludes n=22 from (47), which did not provide age statistics.

ADDUCTOR AND ABDUCTOR STRENGTH

Purpose

The physical demands of soccer, namely acceleration, deceleration, change of direction, and repetitive kicking, place significant load on the hip and groin region. The adductor (ADD) and abductor (ABD) musculature contribute to optimizing multi-planar control during such high-intensity and multidirectional movements. Given these demands, injuries (both time-loss and non-time-loss) are common across the sport (25, 41, 75). Therefore, assessing ADD and ABD strength and unilateral imbalance can provide useful information (73).

Equipment

The hip and groin region is a particularly complex area of anatomy, and no single test can quantify strength in its entirety. As per hamstring strength, multiple tools exist to assess

ADD and ABD muscle strength, and coaches should choose valid, reliable, and practical assessment for their environments. A sphygmomanometer (an instrument commonly used to assess blood pressure) or externally fixed dynamometry devices can be used for a reliable measurement of isometric muscle strength (60, 74). An isokinetic dynamometer may be used, although questionable reliability has been exhibited in comparing eccentric bilateral torque ratios (30). Handheld dynamometers are a practical and reliable solution for both isometric and eccentric strength testing (72), although they may be subject to intertester bias when testers are of different strength (71).

Setup

Given the increased popularity in custom-made hip-strength devices that incorporate an externally fixed dynamometer, the setup and testing protocol for this approach will be outlined as an example. However, many approaches exist.

Testing Protocol

1. The athlete lies supine beneath the device with his or her knees, specifically the femoral medial condyles, aligned between the measurement pads that include the load cells. Currently, no consensus exists on the most suitable position, but joint angles should be kept consistent, and 60 degrees of knee flexion is most common.

2. Perform a warm-up repetition in each direction, at approximately 80% of maximum effort: squeeze inward on the adductor pads for 5 seconds, rest for 5 seconds, and then push outward on the abductor pads for 5 seconds.

3. After the warm-up repetition, instruct the athlete to carry out a maximal effort on each side. Ideally, multiple maximal repetitions are conducted (i.e., 3-5 repetitions) with suitable rest provided in between.

Coaching Tips

- Keep a record of the specific position (i.e., bar height and pad width) required to keep each athlete in a consistent position. The software might provide an option to do this.

- Cue the athlete to keep his or her shoulders and rear on the floor and to keep the arms in a consistent position (e.g., across the chest) throughout the tests.

- Recording and tracking pain on a 0 to 10 scale for each trial can be useful, especially during the rehabilitation process (60).

Descriptive Data

Given the variation in testing equipment, muscle contraction types, joint angles, and ADD and ABD strength assessment measures, it is not possible to provide a concise summary of normative data that encapsulates all approaches. However, descriptive data of peak forces and the ratio between ADD and ABD for two common testing approaches are provided in tables 3.3 and 3.4.

Table 3.3 Normative Values for Male Isometric Adductor and Abductor Strength Using an Externally Fixed Dynamometer Device

Subjects	Age (years) (mean ± SD)	Side	Peak ADD force (N) (mean ± SD)	Peak ABD force (N) (mean ± SD)	ADD:ABD (mean ± SD)
High school– and collegiate-aged soccer athletes (n=31)[a]	17.9 ± 2.4	D	361 ± 110	386 ± 78	0.9 ± 0.2
		ND	370 ± 110	328 ± 24	1.0 ± 0.2
Collegiate-aged Australian Rules Football athletes (n=36)[a]	23.0 ± 3.0	D	347 ± 107	387 ± 83	0.9 ± 0.2
		ND	348 ± 107	377 ± 84	0.9 ± 0.3
Professional soccer athletes (n=195)[b]	24.4 ± 4.7	n/a	267 ± 59	n/a	n/a
Professional Australian Rules Football athletes (n=18)[c]	23.1 ± 2.1	R	382 ± 94	n/a	n/a
		L	381 ± 91	n/a	n/a

ADD = Adductor; ABD = Abductor; D = Dominant; ND = Non-Dominant; R = Right; L = Left

[a] O'Brien et al. (2019).

[b] Wik et al. (2019).

[c] Ryan et al. (2019).

Table 3.4 Normative Values for Male Eccentric Adductor and Abductor Strength Using a Handheld Dynamometer

Subjects	Age (years) (mean ± SD)	Side	Peak ADD torque (nm/kg; mean ± SD)	Peak ABD torque (nm/kg; mean ± SD)	ADD:ABD (mean ± SD)
Collegiate-aged recreational athletes (n=9)[a]	19.5 ± 2.0	D	2.84 ± 0.37	2.15 ± 0.38	n/a
		ND	2.86 ± 0.65	1.93 ± 0.30	n/a
Collegiate-aged elite soccer athletes (n=9)[a]	19.5 ± 1.5	D	2.82 ± 0.18	2.52 ± 0.34	n/a
		ND	2.48 ± 0.14	2.53 ± 0.10	n/a
Semi-professional soccer athletes (n=86)[b]	24.0 ± 4.0	D	2.45 ± 0.54*	2.35 ± 0.33*	1.04 ± 0.18*
		ND	2.37 ± 0.48*	2.25 ± 0.31*	1.06 ± 0.17*
Professional soccer athletes (n=195)[c]	24.4 ± 4.7	D	3.50 ± 0.66	3.23 ± 0.54	n/a
		ND	3.46 ± 0.63	3.20 ± 0.54	n/a

ADD = Adductor; ABD = Abductor; D = Dominant; ND = Non-Dominant

[a] Thorborg, Couppé, et al. (2011).

[b] Thorborg, Serner, et al. (2011).

[c] Wik et al. (2019).

*Isometric muscle actions

POWER TESTS

Power is the product of muscular force and movement velocity. Indeed, muscular power underpins various soccer performance qualities (e.g., kicking, accelerating, turning, jumping, etc.) and remains a staple to soccer fitness assessment batteries.

COUNTERMOVEMENT JUMP (CMJ)

Purpose

The CMJ is widely accepted by soccer strength and conditioning professionals as an assessment of lower extremity power (20, 64, 66). While CMJ height certainly depends on lower extremity power, CMJ height alone might not be a valid indicator of maximal power (see [51] for a review). Regression equations using CMJ height and BM can account for approximately 80% of the variance in peak power (61). Nevertheless, CMJ height remains the most widely used measure of lower extremity power. Interestingly, average CMJ height across teams in the same league has been associated with end-of-season standings (2).

Equipment

A variety of equipment can be used to assess the CMJ, including force platforms, switch mats, and photocell technology. Force platforms can assess CMJ height using different principles, whereas other devices estimate CMJ height from flight time. Coaches should conduct a review of literature to determine the reliability and validity of their chosen device and should be aware of measurement differences between devices and the formulas used to determine jump height.

Setup

Coaches can refer to the manufacturer instructions for their specific measurement technologies.

Testing Protocol

The following protocol is for a CMJ without arm swing, but arm swing (i.e., Abalakov jump) can also be used.

1. After adequate warm-up involving dynamic stretches, allow the athlete to perform three rehearsals using approximately 50%, 70%, and 90% efforts, respectively.

2. During the rehearsal jumps, review proper CMJ technique with the athlete. Ask the athlete to stand motionless with feet hip- to shoulder-width apart and with hands on the hips. Next, ask the athlete to perform a rapid countermovement before jumping into the air.

3. After rehearsal, follow manufacturer guidelines to prepare the testing device for measurement.

4. Instruct the athlete to perform three maximal-effort CMJs, with about 1 minute of recovery between each attempt.

Coaching Tips

- Use consistent language and encouragement across all athletes and jumps.
- Premature foot motion (e.g., a small hop or stepping action) and an inadvertent arm swing can adversely affect reliability.
- Instructing athletes to squat after contact can reduce landing impact and increase safety.
- It might be possible to shorten recovery intervals if doing so does not cause systematic bias.

Descriptive Data

Normative data for CMJ height are shown in table 3.5. To the best of the authors' knowledge, data provided is for the CMJ performed without arm swing. Coaches are also reminded of the variety in equipment and formula used to calculate CMJ height, which might be reflected in the data.

Table 3.5 Countermovement Jump Normative Values Among Soccer Athletes

Subjects	Sex	Age (years) (mean ± SD)	CMJ height (cm) (mean ± SD)
High school–aged athletes (n=307)[a]	F	15.3 ± 1.2	35.4 ± 7.6 (13.6 ± 3.0 in.)
Collegiate and collegiate-aged elite athletes (n=230)[b]	F	20.7 ± 1.8	34.5 ± 9.2 (13.9 ± 3.6 in.)
Professional and international elite athletes (n=61)[c]	F	24.0 ± 2.8	33.2 ± 3.4 (13.1 ± 1.3 in.)
High school–aged athletes (n=498)[d]	M	U15-U19*	35.8 ± 4.9 (14.1 ± 1.9 in.)
Collegiate-aged athletes (n=25)[e]	M	20.2 ± 0.9	40.0 ± 5.0 (15.7 ± 2.0 in.)
Professional athletes (n=258)[f]	M	24.4 ± 4.8	36.1 ± 5.4 (14.2 ± 2.1 in.)

F = Female; M = Male

[a] Emmonds et al. (2018); Pardos-Mainer et al. (2019); Vescovi et al. (2011).

[b] Vescovi et al. (2011); Datson et al. (2014).

[c] Datson et al. (2014).

[d] Deprez et al. (2015); Spencer et al. (2011).

[e] Kuki et al. (2017).

[f] Cometti et al. (2001); Wik et al. (2019).

*Range is provided because age statistics were not indicated by (65). U = Under (represents youth age groups)

GOING FURTHER: CMJ ASYMMETRY

Performing the CMJ using dual force platforms enables determination of bilateral asymmetry, which can support rehabilitation monitoring and decisions about athletes' readiness to return to play after injury. Numerous equations exist for calculating inter-limb asymmetry; therefore, coaches are encouraged to maintain consistency with their approach (7). Assessing asymmetries using the peak values between left and right (e.g., peak takeoff force and peak landing force) is worthwhile, but characterizing asymmetries across portions of the jump (i.e., early, late, and landing phases) can also provide invaluable information (38).

SPEED AND AGILITY TESTS

Speed (i.e., the ability to run fast), change of direction, and agility (see the Agility Assessment sidebar on page 52) are fundamental qualities for soccer athletes. During match play, athletes perform numerous combinations of sprinting and cutting (see 8, 20, 66 for reviews). Linear and curved sprinting are the most common actions performed during attacks on goal, whereas at least one change of direction occurs during approximately 10% of those situations (27). Furthermore, the frequency of high-intensity sprinting and cutting maneuvers tends to increase during critical moments of play (31). Therefore, in addition to assessing single sprint and change-of-direction performance, assessing repeated sprint ability is also important.

There is poor agreement in the published literature about gold-standard assessments for speed, change of direction, agility, and repeated sprint performance (1, 64). Consequently, various protocols have been used (1, 20, 64, 66). Regardless of the protocol used, however, several studies have indicated that these capacities can distinguish between higher and lower levels of soccer athletes (1, 64).

The following tests complement each other by providing the coach with a convenient setup (figure 3.1a) while allowing one to go further with the test results (see the Going Further sidebars on pages 54 and 55). This battery can be implemented in a single testing session, by which the coach would assess the modified 505 first, the 30-meter (33 yard) sprint second, and the 6 × 30-meter (33 yard) repeated sprint last.

Stu Forster/Getty Images

Linear (shown here) and curved sprinting are the most common actions performed during attacks on goal.

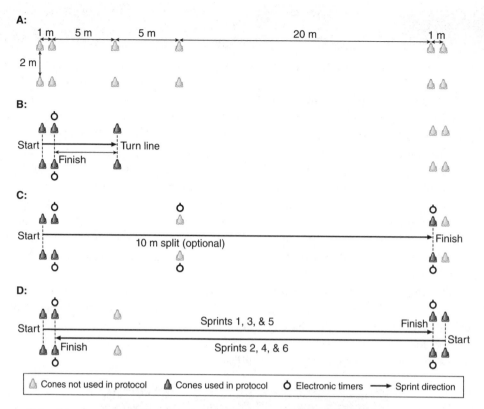

Figure 3.1 Single-session field setup for (a) the modified 505, (b) the 30-meter (33 yards) sprint, and (c) 6 × 30-meter (33 yards) repeated sprint ability test; (d) protocols, drawn to scale.

AGILITY ASSESSMENT

Agility was traditionally defined as the ability to rapidly change direction (63). However, it is now defined as the ability to rapidly change direction while responding to an external stimulus, with the former definition now used for change-of-direction ability (63). Agility assessments using lights, video, and human gestures have been developed and are gaining popularity. While agility tests have not been validated for soccer at this time (1), coaches are encouraged to pay attention to emerging research on this topic.

MODIFIED 505

Purpose

Traditionally, the 505 test has included a 10-meter (11 yard) flying start into the timed 10-meter (11 yard) portion of the test. The modified 505 (m505), which does not include a 10-meter (11 yard) flying start, has recently gained popularity. The m505 is considered a reliable way to assess change-of-direction ability among field-based athletes (29, 67).

Equipment

A tape measure, six cones, and a pair of electronic timing gates

Setup

Figure 3.1a illustrates the setup for the m505 using a 1-meter (1.1 yard) flying start and electronic timers. When more sophisticated electronic timing options (e.g., foot pressure pads or motion start technology) are not available, a 1-meter (1.1 yard) flying start allows the athlete to use a natural beginning posture without premature triggering of the photocells with the torso (33). To reduce error, use a plummet (i.e., a weight attached to a line) to set the eye of each timing gate 1 meter (1.1 yards) directly above the center of each cone (i.e., approximate height of the hip) (33).

Alternative to electronic timers, a handheld timer can be used. While electronic timers elicit greater precision, both options yield reliable results (36). Coaches are encouraged to adapt their protocols according to their available timing technologies.

Testing Protocol

1. After adequate warm-up, allow the athlete to rehearse twice at approximately 70% and 90% efforts, respectively.
2. Instruct the athlete to use a staggered stance with the preferred foot on the start line.
3. Activate the timing gates, and then command the athlete to accelerate maximally to the turn line, to change direction by placing the preferred foot on or past the line and then to maximally accelerate back through the timing gates.
4. Perform at least three trials and allow 2 to 3 minutes of passive recovery between each trial.
5. Record each trial to the nearest 0.01 second.

Coaching Tips

- Encourage athletes to accelerate past the finish line, and make sure other athletes do not obstruct the athlete's deceleration after the test.
- To compare performance in each direction (i.e., asymmetry), at least three trials on each side can be performed in alternating fashion.

Descriptive Data

Table 3.6 displays normative data for the m505 for team-sport athletes.

Table 3.6 Normative Values for Modified 505

Subjects	Sex	Age (years) (mean ± SD)	Time (s) (mean ± SD)
High school–aged soccer athletes (n=52)[a]	F	15.4 ± 2.0	2.92 ± 0.13
Collegiate-aged team-sport athletes (n=74)[b]	F	18.9 ± 1.8	2.93 ± 0.16
Collegiate-aged team-sport athletes (n=99)[c]	M	19.8 ± 2.6	2.69 ± 0.15
Elite rugby league athletes (n=42)[d]	M	23.6 ± 5.3	2.70 ± 0.16

F = Female; M = Male

[a] Pardos-Mainer et al. (2019).

[b] Thomas et al. (2020); Thomas et al. (2018).

[c] Horn et al. (2008); Thomas et al. (2020); Thomas et al. (2018).

[d] Gabbett et al. (2008).

GOING FURTHER: CHANGE-OF-DIRECTION DEFICIT

Coaches can combine a 10-meter (11 yards) split time during the 30-meter (33 yards) sprint (see 30-Meter [33 Yards] Sprint) with the m505 to determine change-of-direction deficit: the difference between the time to complete a change-of-direction task and the time to complete a linear sprint of the same distance (55). By comparing standardized scores between an athlete's 10-meter (11 yards) sprint performance and change-of-direction deficit, a coach can interpret the extent to which the athlete requires linear acceleration and change-of-direction training.

30-METER (33 YARDS) SPRINT

Purpose
The 30-meter (33 yards) sprint is considered a valid and reliable way to assess sprint performance of soccer athletes (1, 66).

Equipment
The equipment for this test includes a tape measure, six to eight cones, and two or three pairs of electronic timing gates.

Setup
Figure 3.1b illustrates the setup for this assessment, and greater detail is provided earlier (see Setup for m505).

Testing Protocol
1. If this assessment will occur in an isolated testing session, include a standardized warm-up and two rehearsals at approximately 70% and 90% efforts, respectively.
2. Allow 2 to 3 minutes of passive recovery after the last rehearsal (or last attempt in the m505).
3. Instruct the athlete to use a staggered stance with the preferred foot on the start line.
4. Activate the timing gates, and then cue the athlete to accelerate maximally and to continue sprinting through the final pair of timing gates.
5. Perform at least three trials, and allow 2 to 3 minutes of passive recovery between each trial.
6. Record each trial to the nearest 0.01 second.

Coaching Tips
- To achieve best results, instruct athletes to sprint past the timing gates before decelerating.
- To increase motivation, ask a teammate to warm up by starting 5 to 10 meters (5-11 yards) ahead of the athlete testing, who can chase the other.
- Motivation can also be inspired by using two test setups and allowing athletes to race during the test. Multiple test setups also can improve group testing efficiency.
- If using more than one test setup, follow the manufacturer's instruction to eliminate interference between device signals.

Descriptive Data

Normative data for the 30-meter (33 yards) sprint are displayed in table 3.7.

Table 3.7 Normative Data for 30-Meter (33 Yards) Sprint for Soccer Athletes

Subjects	Sex	Age (years) (mean ± SD)	Time (s) (mean ± SD)
High school–aged athletes (n=99)[a]	F	15.3 ± 1.6	4.88 ± 0.25
Collegiate athletes (n=19)[b]	F	20.3 ± 1.3	4.64 ± 0.20
Professional athletes (n=23)[c]	F	23 (range: 18-29)*	4.74 ± 0.05
High school–aged athletes (n=442)[d]	M	16.5 ± 1.1	4.43 ± 0.20
Collegiate athletes (n=25)[e]	M	20.2 ± 0.9	4.11 ± 0.16
Professional athletes (n=63)[f]	M	24.5 ± 5.2	4.24 ± 0.17

F = Female; M = Male

[a] Emmonds et al. (2018); Pardos-Mainer et al. (2019).

[b] Lockie et al. (2010).

[c] Krustrup et al. (2010).

[d] Deprez et al., (2015).

[e] Kuki et al. (2017).

[f] Cometti et al. (2001).

*Only mean and range were provided by Krustup et al. (2010).

GOING FURTHER: SPRINT MECHANICAL PROPERTIES

The force–velocity and power–velocity relationships during sprint acceleration (53) can be estimated from the 30-meter (33 yards) sprint using relatively inexpensive technology, such as radar or high-speed mobile phone cameras, and tools that can quickly perform the associated mathematical operations (59). This method has successfully differentiated soccer playing ability (34) and promises to support individual training prescription and evaluation. (Interested readers are directed to Morin and Samozino [52].)

6 × 30-METER (33 YARDS) REPEATED SPRINT ABILITY TEST

Purpose

Repeated-sprint activity involves at least two short sprints (≤ 10 s) interspersed by short recovery intervals (≤ 60 s) and is characterized by sprint-by-sprint fatigue (31). Typical outcome measures for repeated sprint protocols are the total time (s) of all sprints and the percent decrement score, which is considered the most valid index of repeated sprint fatigue (31):

$$\% \text{ Decrement Score} = (TT - IT) / TT \times 100$$

where TT is total time (the sum of all sprint times) and IT is the ideal time (the time of the best sprint multiplied by the number of sprints performed) (31).

There is poor agreement on a gold-standard repeated sprint protocol for soccer. Consequently, protocols vary by distance (e.g., 20-40 m [22-44 yards]), number (e.g., 6-12 sprints), recovery duration (e.g., 15-30 s), active versus passive recovery, and linear versus change-of-direction sprint protocols (e.g., 40 m [44 yards] shuttles). In general, holding other protocol variables constant, longer sprint distance, shorter recovery intervals, active recovery, and change of direction will increase repeated sprint fatigue (31). While coaches are encouraged to explore different repeated sprint protocols, a 6 × 30-meter repeated sprint ability test is described in this section.

Equipment

A tape measure, eight cones, and two pairs of electronic timing gates are required for this assessment. Coaches also need to ensure each sprint begins every 30 seconds using either a stopwatch or a custom audio file, playing device, and loudspeaker.

Setup

The setup for this test extends from the setup for the 30-meter (33 yards) sprint (figure 3.1c).

Testing Protocol

Prior to performing a repeated sprint ability test, at least one maximal-effort 30-meter (33 yards) sprint is required. Performance during this sprint serves as a criterion (i.e., criterion sprint) to validate the repeated sprint ability test. Specifically, the first sprint in the repeated sprint ability test must be within 2.5% to 5% of the criterion sprint (table 3.8). For this reason, the authors recommend performing the 30-meter (33 yards) sprint during the same testing session and using the best time as the criterion sprint. If this is not possible, refer to the 30-meter (33 yards) sprint protocol to perform at least one criterion sprint before conducting the 6 × 30-meter (33 yards) repeated sprint ability test.

1. Allow two to three minutes of passive recovery after performing the criterion sprint.

2. During the criterion sprint recovery interval, determine the criteria for the first sprint of the repeated sprint ability test (table 3.8).

3. Instruct the athlete to initiate a staggered stance with the preferred foot on the start line, and play the custom audio file (if used).

4. Activate the timing gates, and then cue the athlete to accelerate maximally through each pair of timing gates according to the audio file. If not using an audio file, start a running clock when the athlete initiates the first sprint.

5. Allow the athlete to decelerate past the timing gates using as much distance as necessary, and then have him or her walk back to prepare for the next sprint.

6. During the recovery interval between the first and second sprints, confirm that the first sprint time was completed within the allowable time (table 3.8). If not, restart the test after a two- to three-minute rest.

Table 3.8   Validity Criteria for the First Sprint in a Repeated Sprint Ability Test

Criterion sprint	2.5% Validity criteria		5.0% Validity criteria	
(s)	Time difference (s)	First sprint time (s)	Time difference (s)	First sprint time (s)
4.00	0.10	4.10	0.20	4.20
4.10	0.10	4.20	0.21	4.31
4.20	0.11	4.31	0.21	4.41
4.30	0.11	4.41	0.22	4.52
4.40	0.11	4.51	0.22	4.62
4.50	0.11	4.61	0.23	4.73
4.60	0.12	4.72	0.23	4.83
4.70	0.12	4.82	0.24	4.94
4.80	0.12	4.92	0.24	5.04
4.90	0.12	5.02	0.25	5.15
5.00	0.13	5.13	0.25	5.25

7. Each remaining sprint will begin every 30 seconds, and the athlete will start 1 meter (1 yard) behind the timing gates on either side of the test setup. Approximately 5 seconds before each sprint, ask the athlete to reset into the same staggered stance.

8. Record performance of each sprint to the nearest 0.01 second.

Coaching Tips

- Repeated sprint ability tests are extremely demanding. Consistent and vigorous verbal encouragement is highly encouraged.
- Instruct athletes to continue sprinting past the timing gates because early deceleration will reduce test reliability.
- Coaches should determine if a 2.5% or 5.0% validity criterion is best suited for their team, based on their chosen protocol.
- Using a running clock can increase human error during the protocol. If using a stopwatch, eliminate all potential distractions to ensure that each sprint occurs every 30 seconds.
- Coaches can use lap mode on the electronic timing device to recall the times of each sprint after the protocol, or they can write down the times as the test proceeds.

Descriptive Data

Table 3.9 displays normative data for repeated sprint ability among soccer and futsal athletes.

Table 3.9   Performance Data for Repeated Sprint Ability Test

Subjects	Age (years) (mean ± SD)	Protocol	Total time (s) (mean ± SD)	Decrement (%) (mean ± SD)
Female collegiate soccer athletes (n=19)[a]	20.3 ± 1.3	6 × 20 m (22 yards), every 15 s with active recovery	22.3 ± 1.0	8.4 ± 5.5
Female elite soccer athletes (n=19)[b]	18.1 ± 2.9	6 × 20 m (22 yards), every 15 s with active recovery	21.9 ± 1.3	6.5 ± 2.1
Female semi-professional futsal (n=13)[c]	21.8 ± 2.5	8 × 30 m (33 yards), 25 s recovery	41.8 ± 1.7	4.7 ± 1.8
Female professional futsal (n=14)[c]	21.1 ± 2.3	8 × 30 m (33 yards), 25 s recovery	41.1 ± 1.9	4.9 ± 2.2
Male high school–aged soccer athletes (n=55)[d]	U15-U18*	6 × 30 m (33 yards), every 30 s	26.8 ± 0.8	n/a
Male elite soccer athletes (n=18)[e]	23 ± 4	6 × 30 m (33 yards), every 20 s	26.9 ± 0.7	3.9 ± 1.2

[a] Lockie et al. (2018).

[b] Gabbett (2010).

[c] Ramos-Campo et al. (2010).

[d] Spencer et al. (2011).

[e] McGawley and Andersson (2013).

*Range is provided because age statistics were not indicated by Spencer et al. (2011). U = Under (represents youth age groups)

High-Intensity Aerobic Endurance Capacity

Aerobic fitness is positively related to soccer performance, and improving this capacity can enhance physical (e.g., distance covered, work intensity, and number of sprints) and technical (e.g., number of involvements with the ball) match outcome measures (35). Given the intermittent demands of soccer, research recommends the use of intermittent beep tests over tests that are continuous in nature, such as the multistage fitness test, 1.5-mile (2.4 km), or 12-minute run (77).

YO-YO TEST

Purpose

Field tests are an appealing approach to assessing physical capacities, given the practicality of testing large groups and lack of specialist equipment in comparison to laboratory testing. However, such field tests should be determined as valid, reliable, and relevant to the sport in question. In soccer, the yo-yo tests have been developed to assess the ability to repeatedly and intermittently perform intense exercise (4).

Two main variations of the yo-yo test exist, the intermittent endurance (YYIE) and the intermittent recovery (YYIR) tests, each with two difficulty levels, plus a children's version (YYIR1C). The differences between these tests are outlined in table 3.10. In brief, the YYIE tests are more aerobically taxing, while the YYIR tests are more aerobic-anaerobic-related (79). It has been recommended that athletes with younger ages or training histories begin with the YYIE, progressing from level one to two. Alternatively, elite and more experienced athletes are recommended to undergo the YYIR level two (77).

Table 3.10   Differences in Test Setup in Yo-Yo Intermittent Tests

Test	Level	Beginning speed (km/hr)	Speed increments (km/hr)*	Running distance (m)	Recovery distance (m)	Recovery time (s)
Endurance test (YYIE)	1	8 (5.0 mph)	0.25 (0.16 mph)	2 × 20 (22 yards)	2 × 2.5 (2.7 yards)	5
	2	11.5 (7.1 mph)	0.25 (0.16 mph)	2 × 20 (22 yards)	2 × 2.5 (2.7 yards)	5
Recovery Test (YYIR)	1	10 (6 mph)	0.5 (0.3 mph)	2 × 20 (22 yards)	2 × 5 (5.5 yards)	10
	2	13 (8 mph)	0.5 (0.3 mph)	2 × 20 (22 yards)	2 × 5 (5.5 yards)	10
Children's test (YYIR1C)	1	10	0.5 (0.3 mph)	2 × 16 (17 yards)	2 × 4 (4.4 yards)	10

*Speed increments will initially increase at a faster rate but approximately one minute into each test will start to increase consistently by the increment shown.

Equipment

A test recording sheet, tape measure, set of cones, audio file of the test of choice, and a method for playing the track aloud

Setup

Figure 3.2a-b illustrates the setup for the YYIE and the YYIR. Note that the start line should be wide enough for the testing group to run in lanes that are 1 to 2 meters (1.1-2.2 yards) apart (marked by cones). Ensure the audio device used to play the track can be heard across the entire testing area.

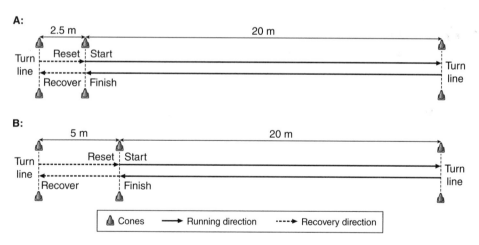

Figure 3.2   The setup and protocols for (a) the YYIE and (b) the YYIR. Note that the children's version is not shown, but the running distance would be set to 16 meters (17 yards).

Testing Protocol

1. After an adequate warm-up, explain the protocol to the athletes and answer any questions they may have. If necessary, play the first 60 seconds of the audio file to familiarize the athletes with the specific sounds before setting the audio file back to the beginning.

2. Instruct the athletes to line up behind the start line (see figure 3.2), and then play the audio file.

3. Athletes start jogging toward the turn line, ensuring they reach the line before the beep while still maintaining their pace with the audio track. They then turn and jog back to the start/finish line again before hearing the beep.

4. The athletes walk to the recovery turn line and then back to the start line to reset before the next beep.

5. Speed increases during subsequent levels. The athletes continue progression until volitional exhaustion or until they twice fail to reach the front line in time.

6. Record the total distance (m) covered during the running portion (i.e., number of shuttles multiplied by 20) as the athlete's score.

Coaching Tips

- Integrating the start of the test into the warm-up (e.g., first four running bouts) can assist with preparation and familiarization.

- Lining athletes up according to ability can motivate greater effort and competition during testing.

- Running too fast during early stages causes undue fatigue. Tell the athletes to slow down if they reach the lines notably before the relevant beep.

Descriptive Data

Normative data taken from a systematic review (62) of the yo-yo tests are given in table 3.11.

Table 3.11   Normative Data for the Yo-Yo Tests

Protocol	Sex	Classification	Subjects	Distance (m) (mean ± SD)
YYIR level 1	F	Amateur	19	920 ± 322 (1,006 ± 352 yards)
	F	Sub-elite/elite	212	1,197 ± 502 (1,309 ± 549 yards)
	M	Amateur	340	1,743 ± 529 (1,906 ± 579 yards)
	M	Sub-elite	802	1,891 ± 466 (2,068 ± 510 yards)
	M	Elite	429	2,126 ± 456 (2,325 ± 499 yards)
	M	Top-elite	288	2,302 ± 509 (2,517 ± 557 yards)
YYIR level 2	F	Sub-elite	62	502 ± 159 (549 ± 174 yards)
	F	Elite	16	634 ± 155 (693 ± 170 yards)
	M	Amateur	329	740 ± 353 (809 ± 386 yards)
	M	Sub-elite	605	874 ± 300 (956 ± 328 yards)
	M	Elite	253	866 ± 224 (947 ± 254 yards)
	M	Top-elite	239	1,047 ± 322 (1,145 ± 352 yards)
YYIE level 1	F	Sub-elite	22	2,388 ± 1,027 (2,612 ± 1,123 yards)
	M	Amateur	18	3,044 ± 442 (3,329 ± 483 yards)
	M	Elite	97	1,890 ± 457 (2,067 ± 500 yards)
YYIE level 2	F	Amateur	46	1,261 ± 449 (1,379 ± 491 yards)
	F	Sub-elite	19	994 ± 373 (1,087 ± 408 yards)
	F	Elite	184	1,645 ± 557 (1,799 ± 609 yards)
	M	Amateur	293	1,059 ± 389 (1,158 ± 425 yards)
	M	Sub-elite	32	2,539 ± 677 (2,777 ± 740 yards)
	M	Elite	180	1,685 ± 535 (1,843 ± 585 yards)
	M	Top-elite	203	2,428 ± 531 (2,655 ± 581 yards)

F = Female; M = Male

Note: According to (62): Amateur = non-professional, regional level; Sub-elite = semi-professional, national level; Elite = professional, national level; Top-elite = international, professional level.

Adapted from B. Schmitz et al., "The Yo-Yo Intermittent Tests: A Systematic Review and Structured Compendium of Test Results," *Frontiers Media S* 9 (2018): 870. Distributed under the terms of the Creative Commons Attribution 4.0 International License. (http://creativecommons .org/licenses/by/4.0).

30-15 INTERMITTENT FITNESS TEST

Purpose

The 30-15 intermittent fitness test (30-15 IFT), originally proposed by Buchheit (12), has become a popular alternative to the yo-yo tests, in particular because of its use in training prescription (see the Going Further: Prescribing Interval Training From Field Tests sidebar).

Equipment

A test recording sheet, tape measure, cones (or other line marking options), the 30-15 IFT audio file, an audio device, and a loudspeaker that can be heard across the testing space

Setup

See figure 3.3 for the setup for the 30-15 IFT.

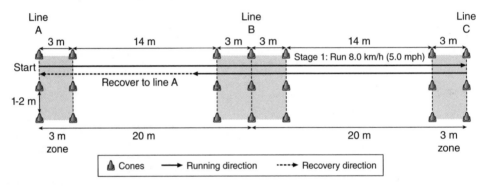

Figure 3.3 30-15 intermittent fitness test.
Data based on Buchheit (2008).

Testing Protocol

The 30-15 IFT involves progressively faster 30-second shuttle runs interspersed by 15 seconds of recovery, between two lines marked 40 meters (44 yards) apart. An audio file helps guide athletes' pace and is calibrated to the speed of each 30-second interval. The first interval begins at a jogging speed of 8.0 kilometers per hour (5.0 mph), and each subsequent stage increases by 0.5 kilometers per hour (0.3 mph). The total running distance of each interval is corrected by a factor of 0.7 seconds per change of direction. Athletes advance stages until they can no longer keep up with the pace. Following are more detailed instructions:

1. After an adequate warm-up, explain the protocol to the athletes and answer any questions they may have. If necessary, play the first 60 seconds of the audio file to familiarize the athletes with the specific sounds before setting the audio file back to the beginning.

2. Instruct the athletes to line up behind line A (see figure 3.3), and then play the audio file.

3. Athletes begin the first interval using the beeps played from the audio file to maintain their pace. Specifically, they run back and forth between lines A and C, and they should pass through each 3-meter (3.3 yards) zone associated with lines A, B, and C (gray shaded areas in figure 3.3) with the sound of each beep.

4. A different type of beep indicates when to stop running, and the athletes have 15 seconds to walk to the next line, where they will wait for the start of the next interval. For example, if the 30-second interval ended after they crossed line B, they would walk in the same direction to line A or C.

5. Running speed increases during each subsequent stage. Athletes continue progression until volitional exhaustion or until they cannot reach the 3-meter (3.3 yards) zones associated with each line on three consecutive beeps.

6. Record the running speed (km/h) achieved during the last completed stage (V_{IFT}).

Coaching Tips

- Motivate greater effort and competition by letting athletes of similar ability run next to each other.

- Running too fast during early stages causes undue fatigue. Tell the athletes to slow down if they exit a zone before the relevant beep.

- Encourage the athletes to establish a consistent running pace so that they do not have to continually speed up or slow down as they pass through each zone.

- For best results, encourage athletes to push themselves until they miss the 3-meter (3.3 yards) zones three times rather than giving up early.

GOING FURTHER: PRESCRIBING INTERVAL TRAINING FROM FIELD TESTS

Maximal aerobic speed (MAS) represents the minimal speed that elicits maximal oxygen uptake (6). Corrective equations can be used to estimate MAS from continuous (5) or intermittent running field tests (16, 24). Coaches can adapt those estimates to prescribe individualized interval training programs. As outlined in this chapter, however, the physical determinants of soccer performance extend beyond aerobic capacity alone. Interestingly, the speed reached at the end of the 30-15 IFT (V_{IFT}) considers the metabolic requirements to perform high-intensity intermittent activity involving changes of direction. Buchheit has provided guidelines on how to use V_{IFT} to prescribe individualized training using various interval training protocols (12, 13).

Descriptive Data

Descriptive data for the velocity at the end of the 30-15 IFT (V_{IFT}) for female and male athletes is shown in figures 3.4 and 3.5, respectively.

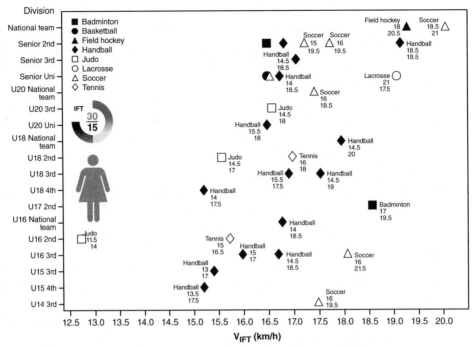

Figure 3.4 30-15 IFT performance among female athletes of different age, sport, and playing standard.

Adapted by permission from P. Laursen and M. Buchheit, *Science and Application of High-Intensity Interval Training* (Champaign, IL: Human Kinetics, 2019), 28.

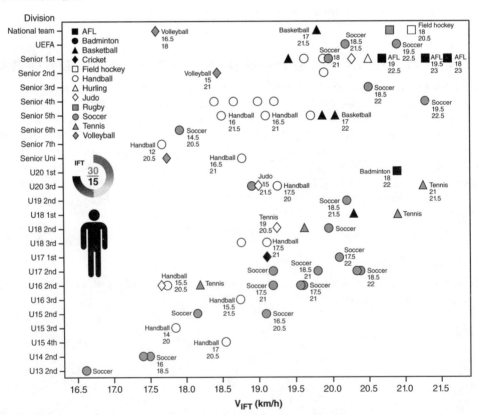

Figure 3.5 30-15 IFT performance among male athletes of different age, sport, and playing standard.

Adapted by permission from P. Laursen and M. Buchheit, *Science and Application of High-Intensity Interval Training* (Champaign, IL: Human Kinetics, 2019), 28.

GOING FURTHER: RETURN TO SPORT

A comprehensive fitness battery can be used to monitor progress during rehabilitation and to aid decisions about an athlete's readiness to return to sport. By using a battery of tests, both ability (relative to trained healthy baselines) and symmetry should be considered. For example, an athlete who has successfully restored strength, power, and symmetry but not high-intensity aerobic endurance capacity might be able to participate fully for short durations. Conversely, an athlete who has restored high-intensity aerobic endurance capacity but not speed and change-of-direction performance might safely participate during activities that do not require full-speed efforts. In conjunction with the fitness profile, the on-field progressions can be developed from typical practice and match activity demands if tracking technology is available.

CONCLUSION

This chapter has outlined evidence-based assessments of the physical capacities required to perform in soccer, specifically across strength, power, speed, agility, and high-intensity aerobic endurance capacity. Such data collection can facilitate individual training prescription, training program evaluation, injury risk reduction and can monitor readiness and rehabilitation (see the Return to Sport sidebar above), return to training and participation, and talent recruitment and selection. Often, multiple assessment methods, equipment, and protocols exist. It is the coach's responsibility to determine the most suitable method for his or her individual environment, along with ensuring assessments are conducted in a consistent and reliable manner. Finally, it is important to acknowledge that often the data provided by such tests provide a vehicle to build a relationship between the coach and athletes.

4

SPORT-SPECIFIC PROGRAM DESIGN GUIDELINES

MEGAN YOUNG, GARGA CASERTA, AND MATT HOWLEY

Soccer involves a variety of physical and performance demands across a range of positions. To successfully respond to those demands, soccer athletes need to follow a resistance training program. Important tenets serve as the foundation and framework of a well-designed program. The objective of this chapter is to describe the principles and guidelines that are integral to developing an effective resistance training program for the soccer athlete.

SPECIFICITY, OVERLOAD, AND ADAPTATION

The first step in the program design process is to define the principles on which the program will be based. Three principles are universal to resistance training and must be considered. The first principle explains the body's ability to repair and improve (i.e., adapt) tissues that were put under a specific stress (i.e., demand), if given time to recover following the stimulus. This is often referred to as the **SAID principle** (specific adaptation to imposed demands), described in chapter 1. Training stress is necessary for a program to be effective; however, a lack of balance between the stress imposed by the program and the athlete's ability to cope with it can lead to negative responses (16). This principle then leads to the next two universal principles describing specificity and progressive overload.

Specificity relates to the type of stimulus; to elicit an adaptation, the stimulus applied must be specific to the adaptation desired. If the goal of a program is to increase the overall strength of an athlete, the stress caused by the exercise program must demand a higher level of strength than the athlete is accustomed to. For example, if strength is the specific goal, increasing the amount of load lifted in an exercise would lead to a demand for higher levels of force production, thus stimulating the body to adapt to such demand. If the goal is to improve muscular endurance, increasing the number of repetitions performed or the duration of the activity might be an appropriate stimulus. Athletes with a lower training age (see the Training Age section on the following page) might benefit with less specificity in training; however, as training age increases, the need for specificity also increases (12). Along with being specific, resistance training must also be progressive to cause continuous adaptations to occur.

The **progressive overload** principle describes the process of incrementally increasing the specific stress from a level with which the athlete is capable of coping, in the direction of the desired result (specificity) and toward a level to which the athlete is not accustomed. Using the strength example above, this principle now will guide the coach to design the program so that the athlete is overloaded with a progressively increasing strength demand to create the necessary tissue adaptation and tolerance required to become stronger. This principle also requires that increases in load are great enough to drive adaptation, but not so great that the athlete cannot recover prior to the next training session. The greater the overload, the longer the athlete might need to recover. This mistake in prescription of overload paired with lack of sufficient recovery causes overreaching. Excessive or prolonged overreaching can lead to health and wellness issues or, in more extreme cases, injuries. It is the role of strength and conditioning professionals to assess the appropriate starting point for each athlete and to use their experience and academic research findings to determine the optimal extent of progressive overload that results in the desired adaptation.

The concept of progression in training can be observed from a variety of perspectives. For example, resistance training exercises can be progressed within a skill perspective, from simple to more complex in execution. Within this movement progression framework, early exercises in these progressions can be seen as precursors to later ones, with the purpose of allowing athletes to learn complex movements in bite-sized segments they can handle prior to taking on the more advanced tasks. Learning the skills required to perform a barbell front squat, for example, will facilitate the learning of the catch phase of the hang clean. Also, performance of a Romanian deadlift (RDL) with proficiency can be a precursor to the introduction of kettlebell swings, which demand more coordination, rhythm, and speed of movement from the athlete.

The manipulation of movement progression framework also can be seen within the concept of **phase potentiation**. This concept refers to a higher-level perspective of the program design process, looking at the different phases of training that make up a mesocycle. Prior to driving a hypertrophic muscular response, there might be benefits in focusing on causing metabolic adaptations in athletes to increase their work capacity first. Since hypertrophy demands a certain level of work capacity, ensuring this level can be met is a reasonable initial target goal. The same concept can be applied to improving force-generating capacities during a program's strength phase prior to focusing on the rate of force development during the subsequent power phase.

RESISTANCE TRAINING PROGRAM VARIABLES

In addition to specificity, overload, and adaptation, a well-designed resistance training program needs to address exercise selection, training frequency, exercise order, intensity, volume, and rest periods.

Exercise Selection

When deciding on exercise selection, it is important to consider the major aspects influencing selection as they relate to the individual athlete's needs. Biological information about the athlete, as well as the experiences and environment to which athletes have been exposed, might influence the type of exercises used. Also, exercises that are best suited to drive adaptations desired within each phase of training within the program's periodization strategy should be considered.

Training Age

The amount (length) of an athlete's experience and training, referred to as **training age**, can influence an athlete's ability to perform and benefit from a resistance training program. If trained and experienced athletes have been training consistently for many weeks, months, and years without long periods of detraining, they would have built stress tolerance and should be able to handle higher levels of stress. For example, professional athletes might have had many years of resistance training experience, allowing them to perform more complex exercises. Note, though, that not all professional athletes have been exposed to regular resistance training, and, further, just because an athlete excels in his or her sport, he or she can still have a low training age with regard to resistance training.

For athletes with low training age, it is important to emphasize the technical development of resistance training. Self-limiting exercises that challenge athletes' coordination, balance, timing, and mobility are well suited for this purpose and will work well as teaching tools for the athletes' introduction into the program. Since athletes with lower training age will also likely have lower tolerance to the stress of resistance training, a relatively lower volume and load is needed to elicit a response.

Injury History and Current Status

Previous injuries can affect exercise selection based on limitations they might develop for the injured segment. If an athlete communicates a history of lower leg injuries, further consideration should be put toward understanding the appropriate starting point for leg strength exercises during a needs-based assessment and movement analysis. Communication with the medical providers is critical when dealing with a current injury to collaborate on phases of return to best address the athlete's needs. The athlete should be able to continue performing a resistance training program throughout rehabilitation, as long as the exercises in the program do not interfere with the recovery from the specific injury.

Phases of Training

Different phases of training relative to the planning of resistance training for soccer athletes are highlighted in the Periodization section later in this chapter. However, as it relates to exercise selection, we will focus on the outcomes that might be highlighted within these phases and the types of exercises that might be best suited for them.

Strength Exercises   Early variations of compound knee- and hip-dominant lower body patterns as well as upper body pushing and pulling exercises should be used. These self-limiting exercises allow for the development of these specific movement patterns safely but also challenge the athlete's total body coordination and postural alignment. These variations affect athletes' balance and coordination to create favorable conditions for the athlete to achieve optimal positions. For example, in the hip-dominant variations, a trap bar deadlift allows for the load to remain in line with the athlete's center of gravity, versus a standard deadlift in which the load is shifted in front of the center of gravity. Single-leg variations allow for common early asymmetries to be addressed prior to the introduction of bilateral movements with heavier loads. The use of hanging (i.e., a dead hang) and suspended inverted rows allows athletes to build tolerance and strength prior to performing pull-ups loaded with their total body weight.

- *Knee-dominant focus:* single-leg squat, rear foot–elevated split squat, goblet squat
- *Hip-dominant focus:* glute bridge, single-leg RDL, kettlebell or trap bar deadlift
- *Upper body pushing focus:* push-up, one-arm bench press, one-arm incline or landmine press, dumbbell shoulder press
- *Upper body pulling focus:* dead hang, lat pulldown, suspended inverted row, one-arm bent-over row

For the purpose of clarity, the definition of jumps, hops, and bounds follow:
- *Jumps:* double-leg take-off, double-leg landing
- *Hops:* single-leg takeoff, single-leg landing (same leg)
- *Bounds:* single-leg takeoff, single-leg landing (opposite leg)

Power Exercises   Plyometric and medicine ball exercises are effective introductions to power or explosive resistance training exercises because they allow the athlete to learn strategies for absorbing and tolerating landing impact, generating force against the ground, and transferring force through the whole body.

- *Introductory-level plyometric exercises (i.e., landing and non-stretch-shortening cycle initiations; see chapter 1):* drop squat, single-leg drop squat, weight shift, quick stability bounds
- *Medicine ball exercises:* granny toss, squat to overhead throw, chest pass, overhead slam, rotational tosses and passes

For athletes who have developed an initial level of impact tolerance and absorption, it is possible now to progress toward stressing the tissue stiffness and its elastic response. Plyometric and loaded ballistic exercises are an effective way to do so. The multidirectional initiation of the hops and bounds allow the athlete to optimize alignment and angles of force application through the lower body and the ground. It also allows for maintenance of stiffness and health of the lower leg, including arch of the foot, ankle, and the muscles and tissues related to the Achilles tendon. The linear bounding and pogo jumps are an opportunity for the athlete to develop the ability to generate vertical force at a high rate of force development to enhance stiffness of the lower leg and decrease ground contact time during sprinting. These movements can be integrated into the preparation process within soccer practices or practiced in the weight room as part of the resistance training program:

- *Linear plyometric exercises:* countermovement and continuous jumps, hops, and bounds; variations of the former exercises that are performed onto boxes (if limitations on landing impact are needed) or over hurdles (if impact limitations are not needed)
- *Ballistic exercises:* kettlebell swing, dumbbell or barbell squat jump, plyometric push-up, push jerk

Advanced Strength Exercises and Strength–Power Exercise Combinations

As athletes reach an advanced training age and need high levels of stress to continue driving adaptations, resistance training exercises have to stress the neuromuscular system specifically and with higher intensity. This validates the need for teaching techniques early in the process so athletes can rely now on higher-complexity exercises that offer an increased level of intensity. Considering the force–velocity curve, exercises that maximize force generation can be paired with exercises performed at high velocities to further stimulate the central nervous system (CNS) to adapt to moving powerfully. Also, by definition, a focus is needed on the speed in which movements are performed. This type of neuromuscular potentiation can be highly effective in driving intensity but not appropriate for athletes who have not yet developed a high level of tolerance to resistance training. Advanced variations that allow for heavier loading include the following:

- *Total body strength and power exercises:* clean pull, push press, drop snatch
- *Lower body strength exercises + ballistic exercises:* deadlift + kettlebell swing, back squat + squat jump
- *Upper body strength exercises + ballistic exercises:* pull-up + medicine ball overhead slam, bench press + plyometric push-up

Advanced Power Exercises To continue progressing the power-based exercises, physics variables must be manipulated. To increase the eccentric stress during loading for a jump, for example, the athlete can drop from a box that is higher than his or her maximum vertical jump height. This would overload the athlete with a higher-impact stress than what he or she is accustomed to. Another possible variation is to increase the lever length around a movement. For example, performing linear bounds with a straight leg would increase the force generated around the hips during the leg swing. Olympic weightlifting exercises are very effective in developing power; however, they are highly technical and should be progressed as skill is improved over time:

- *Advanced plyometric exercises:* drop jump and hop, continuous straight-leg bound
- *Olympic weightlifting movements*: clean, jerk, and snatch

Training Frequency

Training frequency considers the number of exposures to a stimulus within a microcycle (commonly a week long) (3). Many factors affect the frequency that athletes require to improve their physical qualities or maintain those that have been developed from previous training cycles. The athletes' training status, injury history, phase of the season, projected on-field training stress, exercise type, and training goals are all specific factors (15), along with non-specific factors such as travel and academics for certain populations. These all affect the strength and conditioning professional's ability to plan and prescribe resistance training across the course of the year.

The exposures to resistance training that an athlete requires to achieve desired physical development goals will change throughout a yearly training plan. The athlete's training status and level of competition (e.g., high school, academy, college, or professional) are determining factors in their level of preparedness as it pertains to training frequency. As athletes become more proficient and adapt to the training program, athletes should be progressed accordingly, because having periods of infrequent or inconsistent training will hinder adaptation and affect performance. Less frequent training leads to athletes suffering from delayed onset muscle soreness, which will negatively affect their sport performance. Therefore, it is important to keep consistency with training throughout demanding periods that take into consideration a game schedule, training, planned breaks, academics, and personal factors. Keeping this consistency enables an athlete to keep building or, in the least, maintain strength and power qualities even if exposures to training are short in duration and low in volume and intensity. For example, in professional soccer athletes one session per week during the in-season is typically sufficient to maintain strength and speed performance following a preceding preparatory (preseason) period (13). For youth soccer athletes, though, jumping performance was improved irrespective of a training frequency of one or two sessions a week (9). However, two training sessions per week (i.e., not just one) were needed to improve linear sprint speed and change-of-direction ability, showing that a greater frequency could result in greater physical outcomes for youth soccer athletes (9).

As mentioned earlier, smaller exposures can help with this while also maintaining strength and power qualities. Also, athletes who are not exposed to a significant amount of game-playing time need additional resistance training and conditioning sessions. It is important to remember with such athletes a rapid increase in frequency could have a detrimental impact and possibly lead to increased soreness or even injury, so building in planned additional work across a period of time to help with their physical development and preparedness is strongly encouraged.

Exercise Order

When constructing a resistance training program, it is imperative that the strength and conditioning professional understands the physical demands of soccer, the goals that apply to the phase of training, and the environment in which the session will be performed. These elements will drive the order in which the exercises will be performed to enable the soccer athlete to optimize the desired outcomes. The order of exercises within a resistance training session significantly affects lifting performance and the strength and power adaptations derived through resistance training (10). Further, the goals of the resistance training session will ultimately dictate the order in which exercises are performed (10).

Generally, the resistance training exercises should be sequenced within a session beginning with those that have the highest CNS demand, fine motor coordination, and a high requirement for force production and ending with those that have the lowest CNS demand, little need for fine motor coordination, and a low requirement for force production (17). By following this arrangement, the initial exercises are performed in a state of lower fatigue, therefore providing the athlete with a better chance to achieve the desired adaptation.

Following these guidelines, exercises aimed at developing power such as the Olympic lifts or their derivatives (or plyometric-based movements) should take priority within the training session and be performed first in a session. These exercises are very complex in nature and require maximum effort and high levels of CNS activation.

Multi-joint, non-power core exercises that involve the recruitment of many muscle groups should be performed next. The back squat and deadlift for the lower body and the bench press, chin-up, and shoulder press for the upper body (and all of their respective derivatives) are common choices. These exercises are generally programmed with the intent of developing strength, and they require the highest level of muscle activation to complete and are very taxing on the athlete, requiring adequate rest intervals between sets.

Finally, single-limb or single-joint assistance exercises (e.g., biceps curl, triceps extension, leg curl, leg extension) should be programmed last within the resistance training session. These exercises are generally programmed with higher volumes at lower intensities due to the nature of the exercises and their goals (e.g., hypertrophy, muscular endurance, injury prevention, or movement efficiency).

Also, multi-joint, non-power core exercises and assistance exercises can be performed in a **superset** (i.e., two or more exercises that train opposing muscles groups that are performed without a rest interval between them), such as the following:

- *Upper body superset:* pairing a pushing movement (e.g., a push-up) with a pulling movement (e.g., an inverted row)
- *Upper body-lower body superset* (e.g., a push-up paired with a Nordic curl)

Intensity

The most common method of assessing the intensity of an exercise is by the weight (commonly referred to as *load*) lifted. This variable is the most individual for each athlete; the strength and conditioning professional can use a variety of methods to gain a specific understanding of intensity for each athlete. Maximum strength testing, the autoregulatory progressive resistance exercise (APRE) protocol, and velocity-based training (VBT) are methods from which information can be gathered to understand exercise intensity.

Maximum Strength Testing

The load to be lifted for an exercise can be calculated (i.e., it is a percentage) from an athlete's **one repetition maximum,** which is the most weight an athlete can lift in a certain exercise for one repetition (referred to as the **1RM**). The 1RM testing protocol and an explanation of how to determine loads based on the relationship between the relative load lifted and the number of repetitions that can be performed (i.e., the %1RM method; e.g., six repetitions can typically be performed at 85% of the 1RM) is described in reference 15. Because maximum strength testing places significant stress on the athlete, it is becoming less favored among strength and conditioning professionals, in that it carries a higher degree of risk, particularly to inexperienced, untrained individuals. An alternative is to determine the maximum number of repetitions that can be performed in an exercise with a certain amount of weight; this is termed the **repetition maximum** (RM). For example, a 6RM is the most weight that can be lifted for six repetitions, and because multiple repetitions can be performed, the load lifted is lighter than a 1RM.

A relationship exists between the RM loading and the goal of training. If the goal is to increase strength, the RM is typically six or fewer using 85% of the 1RM or greater; if the goal is to increase muscle size, use 6-12RM loads at 67% to 85% of the 1RM; and when training for local muscular endurance, the RM is 12 or more using 67% or less of the 1RM (15).

Autoregulatory Progressive Resistance Exercise Protocol

The APRE protocol (consult references 6 and 8 for more detail) enables the strength and conditioning professional or athlete to gain information during a given training session (or, more specifically, during a given exercise) and then make adjustments to the load based on how many repetitions can be performed in that exercise on that day of training. Instead of the %1RM method, in which an athlete lifts a load for a prescribed number of repetitions, the APRE protocol involves the athlete working up to a weight. That is, the athlete completes the maximum number of repetitions with that load (i.e., until failure), then makes a load adjustment based on a certain RM goal (e.g., 3RM, 6RM, or 10RM) and then again performing repetitions until failure. The athlete's next training session uses the load of the final set, with any needed adjustment made. The benefit of this approach is that the athlete can autoregulate the amount of weight lifted during a given session. Because athletes respond to stimuli at different rates, providing the athlete the autonomy to autoregulate can help to maximize adaptation over the training cycle.

Velocity-Based Training

Velocity-based training (VBT) for trained athletes as it pertains to resistance training is a viable option to measure intensity. VBT methods help to guide strength and conditioning professionals to determine the optimal load for resistance training using velocity at which an athlete can move the load independent of 1RM (7). Figure 4.1 provides suggested speeds at which an

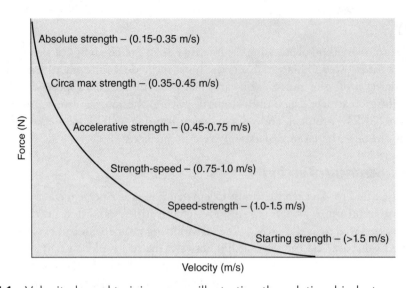

Figure 4.1   Velocity-based training curve illustrating the relationship between the desired adaptation and the associated bar velocities during resistance training.

Reprinted by permission from D.N. French, "Advanced Power," D.N. French, in *Developing Power*, edited by National Strength and Conditioning Association by Mike McGuigan, editor (Champaign, IL: Human Kinetics, 2017), 191; Adapted by permission from M. Kuzdub, "Introductory Guide to Velocity Based Training," *Breaking Muscle* (2015). breakingmuscle.com.

exercise should be performed to elicit the desired adaptation (1). Using the feedback of the VBT device enables the strength and conditioning professional to easily assess the intensity of the exercise and subsequently adjust the load being lifted to help the athlete achieve the intensity to elicit the desired resistance training adaptation.

Volume

Volume is one of the most important variables within a resistance training program as it pertains to developing specific physical qualities. Volume within a resistance training program can be assessed in two ways.

Repetition-Volume

When programming using body-weight exercises, **repetition-volume** is the total number of repetitions performed during a training session. For example, three sets of 10 repetitions for exercise 1 and two sets of 20 repetitions for exercise 2 yields a total repetition-volume of 70 repetitions.

Volume-Load

When completing exercises with added resistance, the **volume-load** method is commonly used, in which the total number of sets is multiplied by the number of repetitions performed per set, which is multiplied by the weight lifted per repetition (15, 17). For example, three sets of 10 repetitions with 100 pounds (45 kg) for exercise 1 and two sets of 20 repetitions with 25 pounds (11 kg) for exercise 2 yields a total volume-load of 4,000 pounds (1,818.2 kg, when converted from 4,000 pounds using 1 kg = 2.2 pounds). In instances where an athlete performs a different number of repetitions or uses a different weight each set, each set is calculated individually and added together to obtain the total session volume. No matter the method used, it is important that the strength and conditioning professional is able to quantify the total work completed by an athlete in a training session.

Cautions Regarding the Effect of Resistance Training Volume

In conjunction with this, it is important to evaluate all exercises, specifically multi-joint exercises, and their respective volumes on an exercise-by-exercise basis to determine how much stress will be placed on specific muscle groups during a training session. Coaches and strength and conditioning professionals need to remember that the stress placed on an athlete's body during a resistance training session is only a portion of the stress that is placed on the athlete. During any given microcycle, resistance training is only one of the multiple stressors an athlete has to handle; it is important that the resistance training program does not affect an athlete's sport performance and that it is properly planned in light of the on-field training and the game schedule. To ensure this occurs, consistent communication between the support staff and the coaching staff is key throughout the training process.

Factors Affecting Resistance Training Volume

Volume assignments also depend on the goal or phase of the training program, that is, whether the goal is primarily strength, power, hypertrophy, or muscular endurance (table 4.1). The volume is dictated significantly by the outcome that the athlete is trying to achieve (15).

In addition to the goal of the resistance training program, athletes' training age and history, along with their game participation, are factors to assess when programming for individual athletes. Those who do not participate in games or play significantly fewer minutes generally could be subjected to more volume to help with their athletic development, while athletes who see significant time during games but have a detailed training history are often able to withstand greater volumes in season compared to those who do not. When athletes are required to peak for sport performance the quantity of training volume generally should be reduced. During these times, it is advisable to maintain small exposures to intense work in the training program, however, in an attempt to maintain the desired physical qualities.

Table 4.1 Volume Assignments Based on the Training Goal

Training goal	Goal repetitions per set	Sets*
Strength	≤6	2-6
**Power:		
Single-effort event	1-2	3-5
Multiple-effort event	3-5	3-5
Hypertrophy	6-12	3-6
Muscular endurance	≥12	2-3

*These assignments do not include warm-up sets and typically apply to core exercises only.

**Based on weightlifting-derived movements (e.g., clean and snatch). The load and repetition assignments shown for power in this table are *not consistent* with the %1RM–repetition relationship. In nonexplosive movements, loads equaling about 80% of the 1RM apply to the two- to five-repetition range.

Reprinted by permission from J.M. Sheppard and N.T. Triplett, "Program Design for Resistance Training," in *Essentials of Strength Training and Conditioning,* National Strength and Conditioning Association by G.G. Haff and N.T. Triplett, editors (Champaign, IL: Human Kinetics, 2016), 463.

Rest Periods

The time between exercises, sets, and workouts are effectively rest and are the periods when recovery and adaptations occur. This is an important yet sometimes overlooked consideration when designing and executing training programs. Various factors might influence the duration of rest between exercises, including the athlete's training status, the relative load lifted, and the type of movement and muscle recruitment the exercises demand.

Less conditioned athletes might need longer rest periods between sets of an exercise based on physiological factors, but shorter durations show similar results because the stimuli required to elicit adaptations is lower anyway (2). However, as training age develops and the demand for specificity and overload increases to cause further adaptations, rest period length has a greater impact on the athlete's results (e.g., longer rest periods [3-5 minutes] are needed to effectively improve muscular strength) (14, 15).

Differences in the type of stimuli being applied also lead to differences in rest period length. For example, the deadlift exercise involves contributions from many muscle groups, so it requires a longer rest period compared to the biceps curl exercise that trains a relatively small amount of muscle mass, especially if the relative load lifted is much greater (and it can be because the deadlift is a multi-joint exercise and the biceps curl is a single-joint exercise). Since the desired adaptation is more related to neuromuscular activation versus energy production, a longer rest period allows the body to be more thoroughly recovered to ensure the next set can be performed at a high level of intensity to maximize the stimuli.

For muscle hypertrophy, since metabolic demands and physiological responses likely play a role in driving adaptations, a somewhat shorter rest period will be more effective; recommendations range from 30 to 90 seconds (15). However, other factors used to maximize the hypertrophy stimulus must be considered. Since larger movements with higher metabolic demands are often used to drive the hypertrophic response, it is important to consider the demands imposed when deciding what rest periods are appropriate and effective.

For muscle endurance training, shorter rest duration ensures metabolic systems are stressed, which in turn drives adaptations in this direction. Recommended rest periods are often 30 seconds or less between sets (15).

There are practical applications of rest periods that can influence program design. Since time limitation is often an issue within resistance training for soccer, pairing two or more exercises can be a time-efficient strategy. A **combination set** can be designed by following a major exercise such as the deadlift, which requires three to five minutes of rest, with a mobility exercise of relatively low intensity within the period of rest between sets of the deadlift. Another strategy is to superset a lower body exercise with an upper body exercise, since the specific muscles stressed during one exercise are actively resting during the other (see the Exercise Order section for examples). These active recovery strategies can lower the total duration of rest needed due to the increased blood flow and energy substrate delivery to affected muscles.

It is also important to consider the recovery needs between the cycles of a periodized training program. A common strategy is to drop the volume and load at preplanned times (called *unloading, underloading,* or *deloading*), such as every four weeks. This allows athletes working with high levels of stress to recover more thoroughly (and reduce the risk of overtraining) so they can continue to adapt and progress their program.

In soccer, periodization systems for practice can also follow a cycle of overload and underload periods, so prescription in the weight room should be well aligned with the big picture of all stresses to which athletes are exposed. In the high school and collegiate setting, other stressful periods should be considered, such as finals week and testing dates when the athlete might already be overloaded from physiological and psychological demands and might not be maximizing recovery with proper sleep, hydration, and nutrition strategies.

In summary, when planning any type of stimuli to drive an adaptation, recovery from that stimuli also should be planned as part of the adaptation process. Be it between sets of an exercise, after several microcycles, or between entire phases of training, an appropriate recovery response to the stress should be considered and included in the program design.

PERIODIZATION

Periodization involves manipulating aspects of the training program such as sets, repetitions, specificity of the exercises performed, the resistance used, the rest interval time, training frequency, or exercise tempo while minimizing the risk of overtraining (11, 15). A training plan template that encompasses the entire training process, generally the whole year, helps guide when certain physical parameters might take on greater focus within the training program. The overall goal of a periodized training program is to apply the appropriate amount of stress to the individual to drive the desired adaptation response while not compromising on-field performance.

Planning Training Phases

Within a yearly cycle, soccer teams generally participate in four phases of training: off-season, preseason, in-season, and postseason. Each phase consists of a different number of microcycles that together make up the phase of training or mesocycle. Breaking down the training plan into mesocycles, and subsequently microcycles, helps with planning to ensure appropriate doses are delivered during the training process. Each microcycle within a training cycle provides the opportunity for exercise modification, specific planning of loading, and the ability to tailor the training program to each athlete's needs. These modifications can be related to other variables such as on-field training load and game minutes.

Planning in a longitudinal fashion enables progression and continual athletic development across the course of the year. Depending on the team's status or age group of athletes, the strength and conditioning professional needs to factor in key landmarks such as international windows, bye weeks for professional players, exam periods or vacation periods for high school and college soccer athletes, and periods of high sport-specific loads such as games or carnivals as it pertains to academy athletes. These landmarks can act as preplanned recovery or deload periods of resistance training. However, it is important to remember—especially in the case of academy soccer athletes—the stress placed on the body is increased due to the higher number of games compared to normal. Planning around such periods and working with the sport coach is integral in appropriately loading the athlete and driving adaptation on each side of such periods within the yearly cycle. Further, planning recovery into microcycles to provide periods when the volume and intensity are lower can promote supercompensation as well as allow the muscle tissue to recover, adapt, and be prepared for the upcoming stimulus.

Types of Periodization

Many types of periodization have been implemented across a variety of sports. Often, the philosophy of the strength and conditioning professional helps shape the periodization model used. Additionally, the training age and level of the athlete can influence the type of periodization strategy applied to the training program. The goal of a periodized training program is to optimize the principle of overload and help the neuromuscular system adapt to the unaccustomed loads or stressors (11).

Linear periodization is a common type of periodization strategy that starts with a period of high-volume, low-intensity training while gradually shifting to programming in which exercises are performed using lower volumes and higher intensities (4). Linear periodization is commonly used with developing athletes so they can begin by learning the exercise under low loads while performing a higher number of repetitions (that help with the motor skill development) and then progress over time to higher loads and lower volume as they become more proficient at performing the movement. Using this model of periodization, athletes sequentially gain strength as volume decreases.

Another periodization strategy is **block periodization**, in which there is a primary focus on a specific goal during each training cycle. In other words, each phase of a block periodization program is characterized by having most of the training program dedicated to a specific goal of the training program; a block would not address hypertrophy, strength, and power in the same cycle—those goals instead would be the focus of separate, sequenced blocks (e.g., a period of hypertrophy followed by strength followed by power) (5). Block periodization is commonly implemented with athletes who are training for longer-term goals and are aiming to peak once or multiple times across a competition season.

Nonlinear periodization, also referred to as *undulating periodization*, has become more adopted within sports that involve long in-season periods. This type of periodization can be adapted on a week-to-week or day-to-day basis, which is commonly referred to as *daily undulating periodization*. Undulating periodization allows for the strength and conditioning professional to adjust volume and intensity on a week-to-week or day-to-day basis rather than doing so over a period of months (4). This model also allows for qualities to be trained across different days within the microcycle or within sessions of the microcycle. An undulating periodization model is generally suited to advanced academy or collegiate and professional athletes. Such a model is generally not suited to younger inexperienced, developing athletes.

More recently, soccer teams at the collegiate and professional levels are implementing a **concurrent model of periodization**. In the previously mentioned periodization models, on-field goals within the periodization model are generally mirrored with composite goals, which are aimed to be developed in the resistance training program. In the concurrent periodization model, the strength and conditioning professional looks to develop multiple fitness qualities within the same microcycle. Such an approach is appropriate for a sport like soccer, in which, in the professional environment, the preparatory period is very short (generally 3-8 weeks) and the in-season (competition period) lasts between 5 and 10 months in some instances. Because performance in the sport itself is always the primary objective, being able to concurrently drive the adaptation as it pertains to aerobic and anaerobic fitness as well as strength and power is critical to the athletes' performance across a long competition period.

SPORT-SPECIFIC GOALS OF A RESISTANCE TRAINING PROGRAM

The primary goal of a sport-specific training program—of any type—is to prepare athletes to handle the unique demands of their sport. As explained, the program should apply specific stimuli that overload the involved tissues and cause an adaptation that will enhance the athlete's ability not just to tolerate the stress, but to perform optimally.

Visionhaus/Getty Images

Contact between athletes creates another physical demand beyond sprinting and jumping.

Strength and Power

Soccer is a multifaceted sport that has many physiological requirements, but a primary focus of a resistance training program is to develop strength and power, and this in and of itself can help reduce the likelihood of injury. Many of the physical qualities required in soccer can be developed during on-field resistance training; however, off-field resistance training for strength and power development is critical to aiding in injury prevention, decreasing injury risk factors, developing more resilient athletes, and improving sport performance.

Movement Skill

Beyond strength and power, soccer also has a physical demand related to sprinting, as well as occasional jumping and contact between athletes. **Movement skill** is a term used to describe the various mechanics within a sport that, in the case of soccer, are related to acceleration, maximum velocity, deceleration, and transitions (changing directions). (For more detail, see pages 11-13 in chapter 1 and pages 19-25 in chapter 2.)

When assessing specific movement skills, it is possible to recognize which muscle groups are primarily stressed during execution of those skills. For example, as velocity increases during high-speed running, the overall posture of the sprinter becomes progressively more vertical to the ground, and so does the direction of force application in each stride. This position, in general, leads to ground contact happening slightly in front of the hips, with a pattern of force generation very similar to that in hinging or hip-dominant exercises. So, as velocity increases, so does the stress placed on the posterior chain muscles, including the calves, hamstrings, glu-teals, and spinal erectors. A similar assessment can be made during deceleration and transition to acceleration, especially if it involves change in direction. Anterior chain muscles such as the quadriceps, hip flexors, and lower abdominals are primarily stressed. During deceleration, a pattern very similar to a forward lunge and other knee-dominant exercises is observed, with force being applied forward into the ground to drive the body backward and to decrease the inertial force of the athlete's forward momentum. Since these muscle groups work together and with complex sequences of activation and synchronization, it is essential that compound resistance training exercises, with similar patterns of movement, are prescribed to address these muscle groups to help prepare the athlete to handle the demands of these sport-specific movement skills.

Force–Velocity Profile

Test results from the assessments described in chapter 3 can provide details to the strength and conditioning professional about an athlete's physical attributes. For example, because strength and power are two key physical qualities of soccer athletes, assessing how an athlete creates force along the force–velocity curve (i.e., the athlete's force–velocity profile) provides the strength and conditioning professional with a detailed overview about the athlete's physical characteristics, which is key in designing an individualized resistance training program.

As shown in figure 4.1 on page 74, the force–velocity curve displays velocity on the vertical (i.e., y-axis) and force on the horizontal (i.e., x-axis). Training for strength involves lifting heavier loads at slower speeds (i.e., the upper left part of the curve), and training for speed involves lifting lighter loads at faster speeds (i.e., the lower right part of the curve). A global goal of training for the soccer athlete is to incorporate training for all aspects of the force–velocity curve, thereby shifting the force–velocity curve favorably up and to the right. Moving the curve in this direction indicates improvements in both strength and power (an expression of strength-speed) because the athlete would be lifting heavier loads by producing more force and be able to move those loads at a faster speed by generating more power. If an athlete's underlying deficiency is strength and force production, a resistance training program that is designed around the premise of strength-speed or maximal resistance training is recommended. For an athlete who lacks power or the ability to generate force quickly, a maximum velocity or speed-strength-focused resistance training program would help achieve those desired outcomes. In athletes with a low training age or who lack overall strength and power characteristics, training the entire force–velocity curve is most favorable to help improve overall athletic development.

Position-Specific Programming

Movement capacities of field athletes are similar; they are required to sprint, change direction, compete in the air, and adhere to tactical principles. Thus, the overall philosophical approach to the development of the resistance training program should be similar. Most coaches and strength and conditioning professionals generally develop a base template and then make adjustments as needed based on their athletes' individual factors such as injury history, movement compensations, body type, and training age.

Goalkeepers, on the other hand, have a significantly reduced running volume and movement demands in comparison to field athletes and rely much more on power, quickness, and reaction abilities, often leading to high ground impact due to diving. As a result, their programs usually differ quite significantly from field athletes'. Goalkeepers have a greater need for strength and power development as well as a greater need for hypertrophy work since the increased muscle mass works as the athlete's body armor against ground impact. Also unique to the position is a higher demand for upper body strength when throwing the ball in distribution as well as for

Goalkeepers have an elevated need for upper body strength to throw the ball in distribution and for stopping shots.

shot stopping. The latter requires high levels of strength at extreme ranges since often contact with the ball is made at full extension and with feet off the ground, which greatly increases the stress put on the distal segments. Therefore, specific shoulder work to ensure proper overhead flexion and extension is necessary.

The force–velocity curve has applications for position-specific programming. For example, a goalkeeper who performs many plyometric-based movements during sport-specific training might have a well-developed velocity end of the force–velocity curve but perhaps less absolute strength. A program that focuses on maximal strength and strength-speed would be advantageous in helping this athlete develop the entire force–velocity curve. For a field athlete who displays good strength in shielding athletes from the ball and battling to win the ball from the opposition but infrequently reaches maximum velocity while running would benefit from a program targeting speed-strength and velocity training in the gym. This would help the athlete develop an ability to produce force more quickly, which can translate to improved sprint speed.

CONCLUSION

In summary, program design is a complex process involving a great number of variables both on the side of the athletes and their needs as well as the technical nuances of exercise biomechanics and physiology. The strength and conditioning professional should gather as much relevant information about the athlete as possible, perform a thorough needs analysis, and apply well-rounded knowledge in athletic development and sports insights, while adhering to the basic principles of strength and conditioning to design appropriate programs for athletes. Considerations should be given to different environments, from youth to professional teams, as well as the seasons within a year and other external factors affecting each athlete's well-being.

PART II

EXERCISE
TECHNIQUE

5

TOTAL BODY EXERCISE TECHNIQUE

SCOTT CAULFIELD AND BRYAN MANN

Resistance training using total body exercises is effective for improving athletic movement abilities in soccer athletes. Total body exercises are also important for training economy, meaning athletes can get more done in less time using fewer exercises.

The ability to control one's body and create and absorb force, such as starting and stopping and changing direction, is crucial for soccer athletes of any position. Moving the body efficiently in all three planes of motion to sprint, stop, laterally shuffle, crossover run, and backpedal, and so on requires strength. Resistance training using total body exercises can be an excellent way to help create the foundation for these abilities.

Exercises that use both lower and upper body in coordination are not only good for building strength throughout the body but also typically involve athletic movements such as the Olympic-style weightlifting movements and derivatives. While the true Olympic weightlifting movements are performed from the floor, strength and conditioning professionals working with team sport athletes often use the Olympic derivatives, which can be used for control, stability, and moderate increases in strength. The "hang" and "power" variations included in this chapter are from the hang position, which means beginning the movement above the knees and catching the bar in the power position, then receiving the bar in an athletic quarter-squat position. Make sure to perform the exercise to its specified intent (i.e., Olympic lift derivatives for speed and power should be performed quickly and exercises for strength and coordination should be performed in a slow and controlled fashion).

For more information regarding other total body exercises and their technique, consult NSCA's professional resources (1, 2).

Exercise Finder

Hang Power Clean 86
Hang Power Snatch 88
Kettlebell Swing 92
Medicine Ball Granny Toss 95
Sled Push 94
Turkish Get-Up 90

HANG POWER CLEAN

Primary Muscles Trained

Gluteus maximus, semimembranosus, semitendinosus, biceps femoris, vastus lateralis, vastus intermedius, vastus medialis, rectus femoris, soleus, gastrocnemius, deltoids, trapezius

Beginning Position

- Stand with the feet placed hip- to shoulder-width apart, with the toes pointed slightly outward.
- Grasp the bar with a closed pronated grip, with the hands spaced evenly, approximately shoulder-width apart (a).
- The arms should be straight with the elbows fully extended and out to the sides.
- Keeping the bar close to the body, slowly squat to where the bar is just above the knees.
- All repetitions begin from this standing position.

Movement Phases

1. Begin the exercise by forcefully extending the hips, knees, and ankles (triple extension) (b).
2. Try to keep the shoulders over the bar and the elbows extended as long as possible.
3. At maximum triple extension of the hips, knees, ankles, flex the elbows and drop into a quarter-squat position to catch the barbell in an athletic position (c). The bar path should remain close to the body throughout the movement.
4. Stand up fully with the barbell resting on the shoulders (d), and then lower the bar under control back to the thighs as in the beginning position.

Breathing Guidelines

Inhale prior to the first pull from the position above the knees, and then exhale once the bar is caught at shoulder height in the quarter-squat position while returning to standing.

Spotting Guidelines

Spotters are not required when performing Olympic lifting derivatives due to the highly technical nature of the exercise and the chance for injury of both the athlete and spotter if trying to assist. Athletes should be taught how to properly miss these exercises to allow them to move safely out of the way of the barbell in the event they are unable to lift the weight.

Exercise Modifications and Variations

This movement can be performed from a power rack with safety pins set at approximately mid-thigh height. Another variation is a pull, which includes the triple extension movements but not catching the barbell at the shoulders.

Coaching Tip

Push the feet into the floor, jump as high as possible, and punch the elbows through to the finish.

Figure 5.1 Hang power clean: *(a)* beginning position; *(b)* extend the hips, knees, and ankles; *(c)* catch; *(d)* end position.

HANG POWER SNATCH

Primary Muscles Trained

Gluteus maximus, semimembranosus, semitendinosus, biceps femoris, vastus lateralis, vastus intermedius, vastus medialis, rectus femoris, soleus, gastrocnemius, deltoids, trapezius

Beginning Position

- Stand with the feet placed hip- to shoulder-width apart, with the toes pointed slightly outward.
- Grasp the bar with a closed pronated grip, with the hands spaced evenly, approximately as wide as when holding the elbows up and abducted measuring from elbow to elbow.
- The arms should be straight with the elbows fully extended and pointing out to the sides.
- Keeping the bar close to the body, slowly squat to where the bar is just above the knees (a).
- All repetitions begin from this standing position.

Movement Phases

1. Begin the exercise by forcefully extending the hips, knees, and ankles (triple extension) (b).
2. Try to keep the shoulders over the bar and the elbows extended as long as possible.
3. At maximum triple extension of the hips, knees, and ankles, flex and rotate the elbows around the bar while dropping into a quarter-squat position to catch the barbell overhead in an athletic position (c-d). The bar path should remain close to the body throughout the movement.
4. Stand up fully with the barbell overhead in an overhead squat position (e), and then lower the bar under control back to the thighs as in the beginning position.

Breathing Guidelines

Inhale prior to the first pull from the position above the knees, and then exhale once the bar is caught overhead in the overhead squat position as you stand up.

Spotting Guidelines

Spotters are not required when performing Olympic lifting derivatives due to the highly technical nature of the exercise and the chance for injury of both the athlete and spotter if trying to assist. Athletes should be taught how to properly miss these exercises to allow them to move safely out of the way of the barbell in the event they are unable to lift the weight.

Exercise Modifications and Variations

This movement can be performed from a power rack with safety pins set at approximately mid-thigh height. Another variation is to use one dumbbell, and the movement can be done by catching the weight in the position previously described or in a deeper squat position if the athlete's mobility and flexibility allows.

Coaching Tip

Push the feet hard into the floor, jump as high as possible, and pull the bar apart overhead to finish.

Figure 5.2 Hang power snatch: *(a)* beginning position; *(b)* shift weight back; *(c)* shrug; *(d)* catch; *(e)* end position.

TURKISH GET-UP

Primary Muscles Trained

Gluteus maximus, semimembranosus, semitendinosus, biceps femoris, vastus lateralis, vastus intermedius, vastus medialis, rectus femoris, rectus abdominis, transverse abdominis, internal obliques, external obliques, deltoids, triceps, biceps, pectoralis major

Beginning Position

- Begin by lying on the floor with the kettlebell by the left shoulder.
- Turn toward the kettlebell and grasp the kettlebell in the left hand with a closed pronated grip and with the kettlebell resting on the back of the left wrist.
- Flex the left hip and knee so that the left foot can be placed flat on the floor approximately 12 to 18 inches (30-46 cm) from the left glute.
- Extend the left elbow so that the arm is fully extended and the kettlebell is now over the shoulder in line with the left elbow and wrist.
- Place the right arm alongside the body on the right side (a).
- All repetitions begin from this position.

Movement Phases

1. Keeping both eyes on the kettlebell, begin by simultaneously pushing into the floor with the flexed left leg and flexing the torso forward, keeping the kettlebell extended at arm's length overhead until reaching a sitting position with the right arm extended and the palm in contact with the floor (b-c).
2. From the sitting position push through the right hand in contact with the floor and the foot of the left leg side so that the hips extend to make a straight line through the right side of the body from the right ankle through the right shoulder (d).
3. With the hips fully extended and the body in an elevated position, bring the left leg under the body so that the knee is resting on the floor under the hip into a half-kneeling position (e).
4. Extend the torso so that the body is in a half-kneeling position, with the kettlebell arm still extended above the body (f).
5. Align the body so that both feet are pointing forward (if needed), and push the left foot into the floor and step the right foot forward to a fully standing position with the kettlebell still overhead (g). Perform the movements in reverse order until lying on the floor again.
6. Carefully switch the kettlebell to the right hand, and perform the exercise in the same manner as described using the opposite hand and leg position.

Breathing Guidelines

Inhale prior to the first upward movement, and then exhale when moving to standing with the kettlebell in the overhead position.

Coaching Tip

Keep the eyes on the kettlebell throughout the exercise and push it into the air as hard as possible to maintain a straight arm.

Figure 5.3　Turkish get-up: *(a)* beginning position; *(b-c)* support on hand; *(d)* lift hips and maximally extend them; *(e)* move right leg back and kneel under the hips; *(f)* lift hand off floor and extend torso upright; *(g)* shift weight to left leg and push into the floor to stand up in a balanced stance.

KETTLEBELL SWING

Primary Muscles Trained

Gluteus maximus, semimembranosus, semitendinosus, biceps femoris, vastus lateralis, vastus intermedius, vastus medialis, rectus femoris

Beginning Position

- Stand over a kettlebell with feet hip- to shoulder-width distance apart and the toes pointed straight ahead or slightly outward.
- Squat down and grasp the horns of the kettlebell with both hands with a closed pronated grip.
- Stand up with the kettlebell so that the arms are in front of the body and the kettlebell is hanging between the legs (a).
- All repetitions begin from this position.

Movement Phases

1. Initiate movement in the swing by flexing the hips and knees while passing the kettlebell back through the legs as if hiking a football (b).
2. Keep the torso rigid and scapulae retracted.
3. After reaching approximately a quarter-squat position forcefully extend the hips and knees to return to standing, and allow momentum to swing the kettlebell upward to a maximum height of shoulder level (c).
4. Swing the kettlebell back through the legs with control while flexing the hips and knees, then reverse momentum forcefully by extending the hips and knees to create a ballistic swinging motion.

Breathing Guidelines

Inhale prior to the first downward movement, then exhale while swinging the kettlebell upward.

Exercise Modifications and Variations

The kettlebell swing can be performed with band resistance by looping a long elastic band through the kettlebell. Stand on one end of a long band, then loop it through the handle of the kettlebell and step on the other end of the band. Follow the movements as previously described with the band around the kettlebell. Another variation is the partner-assisted eccentric overload kettlebell swing. In this variation a partner faces the athlete swinging the kettlebell and provides additional force of the downward movement of the kettlebell that the athlete must control eccentrically.

Coaching Tips

- Push through the heels.
- Keep the head in a neutral position.

Figure 5.4 Kettlebell swing: *(a)* start position; *(b)* swing kettlebell backward; *(c)* swing kettlebell forward.

SLED PUSH

Primary Muscles Trained

Gluteus maximus, semimembranosus, semitendinosus, biceps femoris, vastus lateralis, vastus intermedius, vastus medialis, rectus femoris, soleus, gastrocnemius

Figure 5.5   Sled push.

Beginning Position

- Facing a sled that has handles, flex at the hips to reach forward toward the handles.
- Begin the movement by grasping each handle with a neutral closed grip.
- Step forward with one foot as if walking to begin movement of the sled.
- All repetitions begin from this position.

Movement Phases

1. Extend through the hip, knee, and ankle of the front leg to propel the sled forward.
2. Step through with the trail leg to walk forward while keeping the arms fully extended as the sled moves forward.
3. Fully extend the hip, knee, and ankle of the front leg with each step so that all lower body muscles are engaged throughout the movement.

Breathing Guidelines

Inhale prior to the first stepping movement, then exhale through each step as the sled moves forward.

Exercise Modifications and Variations

The sled push can be performed for strength or speed, and the method of movement is based on the intent. When performed for strength, walking is typically the best method of performance. When performed for speed, lighter loads and sprinting can be used.

The sled drag is a popular variation that involves dragging the sled behind the athlete by holding straps or attaching a belt to the athlete's waist. Another variation is the crossover (lateral) sled drag, which involves a crossover step while holding the strap or having it attached to a waist belt.

Coaching Tips

- Keep the elbows locked out throughout the movement.
- Do not hyperextend the neck during the exercise.
- Ensure that the athlete is not using a load that is so heavy that he or she is unable to move in a straight line. Also, ensure fluidity of movement. If the athlete has an imbalanced ability to move (i.e., left vs. right asymmetry), reduce the load.

MEDICINE BALL GRANNY TOSS

Primary Muscles Trained

Gluteus maximus, semimembranosus, semitendinosus, biceps femoris, vastus lateralis, vastus intermedius, vastus medialis, rectus femoris, soleus, gastrocnemius, biceps, anterior deltoids

Beginning Position

- Stand over a medicine ball with the feet hip- to shoulder-width distance apart and toes pointed straight ahead or slightly outward.
- Squat down to grasp the medicine ball in the hands on each side with the palms facing each other (a).
- All repetitions begin from this position.

Movement Phases

1. Forcefully extend through the hips, knees, and ankles to stand up rapidly.
2. When reaching full extension and jumping off the floor, allow the arms to help propel the ball upward.
3. Momentum from the rapid extension should propel the ball upward, and as the ball reaches abdominal to chest height, throw it into the air (b).
4. Allow the ball to fall on its own. Do not try to catch it out of the air.

Coaching Tips

- Drop the hips between the heels when lowering the ball.
- Push the feet as hard as possible into the floor.
- Jump as high as possible, and release the ball at its highest point.

Figure 5.6 Medicine ball granny toss: (a) start position; (b) toss.

6

LOWER BODY EXERCISE TECHNIQUE

SCOTT CAULFIELD AND BRYAN MANN

Lower body strength is key to athletic performance in the sport of soccer, which requires repeated efforts of speed, aerobic endurance, change of direction, and explosive ballistic movements. Athletes with greater lower body strength likely will have improved performance and might have a reduced risk of injury.

Performance is improved because the musculature produces more force per contraction. Newton's third law states that the more force that is applied into the ground, the further the athlete is propelled per stride. Even if the stride rate remains the same, a greater movement velocity is achieved because of the greater distance per stride. The same phenomena has been found for change of direction. Stronger individuals can withstand greater forces, so the deceleration phase is less before reaccelerating in the desired direction. Simply put, they can change direction faster because of their greater strength.

By increasing the strength of the lower body musculature, specifically the hip abductors, hip external rotators, and hamstrings, the likelihood of ACL tears is reduced because hip adduction, hip internal rotation, and tibial anterior translation are all mechanisms of the ACL tear. Increasing strength of those muscles counters the mechanisms of the ACL tear and thus reduces the likelihood of this and other knee injuries. In addition to this, the soft tissue injuries often seen in the sport of soccer, such as strained quadriceps and hamstring muscles, are less likely because the musculature is stronger and more resilient.

Slight changes in the method of performance of these exercises can be done to perform the movement for strength or for power. Strength performance is developed through heavier loads (75% 1RM and greater), and power performance is developed through lighter loads (20%-60% 1RM) with maximal intent (i.e., moving the bar quickly) (4). What is needed depends on the athlete. After possessing the requisite strength levels, those who are constantly fighting for position might benefit from additional strength, but those who are using speed might benefit from more time spent in explosive training. The change in the goal of development is dependent on both the athlete and the time of the year.

In-season training is also crucial for performance and varies based on the needs of the individual athlete. If the athlete requires additional strength, submaximal loading and progressive overload is ideal. If the athlete requires greater speed for performance, focusing their time on explosive exercises enhances their performance. The main determinant of success in soccer is the score board, not what progress was made in the weight room. The strength and conditioning professional should not push the volume and intensity to the point where the athlete will not be recovered for their subsequent games or training sessions. For instance, if the strength and conditioning professional typically performs an **autoregulatory progressive resistance exercise** (APRE) protocol for strength, a single working set with progressing loads each week is sufficient as opposed to the normal two working sets (2). A good rule of thumb is, when trying to progress in-season, only use between 50% and 60% of the total workloads used in the off-season (2).

For more information regarding other lower body exercises and their technique, consult NSCA's professional resources (1, 3).

Exercise Finder

Back Squat 102
Copenhagen Adductor Exercise 114
Eccentric-Only Nordic Leg Curl 111
Forward Lunge. 109
Front Squat 100
Glute-Ham Raise (GHR) Prone Isometric Hold 112
Hip Thrust 104
One-Arm Single-Leg RDL 106
Sliding Leg Curl 108
Split Squat 105
Trap Bar Deadlift 98

TRAP BAR DEADLIFT

Primary Muscles Trained

Gluteus maximus, semimembranosus, semitendinosus, biceps femoris, vastus lateralis, vastus intermedius, vastus medialis, rectus femoris, trapezius

Beginning Position

- Stand in the middle of a trap bar with the feet placed hip- to shoulder-width apart, with toes pointed forward or slightly outward (a).
- Squat down and grasp the handles with a neutral closed pronated grip (b).
- Keep the feet in the middle of the trap bar with the chest up, a neutral spine, and hips slightly higher than the knees.

Movement Phases

1. Begin the exercise by bracing the core; retracting the scapula; and extending the hips, knees, and ankles.
2. Maintain full arm extension throughout the movement.
3. Stand up with the weight until the hips and knees are fully extended (c).
4. Lower the bar slowly by flexing the hips and knees to squat back down to the beginning position.

Breathing Guidelines

A general guideline regarding proper breathing during resistance training is to inhale prior to lifting or during what is known as the concentric phase and then exhaling when passing the **sticking point** during the lowering, or eccentric, phase. Often the sticking point is at or close to the transition between the two phases, and this breathing strategy can apply to nearly every resistance training exercise (1).

Exercise Modifications and Variations

This movement can be performed using one or two kettlebells by placing the kettlebell(s) between or outside of the feet (depending on how many kettlebells are used) and lifting as described above. This movement also can be done using a landmine attachment, with the athlete standing on one side of the bar and using one arm at a time to perform a modified one-arm deadlift.

Coaching Tips

- Align the shoulders vertically with the mid-foot.
- Keep a braced torso position throughout the exercise.

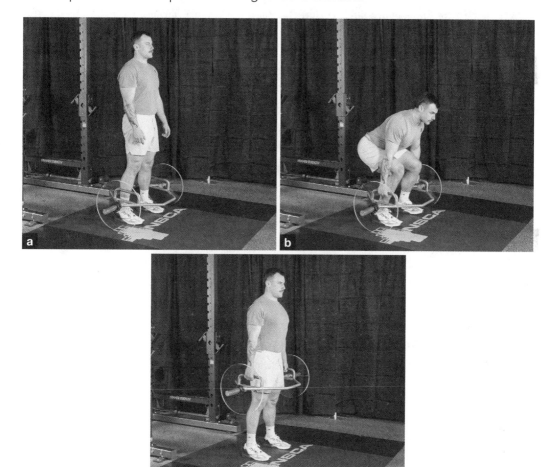

Figure 6.1 Trap bar deadlift: *(a)* beginning position; *(b)* grasp trap bar handles; *(c)* extend to standing position.

FRONT SQUAT

Primary Muscles Trained

Gluteus maximus, semimembranosus, semitendinosus, biceps femoris, vastus lateralis, vastus intermedius, vastus medialis, rectus femoris

Beginning Position

- Place a barbell in a rack at approximately shoulder height.
- Grasp and position the barbell using one of the following two methods:
  1. Parallel-arm position
     - Use a closed pronated grip with hands slightly wider than shoulder-width apart, with the bar resting on the anterior deltoids and the center of the bar close to the neck.
     - Rotate the arms around the bar so that it rests on top of the front deltoids and clavicles. The back of the hands will be just outside of the anterior deltoids on each side.
     - Lift the elbows upward so that the upper arms are parallel to the floor and the anterior deltoids create a shelf on which the bar rests *(a)*.
  2. Crossed-arm position
     - Cross the arms in front of the body close to the bar, and place the opposite hands on the opposite deltoids to keep the bar in place.
     - Lift the elbows upward so that the upper arms are parallel to the floor and creates a shelf on the anterior deltoids *(b)*.
- Lift the bar by extending the hips and knees to take the bar off the rack.
- Take one or two steps back from the rack, and place the feet shoulder-width apart, with toes pointed straight ahead or slightly outward.
- All repetitions begin from this position.

Movement Phases

Spotters

1. Stand at both ends of the bar, with palms facing the bar and thumbs interlocked to provide a strong grip.
2. Once the athlete is ready to lift the bar off the rack, step back with the athlete, and reposition when he or she stops and is ready to perform the movement.
3. As the athlete performs the movement, squat down with him or her, keeping the hands close to the bar end and ready to assist if necessary.

Athlete

1. Squat down by flexing the hips first to sit slightly backward.
2. Continue squatting by flexing the hips and knees until the top of the thighs are parallel or slightly below parallel to the floor *(c)*. (Alternatively, another guideline is to lower until the crease of the hip is below the knee.)
3. Keep a neutral spine by bracing the core and keeping the upper arms parallel to the floor, with the eyes facing forward.

Breathing Guidelines

Inhale prior to lifting the bar, then exhale when passing the sticking point during the upward movement.

Exercise Modifications and Variations

This movement can be performed with a dumbbell held in front of the body, commonly referred to as a *goblet squat*. It also can be performed by holding two dumbbells with a closed neutral grip, resting each dumbbell on the anterior deltoid.

Figure 6.2 Front squat: *(a)* parallel-arm position; *(b)* crossed-arm position; *(c)* squat.

BACK SQUAT

Primary Muscles Trained

Gluteus maximus, semimembranosus, semitendinosus, biceps femoris, vastus lateralis, vastus intermedius, vastus medialis, rectus femoris

Beginning Position

- Place a barbell in a rack at approximately shoulder height.
- Move under the barbell with the bar centered on the upper back and shoulders and the hands holding the bar slightly wider than shoulder-width apart with a closed pronated grip (a).

Movement Phases

Spotters

1. Stand at both ends of the bar, with the palms facing the bar and the thumbs interlocked to provide a strong grip.
2. Once the athlete is ready to lift the bar off the rack, step back with the athlete, and reposition when he or she stops and is ready to perform the movement.
3. As the athlete performs the movement, squat down with him or her, keeping the hands close to the bar end and ready to assist if necessary.

Athlete

1. Squat down by flexing the hips first to sit slightly backward (b).
2. Continue squatting by flexing the hips and knees until the tops of the thighs are parallel or slightly below parallel to the floor (c). (Alternatively, another guideline is to lower until the crease of the hip is below the knee.)
3. Keep a neutral spine by bracing the core and keeping the torso upright, with the eyes facing forward.

Breathing Guidelines

After stepping out of the rack with the barbell, inhale prior to lowering into the squat, then exhale when passing the sticking point during the upward movement.

Exercise Modifications and Variations

The *safety bar squat* is a variation of the back squat that uses a specialty bar with handles in the front, which can be advantageous for athletes with poor shoulder mobility or upper body extremity injuries. This allows loading of the spine and lower body without having to place the hands up by the shoulders.

A *belt squat* is a variation of the back squat that uses a different piece of equipment that eliminates the compressive loading of the spine. It can be advantageous for athletes with poor shoulder mobility or upper body extremity injuries as well as those who have injuries such as a disc herniation and cannot tolerate spinal loading.

Coaching Tips

- Lead with the head and chest out of the bottom of the squat.
- Feel the pressure on the heel and ball of the foot evenly.
- When observing the athlete, pay attention to the knee and foot relationship. The knees should track directly over the second toe, so the coaching tip should match the athlete's performance. For instance, do not tell the athlete to push the knees out if the knees track beyond the pinky toe.

Figure 6.3 Back squat: *(a)* beginning position; *(b)* flex the hips to sit slightly backward; *(c)* squat.

HIP THRUST

Primary Muscles Trained

Gluteus maximus, semimembranosus, semitendinosus, biceps femoris

Beginning Position

- Sit on the floor against the side of a bench with the legs extended perpendicular from the bench. The shoulders and upper back should be able to contact the side of the bench easily in this position.
- Grasp the bar with a closed pronated grip, then roll a barbell with weights loaded on it over the legs in line with the hips so that the bar and bench are both lengthwise compared to the body.
- Press the shoulders and upper back into the bench while keeping the feet flat on the floor positioned under the knees and extending the hips to lift the barbell 1-2 inches (3-5 cm) off the floor (a).
- All repetitions begin from this position.

Movement Phases

1. Push through the heels while extending the hips to make a straight line from the shoulders through the hips and knees (b).
2. Hold at the top position, where the torso and hips are in alignment and perpendicular to the bench.
3. Return to the beginning position by flexing the hips and lowering the bar to the floor.

Breathing Guidelines

Take a breath prior to lifting the bar off the floor, then exhale at the top of the movement when the body is parallel to the floor.

Exercise Modifications and Variations

A single-leg version of this exercise can be performed the same as described above except by holding one foot off the floor so that the foot and leg in contact with the floor must do all the work. To overload this movement, it can be done in any manner, with weight plates, heavy medicine balls, dumbbells, and barbells. For comfort, some athletes prefer to use an Airex pad or something similar under the bar when the load gets heavier.

Coaching Tips

- Push through the feet.
- Fully contract the glutes at the top of the movement.
- Maintain a neutral head position.

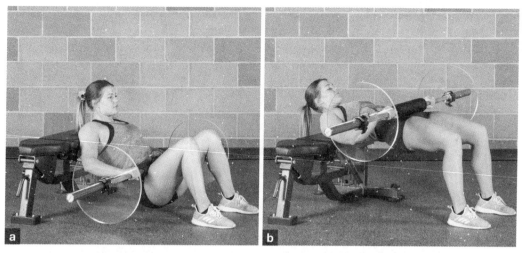

Figure 6.4 Hip thrust: *(a)* beginning position; *(b)* thrust.

SPLIT SQUAT

Primary Muscles Trained

Gluteus maximus, semimembranosus, semitendinosus, biceps femoris, vastus lateralis, vastus intermedius, vastus medialis, rectus femoris, iliopsoas

Beginning Position

- Step forward with one foot as if performing a forward lunge, and keep the feet in this position *(a)*.
- All repetitions are performed from this split stance position.

Movement Phases

1. Squat down by flexing the hips and knees simultaneously.
2. Continue squatting by flexing the hips and knees until the top of the front thigh is parallel or slightly below parallel to the floor *(b)*. (Alternatively, another guideline is to lower until the crease of the hip is below the knee.)
3. The thigh of the trail leg should be approximately perpendicular to the floor.
4. Keep a neutral spine by bracing the core and keeping the torso upright, with the eyes facing forward.

Breathing Guidelines

Inhale prior to lowering the body, then exhale when passing the sticking point during the upward movement.

Exercise Modifications and Variations

Barbell Split Squat

A variation of the split squat can be performed by using a barbell. Place a barbell in a rack at approximately shoulder height. Move under the barbell, with the bar centered on the upper back and shoulders and the hands holding the bar slightly wider than shoulder-width apart with a closed pronated grip. Stand up by extending the hips and knees to lift the bar off the hooks in the squat rack. Take two or three steps back with the feet approximately hip- to shoulder-width apart, then perform the exercise as described above.

Rear Foot–Elevated Split Squat

A rear foot–elevated split squat can be performed by placing the trail leg on a bench behind the athlete so that the shoelaces of the trail leg are in contact with the bench. Using the trail leg and bench for balance, the athlete performs the exercise in the same manner, squatting down until the front thigh is parallel to the floor.

Front Foot–Elevated Split Squat

Place a 25-pound (11 kg) or 45-pound (20 kg) plate on the floor in the rack, then follow the same steps as described for split squat above, except first place the front foot centered on the plate so that it is elevated, creating an increased range of motion.

Coaching Tip

Ensure that the athlete can maintain a vertical torso. If he or she is unable to do that, change the front foot position to closer to the rear foot.

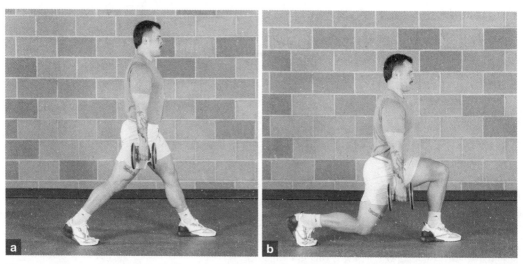

Figure 6.5   Split squat: (a) beginning position; (b) lower into lunge.

ONE-ARM SINGLE-LEG RDL

Primary Muscles Trained

Gluteus maximus, semimembranosus, semitendinosus, biceps femoris, erector spinae

Beginning Position

- Grasp a dumbbell or kettlebell in one hand using a closed pronated grip (a).
- Holding the implement in front of the thigh on one side, shift weight to that leg and slightly flex the hip and knee.
- Allow the hand not holding the implement to rest comfortably along the body.

Movement Phases

1. Flex at the hip and lower the implement, allowing it to slide along the front of the thigh while maintaining a stiff core and retracted scapula.
2. Reach backward with the nonsupport leg by keeping the knee flexed so that at the bottom position the leg is straight behind the athlete *(b)*.
3. Maintain a stiff core, and continue flexing at the hip until the dumbbell or kettlebell has passed the knee and the torso is parallel to the floor.
4. Return to the beginning position and repeat steps 1 through 3 on the opposite side.

Breathing Guidelines

Inhale prior to initiating the lowering part of the movement, and exhale during the upward movement phase.

Exercise Modifications and Variations

Two-Arm Single-Leg RDL

The use of two dumbbells or kettlebells is a variation to load the movement to a greater degree. Perform the movement the same as described above by holding an implement in each hand.

Kickstand RDL

This version is a progression to a single-leg RDL by moving the toes of one foot approximately in line with the heel of the forward foot. The movement is then performed as described above with the main emphasis on the forward hip and leg. This is a great way to progress from two legs to one leg in the RDL exercise.

Coaching Tip

Maintain a neutral spine throughout the movement.

Figure 6.6 One-arm single-leg RDL: *(a)* beginning position; *(b)* bottom position.

SLIDING LEG CURL

Primary Muscles Trained

Gluteus maximus, semimembranosus, semitendinosus, biceps femoris

Beginning Position

- Lie supine on the floor with the floor sliders near the feet.
- Place the heels on the sliders.
- Rest the arms alongside the body on the floor next to the body.

Movement Phases

1. Press the heels into the sliders and extend the hips so that the glutes lift off the floor and the legs are straight (a).
2. Flex the knees to bring the heels toward the glutes.
3. Continue flexing the knees until they are at approximately a 90-degree angle to the body (b).
4. Extend the knees to lower the legs back to the beginning position.
5. Keep the heels in contact with the sliders throughout the movement.

Breathing Guidelines

Inhale prior to initiating the knee flexion movement, then exhale during the downward movement as the knees extend to the beginning position.

Exercise Modifications and Variations

Suspension Leg Curl

Lying on the floor, place the feet in the stirrups of a suspension trainer. Lift the hips and legs off the floor, and flex at the knees to bring the heels close to the glutes. Keep the hips raised off the floor throughout the movement.

Single-Leg Leg Curl

All of the movements described above can be performed using a single-leg variation by keeping the non-working leg off the floor while performing the movement.

Coaching Tips

- Flex the glutes to initiate the movement.
- Keep the hips up throughout the upward movement phase.
- Engage the core to maintain stiffness throughout the exercise.

Figure 6.7   Sliding leg curl: *(a)* beginning position; *(b)* flexed position.

FORWARD LUNGE

Primary Muscles Trained

Gluteus maximus, semimembranosus, semitendinosus, biceps femoris, vastus lateralis, vastus intermedius, vastus medialis, rectus femoris, iliopsoas

Beginning Position

- Grasp a dumbbell in each hand with a closed neutral grip so that the dumbbells rest along the outside of the thighs on each side of the body *(a)*.
- Place the feet approximately hip- to shoulder-width apart.

Movement Phases

1. Take a step forward with one leg.
2. Flex the knee of the stepping leg to absorb the forward momentum, and lower slowly toward the floor.
3. While stepping, allow the trail leg knee to move close to the floor without touching it.
4. Keep the torso rigid, and do not lean forward while stepping forward.
5. At the bottom position, the front thigh should be approximately parallel to the floor, and the trail leg thigh should be approximately perpendicular to the floor *(b)*.
6. Return to the beginning position by pushing back through the forward leg to return to standing.
7. Repeat repetitions on the opposite side.

Breathing Guidelines

Inhale prior to stepping forward, then exhale through the sticking point, stepping back to the beginning position.

Exercise Modifications and Variations

Reverse Lunge

The reverse lunge can be performed by following the same steps as above, except that a reverse step is taken instead of forward. The front knee should be flexed at approximately 90 degrees, and the front thigh should be parallel or slightly above parallel to the floor.

Return to the beginning position by pushing through the front foot and extending the knee and hip to standing.

Lateral Lunge

The lateral lunge can be performed by stepping laterally and sitting back into the movement. The trail foot should remain in contact with the floor, and the trail leg should be straight. Return to the beginning position by pushing through the foot and extending the hip and knee until standing.

Rotational Lunge

The rotational lunge involves a rotation of the trunk during the exercise. This is important because rotation of the trunk is involved in a maximal-effort kick in soccer, and the lunge is a great method to incorporate rotation. This can be done in any plane of movement: frontal, sagittal, or transverse planes. The exercise is performed by stepping back and rotating so that if 12 o'clock is directly in front, the athlete steps toward five and seven o'clock. When the athlete steps into position for the lunge desired, he or she then rotates the torso into and across the leg that performed the lunge. Not only does this help strengthen the obliques, but it helps with the mobility of musculature that is often tight in soccer athletes, such as the hip flexors and hip adductors, by increasing their length during the movement. This might further improve the athlete's mobility and decrease the risk of injury.

Curtsy Lunge

The curtsy lunge is another variation to work through different planes of motion in the lunge. In this version the athlete steps behind the stance or forward leg as if curtsying or bowing to someone in front of them. This version will be felt more in the outside or stance leg hip and glute area.

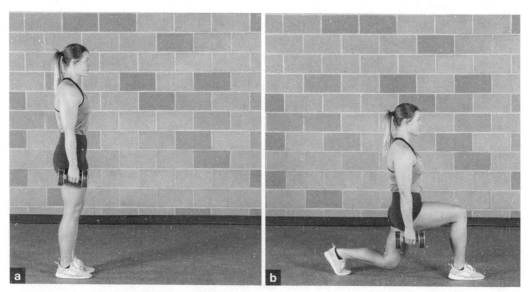

Figure 6.8 Forward lunge: *(a)* beginning position; *(b)* bottom position.

ECCENTRIC-ONLY NORDIC LEG CURL

Primary Muscles Trained

Semimembranosus, semitendinosus, biceps femoris

Beginning Position

- With a partner kneeling behind, kneel upright on a mat or the floor with the knees flexed at approximately 90 degrees and the torso upright (a).
- Keep the ankles flexed and toes in contact with the floor.
- The partner holds the athlete's feet while he or she moves through the exercise.

Movement Phases

1. Maintain a rigid torso while extending at the knees to lower toward the floor.
2. Lower the body as slowly and in as controlled a motion as possible during the downward movement (b).
3. Keeping the hands and arms near the body as if performing a push-up, lower until the hands are in contact with the floor (c).
4. Use the hands and arms to walk the body backward (or vigorously push upward) and pull back to the beginning position.

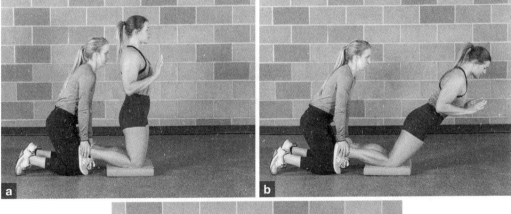

Figure 6.9 Eccentric-only Nordic leg curl: (a) beginning position; (b) downward phase; (c) bottom position.

Breathing Guidelines

Inhale prior to lowering the torso, then exhale through the sticking point, raising back to the beginning position.

Exercise Modifications and Variations

Band-Assisted Nordic Leg Curl

An assisted version of this exercise can be performed by attaching a long band behind the athlete to a piece of equipment, then looping the band over the shoulders or hips in front of the body. Hold the band while performing the movement so that the band assists in pulling the athlete back to the beginning position.

Loaded Nordic Leg Curl

An advanced version of this movement can be performed using external resistance such as a weight plate, dumbbell, or weight vest. Holding the weight in the hands with arms crossed, lower slowly toward the floor and then return to the beginning position. Athletes should drop the weight if they feel they are unable to control their downward movement.

An even more difficult version of this exercise can be done by increasing the lever arm. This will increase the feel of the resistance by holding the weight at arm's length overhead. The athlete first extends the arms straight to bring the weight overhead with the elbows outside the ears and then performs the exercise as described above.

Coaching Tip

Keep the core tight throughout the movement.

GLUTE-HAM RAISE (GHR) PRONE ISOMETRIC HOLD

Primary Muscles Trained

Gluteus maximus, semimembranosus, semitendinosus, biceps femoris, vastus lateralis, vastus intermedius, vastus medialis, rectus femoris, erector spinae, gastrocnemius

Beginning Position

- Get into position on a glute-ham raise machine, placing the legs between the pads so that the knees are flexed to approximately 90 degrees (a).
- The thighs should firmly press against the roller pads on the front of the machine.
- The feet should be placed firmly against the foot plate.
- Brace the core, and cross the arms across the body.

Movement Phases

1. Extend the knees slowly to lower the torso until the body is parallel to the floor (b-c).
2. Keep the torso rigid in the fully extended position and hold a straight line through the body (this is the isometric "hold" position).

Breathing Guidelines

Inhale prior to lowering to parallel then exhale and breathe normally during the hold position.

Exercise Modifications and Variations

Single-Leg Glute-Ham Raise (GHR) Prone Isometric Hold

Athletes can perform a single-leg variation of this exercise by holding one leg above the pads throughout the movement.

Band Glute-Ham Raise (GHR) Prone Isometric Hold

A resisted version of this exercise can be performed by attaching a band to the glute-ham raise machine and holding the band throughout the movement.

Barbell Glute-Ham Raise (GHR) Prone Isometric Hold

An advanced version of this exercise can be performed by holding a loaded barbell during the movement. After getting into position on the glute-ham raise machine, the athlete lowers down to the floor to pick up the bar, then returns to the parallel to floor position and holds for a given duration.

Coaching Tips

- Maintain a stiff core throughout the duration of the exercise.
- Do not flex or extend the head; maintain a neutral spine.
- Push the feet hard into the foot plate.

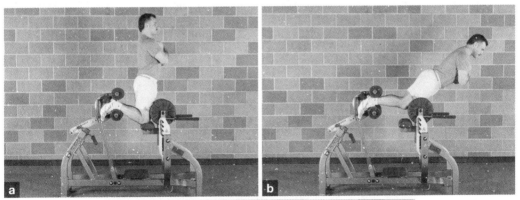

Figure 6.10 Glute-ham raise (GHR) prone isometric hold: *(a)* beginning position; *(b)* downward phase; *(c)* end position.

COPENHAGEN ADDUCTOR EXERCISE

Primary Muscles Trained

Adductor magnus, adductor longus, adductor brevis, pectineus

Beginning Position

- Lie on the floor on one side of the body with the body perpendicular to a bench and the top foot/ankle on top of the bench and the bottom foot/ankle under the bench.
- Stack the feet, knees, hips, and shoulders on top of each other and in vertical alignment.
- Position the elbow of the bottom arm at 90 degrees and directly under the bottom shoulder so that the upper arm is perpendicular to the floor.

Movement Phases

1. Brace the core and lift the hips up until the feet, knees, hips, and spine are in a line. The bottom leg should come up with the torso until the top surface of the bottom foot/ankle touches the underside of the bench (a).
2. Keep the same 90-degree flexed elbow position of the bottom arm with the upper arm of the bottom arm remaining perpendicular to the floor.
3. Allow the torso to eccentrically lower on a 3-second count; the lower foot should not touch the floor, however. Keep the top leg in the beginning position (b).
4. At the bottom of the movement, adduct the top leg to raise the torso and return to the fully lifted position.
5. Repeat repetitions on the opposite side.

Breathing Guidelines

Inhale at the top of the movement prior to getting into position. Exhale during the eccentric portion, and inhale during the concentric portion.

Exercise Modifications and Variations

The intensity can be decreased by flexing the top leg. This shortens the lever arm and makes it easier for the top leg to hold the body into position. Instead of placing the foot of the top leg on the bench, the knee would be placed there.

The intensity can be increased by placing the top foot into a suspension strap when performing the movement. This creates an unstable surface and requires greater proprioception for more contraction of the top leg.

Coaching Tips

- The top adductor works isometrically during the entire movement to maintain the appropriate position, and the bottom leg works concentrically and eccentrically.
- Athletes will most likely forget to breathe during this exercise. Remind them to breathe through the contraction.
- Athletes tend to rotate into a compensation pattern. Try to keep them perpendicular to the floor to target the appropriate muscles.

Figure 6.11 Copenhagen adductor exercise: *(a)* beginning position; *(b)* bottom position.

UPPER BODY EXERCISE TECHNIQUE

IAN JEFFREYS

The role of upper body resistance training in a soccer conditioning program is a much debated and contentious issue. Undoubtedly, it can bring benefits to certain athletes, but similarly, it can incur adaptations that can potentially hinder certain elements of performance. What is crucial is that the potential benefits and drawbacks are considered and related to the direct impact on soccer performance. As a result, decisions require an effective cost-benefit analysis that should include evaluation of an athlete's position and his or her level of performance and playing style. In all likelihood, upper body development will play a far smaller role than lower body development, and even core development, in a soccer athlete's overall program.

COST-BENEFIT ANALYSIS OF UPPER BODY RESISTANCE TRAINING

In general, an effective cost-benefit analysis focuses on two key areas: locomotion and soccer-specific scenarios. In terms of locomotion, soccer is an intermittent high-intensity sport with repeated multidirectional movements and frequent changes in speed and direction, all carried out over a 90-minute period. A clue to the dichotomy of upper body force capacity and especially mass can be traced to Newton's second law of motion. Known as the law of acceleration, the law asserts that the rate of acceleration is dependent on two factors: the force acting on the object and its mass ($F = m \times a$). Here is the dichotomy: upper body resistance training can increase force capacity, which can add to the ability to accelerate the body, but this often is accompanied by an increase in mass, which in turn requires more force to be applied to accelerate the increased mass. The key lies in their proportionality. In reality, the upper body contributes some propulsive capacity but nowhere near that of the lower body. As a result, upper body muscular development is likely to rapidly become a hindrance to speed performance once cross-sectional area is sufficient to provide the forces necessary to accelerate the small upper limbs rapidly and to appropriately tension connective tissue structure to provide stability and force transfer (3).

Another factor to consider is the nature of inertia and the requirement for multiple changes of movement during a soccer game. Inertia refers to the amount of force that is needed to change a body's motion. The greater the amount of motion an object has, the greater its inertia and subsequently the more force needed to change the motion. Given that the amount of motion is a measure of its momentum, which is a product of its mass and its velocity, a body with greater mass requires more force to change its motion. Consequently, greater mass without a concomitant increase in force might result in less of an effective capacity to make the rapid and multiple changes in motion required in soccer. Additionally, given that the body's mass needs to be moved around the field for the duration of the match, it is clear that from a locomotor perspective care needs to be taken with any upper body resistance training program to ensure that the cost-benefit ratio enhances soccer performance.

While locomotor analysis is important it needs to be supplemented with an analysis of soccer performance itself. Interestingly, some of this is based on a number of the same mechanical principles outlined above. When looking at inertia or the resistance to motion, an increased inertia can be beneficial in situations of physical contact (e.g., an athlete is shielding a ball or closing off a space from a set piece). In these instances, force capacity and mass can be beneficial. Similarly, in contact situations such as a heading duel or a tackle, a higher level of momentum potentially can enhance performance. As a result, consideration of the contribution of upper body resistance training should be given to the athlete's playing position and playing style. It is likely that some playing positions (e.g., center back or goalkeeper) require a higher level of upper body development than others (e.g., midfielders or fullbacks). Similarly, a consideration of playing styles within positions is important; for example, some strikers act more as target athletes, requiring the ability to hold up the ball and resulting in many physical battles with defenders, while others depend more on movement and on creating and running into space. Clearly, the requirements for upper body development differ between these styles. Finally, analysis should focus on the strengths and weaknesses of the individual athlete. Athletes who are consistently unable to hold up the ball or lose out in physical contact situations should consider the potential benefits of any upper body development program, although this is always likely to be secondary to a lower body and core development program.

One final consideration, and one often overlooked in traditional needs analysis, is the effect on the athlete's psychological performance. Some athletes equate strength with a certain level of upper body development, and it could be that this brings with it a certain level of on-field confidence. Similarly, some athletes will be willing to engage in upper body training more willingly than lower body training, which might be a consideration when generating the required level of engagement with the overall program.

FOCUS ON FORCE AND FUNCTION

While the focus of upper body development programs often drifts inadvertently onto mass development, the above analysis clearly demonstrates the challenges of this type of thinking. Instead, upper body programs should focus predominantly on the development of force capacities and overall joint function. This can help mediate some of the previous issues, and the focus on function can mitigate some potential injury risks.

Typically, upper body exercises are classified into two major movements—pushing movements and pulling movements—both of which can be further broken down into horizontal and vertical movements. However, this analysis is less useful for soccer, which does not (legally) involve extensive pushing or pulling movements. In these instances, while categorization of exercises as pushing and pulling can be beneficial, a different form of analysis is needed. Given that the key force capacities involve those that generate locomotion and those that benefit contact situations, these can be used as a basis for selecting exercises. The upper body forces that generate locomotion are used to stabilize the core and accelerate the arms. These forces originate in the torso and benefit from a relatively small arm mass. Similarly, contact situations involve force predominantly generated in the legs, through a stable core and supplemented by the torso. Again, the arms play a relatively small role in these situations. Subsequently, the focus of the upper body programs should be on the musculature of the torso rather than the arms.

In terms of injury risk, upper body injuries are far less common than lower body injuries in soccer. However, the joint most at risk of injury in the upper body is the shoulder. Being a ball and socket joint, the shoulder allows movement in multiple planes, which brings benefits in relation to movement but at a potential cost—some risk of injury. As a result, ensuring the shoulder joint functions effectively and has a suitable level of strength can be an important part of a performance program, especially for athletes prone to this type of injury. The exercises in this section include some designed exclusively for shoulder function.

EXERCISE SELECTION

The exercises in this section have been listed in terms of three major functions: pushing, pulling, and activation. Within each, a number of options are listed. In choosing the best option consideration should be given to the major goal of the exercise. As discussed earlier, mass alone is unlikely to be the best goal option in the majority of soccer athletes. As a result focus generally should be either on developing force capacity or more functionality. Some exercises such as the prone Y's are designed specifically to enhance movement function and therefore are best carried out with generally lower loads, focusing on the functioning of the joint and the associated musculature. Other exercises can have a number of goals and thus have multiple options. So, for example, a traditional bench press is probably the best option if the goal is to develop maximal force capacity in a horizontal push. However, switching this to a one-arm dumbbell press switches the emphasis from maximal force production onto the ability to apply force in a more compromised position, with additional emphasis placed on the ability to stabilize the torso. Having a clear goal is crucial to selecting the most appropriate exercise from the following menu.

For more information regarding other upper body exercises and their techniques, consult NSCA's professional resources (1, 2).

Exercise Finder

Bench Press 121

Bent-Over Row. 129

Dumbbell Bench Press. 123

Face Pull 139

Inverted Row 138

Lat Pulldown (Neutral, Pronated, and Supinated Grip) 137

One-Arm Dumbbell Bench Press. 125

One-Arm Dumbbell Row (Three Points Supported). 132

One-Arm Dumbbell Row (Hand and Knee Supported) 131

One-Arm Landmine Overhead Press 126

Prone T 142

Prone W 143

Prone Y 140

Pull-Up (Neutral, Pronated, and Supinated Grip) 135

Push-Up 120

Shoulder Press. 128

Standing Cable Row 134

Two-Arm Dumbbell Row (Head Supported) 133

PUSHING EXERCISES

PUSH-UP

Primary Muscles Trained

Pectoralis major, anterior deltoids, triceps brachii

Beginning Position

- Assume a position face down, with the feet on the floor, the arms fully extended, and the hands directly under the shoulders (a).
- Ensure a neutral spine alignment, with a virtual straight line aligning the ears, shoulders, hips, knees, and ankles.

Movement Phases

1. Lower the body in a single movement so that the alignment is maintained.
2. Make sure the body moves as a whole segment, maintaining alignment throughout.
3. Finish the downward movement when the chest is almost touching the floor (b).
4. Extend the arms to push the body back to the beginning position.
5. Repeat for the desired number of repetitions.

Breathing Guidelines

Take a breath in at the start of the movement. Continue this inhalation or hold the breath during the eccentric phase (descent). Exhale during the concentric phase (ascent).

Exercise Modifications and Variations

A challenge of the push-up is that some athletes are unable to perform sufficient quality repetitions, whereas for others it quickly becomes easy to perform a high number of repetitions. For this reason, a series of regressions and progressions are needed. Using incline or decline versions of the standard push-up provides one method of achieving this.

Regressions can be used when the required number of repetitions cannot be performed with good technique. Simple regressions can use a series of inclines, where boxes or bars are set at different heights, decreasing the resistance and allowing more repetitions to be performed. The higher the height, the easier the exercise.

Decline push-ups, where the feet are raised onto a box or bench, can increase the resistance, providing more challenge to the athlete. The greater the decline, the greater the challenge. The use of additional load placed on the upper body also can provide progression, as can the use of different hand widths.

Coaching Tip

Focus on technique from the start. Athletes tend to adopt poor form in order to perform more repetitions. Moving the body as a whole also benefits the musculature of the torso and has the benefit of core engagement.

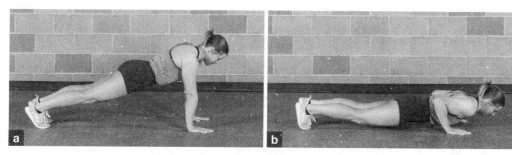

Figure 7.1 Push-up: *(a)* beginning position; *(b)* bottom position.

BENCH PRESS

This is the primary horizontal pushing exercise.

Primary Muscles Trained

Pectoralis major, anterior deltoids, triceps brachii

Beginning Position

- Lie supine on a sturdy bench with five points of contact on the bench (head, shoulders, and hips).
- Retract the shoulder blades as if squeezing them together.
- These positions engage the back, which should maintain its natural curvature (i.e., the back will arch naturally and will not be in contact with the bench).
- The eyes should be below the racked bar, and the feet should be flat on the floor.

- Rack the bar at a height so that the arms are slightly flexed when the hands grip the bar.
- Use a closed pronated grip slightly wider than shoulder-width apart.
- Either unassisted or with help from a spotter, lift the bar from the rack to a position with the bar over the chest, the arms fully extended, and the wrists locked (a).

Movement Phases

1. Lower the bar under control so that it touches the chest gently at approximately mid-chest level. The forearms should be perpendicular to the floor at this point (b).
2. Maintaining the five-point position, push the bar up until the elbows are fully extended; do not excessively arch the back or bring the chest to meet the bar. The bar path is up and slightly back.
3. Repeat for the required number of repetitions.

Breathing Guidelines

Take a breath in when the arms are extended to set the upper body. This inhalation can continue through the eccentric phase, with exhalation through the concentric phase. With high loads the breath can be held during the eccentric phase, then exhale once the sticking point is passed on the concentric phase.

Spotting Guidelines

(*Note*: A spotter is recommended for this exercise, despite not being pictured.) Stand using a staggered stance in a position behind the athlete near to the bar until the athlete gives his or her instruction. Ask the athlete whether he or she requires spotting to lift the bar into position and approximately how many repetitions he or she is likely to complete. If assistance is required to get the bar to the start position, coordinate the movements helping the athlete lift the bar to the start position. Importantly, during the performance of the exercise keep the hands close to, but never touching, the bar, and do not distract the athlete. Be ready to assist at any time but especially during the final repetitions; the athlete's initial repetition range will provide some guidance as to when this might occur. At the end of the set grip the bar with the hands in an alternate grip position inside the athlete's hands, and help him or her guide it back to the racks.

Figure 7.2 Bench press: (a) beginning position; (b) bottom position.

Exercise Modifications and Variations

This exercise can be performed on a standard flat bench or on a range of inclines. Using an incline typically switches the emphasis to the upper portions of the pectoral muscles. The performance on the incline bench press is almost identical to the flat bench press except that the bar contacts the upper chest rather than at nipple level.

A range of grips can be used to alter the primary stress. Wider grips generally switch more emphasis onto the pectoral muscles, while narrower grips switch the stress to the triceps.

Coaching Tip

This exercise probably provides the greatest potential for the development of upper body pushing strength and for mass in the associated musculature. However, "how much you can bench" can become an obsessive score for an athlete, especially if it is tested as the indicator of upper body strength. Care should be taken to weigh the costs and benefits of greater strength and mass (see the section Cost-Benefit Analysis of Upper Body Resistance Training). Heavy bench pressing can place a great deal of stress on the shoulders, and this needs to be considered in any overall analysis.

DUMBBELL BENCH PRESS

Primary Muscles Trained

Pectoralis major, anterior deltoids, triceps brachii

Beginning Position

- Grip two dumbbells with a closed pronated grip.
- Lie back onto a bench, simultaneously bringing the dumbbells to rest on the upper chest.
- Use the same five-point position as for the standard bench press, with the feet flat on the floor.
- Either unassisted or with the help of a spotter, bring the dumbbells to a position where the arms are fully extended and the wrists are locked (a).

Movement Phases

1. Lower the dumbbells simultaneously under control so that they touch the chest gently at approximately nipple level (b). The forearms should be perpendicular to the floor at this point. This movement will see the dumbbells move down and slightly out.
2. Maintaining the five-point position, push the dumbbells up until the elbows are fully extended. Do not excessively arch the back or bring the chest to meet the dumbbells.
3. Repeat for the required number of repetitions.
4. At the end of the set return the dumbbells first to the upper chest and then to the floor.

Breathing Guidelines

Take a breath in when the arms are extended to set the upper body. This inhalation can continue through the eccentric phase, with exhalation on the concentric phase. With high loads the breath can be held during the eccentric phase, then exhale once the sticking point is passed on the concentric phase.

Spotting Guidelines

(*Note*: A spotter is recommended for this exercise, despite not being pictured.) Ask the athlete whether he or she requires spotting to lift the dumbbells into position and approximately how many repetitions he or she is likely to complete. Stand in a position behind the athlete, and if assistance is required, grasp the athlete's forearms near the wrist and assist him or her in getting the dumbbells to arm's length. Do not distract the athlete during the performance of the exercise but be ready to assist if needed, especially during the final repetitions.

Exercise Modifications and Variations

This exercise can be performed on a standard flat bench or with a series of inclines. As with the barbell press, the incline switches the emphasis to the upper portion of the pectoral muscles.

Further variation can be achieved through the use of a neutral grip, in which the hands face each other.

Additionally, variety can be achieved by alternating movement. Here, rather than both dumbbells being pressed at the same time, one dumbbell is moved at any time. Even further, variety can be provided by the position of the non-moving dumbbell. This can be held on the upper chest or at arm's length.

Coaching Tip

The use of dumbbells allows for a greater variation in the movement performance and for a greater range of motion to be achieved. One challenge is having a sufficient progression of dumbbells. Some facilities only have limited dumbbells, so the move from one to the next can often be too large.

Figure 7.3 Dumbbell bench press: (a) beginning position; (b) bottom position.

ONE-ARM DUMBBELL BENCH PRESS

Primary Muscles Trained
Pectoralis major, anterior deltoids, triceps brachii

Beginning Position

- Grip a single dumbbell with a closed pronated grip.
- Lie back on a bench, simultaneously bringing the dumbbell to rest on the upper chest.
- Use the same five-point position as for the standard bench press, with the feet flat on the floor.
- Either unassisted or with the help of a spotter, bring the dumbbell to a position where the arm is fully extended and the wrist is locked (a).

Movement Phases

1. Lower the dumbbell under control so that it touches the chest gently at approximately nipple level (b). The forearms should be perpendicular to the floor at this point.
2. Maintaining the five-point position, push the dumbbells up until the elbows are fully extended. Do not excessively arch the back or bring the chest to meet the dumbbells.
3. Repeat for the required number of repetitions.

Breathing Guidelines

Take a breath in when the arms are extended to set the upper body. This inhalation can continue through the eccentric phase, with exhalation on the concentric phase. With high loads the breath can be held during the eccentric phase, then exhale once the sticking point is passed on the concentric phase.

Figure 7.4   One-arm dumbbell bench press: (a) beginning position; (b) bottom position.

Spotting Guidelines

(*Note*: A spotter is recommended for this exercise, despite not being pictured.) Ask the athlete whether he or she requires spotting to lift the dumbbell into position and approximately how many repetitions he or she is likely to complete. Stand in a position behind the athlete, and if assistance is required, grasp the athlete's forearm near the wrist and assist him or her in getting the dumbbell to arm's length. Do not distract the athlete during the performance of the exercise, but be ready to assist if needed, especially during the final repetitions.

Exercise Modifications and Variations

As with the other pressing exercises, this can be performed on a range of inclines. Additionally, it can be performed with a pronated or neutral grip.

Coaching Tip

This exercise is useful in simultaneously challenging stability and pressing force. Some athletes are able to use a heavier dumbbell in this exercise than when two dumbbells are pressed simultaneously. This seems to be related to the ability to put all of their volition into lifting the one dumbbell rather than splitting this between two. However, this relies on their ability to stabilize the torso.

ONE-ARM LANDMINE OVERHEAD PRESS

Primary Muscles Trained

Pectoralis major, anterior deltoids, triceps brachii

Beginning Position

- Place a loaded bar in a landmine attachment.
- Lift the bar until it rests on the shoulders.
- Stand with feet shoulder-width apart in a staggered stance with the knees slightly flexed.
- Transfer the bar to one hand (a).

Movement Phses

1. Press the weight forward and up in line with the shoulder until the elbow is fully extended (b).
2. Lower the weight to the beginning position.
3. Repeat for the required repetitions.

Breathing Guidelines

Inhale at the start of the exercise, and continue to inhale or hold the breath during the eccentric (lowering) portion of the exercise. Exhale during the pushing (concentric) portion of the exercise.

Exercise Modifications and Variations

The exercise can be performed in a kneeling or half-kneeling position or as a two-arm press. It can also be performed more as a total body push rather than an isolated upper body push. If a landmine is not available, a similar effect can be achieved through an incline dumbbell press, with the incline set at a steep angle.

Coaching Tip

Be clear what the goal of the exercise is. If the aim is to develop a total body push, the legs can be incorporated into the exercise. However, if the aim is to isolate the pushing movement, the action should be limited to the instructions above.

Figure 7.5 One-arm landmine overhead press: *(a)* beginning position; *(b)* extended position.

SHOULDER PRESS

This is the primary vertical pushing exercise.

Primary Muscles Trained

Anterior deltoids, medial deltoids, triceps brachii

Beginning Position

- Set up a bar in a rack so that it is at upper chest level.
- Position the body under the bar as if setting up for a front squat, with the bar resting on the clavicles and the arms perpendicular to the floor.
- Grip the bar with a closed pronated grip, slightly wider than shoulder-width apart.
- Straighten the legs to raise the bar from the rack, and step back (a). (Note: A spotter is recommended for this exercise, despite not being pictured.)

Movement Phases

1. Maintain an upright posture throughout the exercise, and avoid the temptation to lean back.
2. Press the bar overhead, flexing through the deltoids and extending the arms to raise the bar to the beginning position.
3. Pull the head slightly back as the bar passes in front of the face, returning it to its neutral position once this is done.
4. The bar should be directly over the crown of the head at the end of the exercise (b).
5. Flex the arms, returning the bar to the beginning position.
6. Repeat for the required number of repetitions.

Breathing Guidelines

Take a breath in just before initiating the movement to set the upper body phase. Exhale as the bar is raised and especially once the sticking point is passed. Inhale during the eccentric (lowering) phase.

Exercise Modifications and Variations

This exercise can be performed in a seated position. Typically, this results in less load being used. Additionally, the beginning position is sometimes reversed so that the arms are fully extended at the beginning and the bar is first lowered to the clavicles before being extended. This can be performed with a generally upright bench providing support or without a back support, which places more stress on the ability to maintain posture.

Dumbbells can be used as an alternative to barbells. These also allow for the alternating of pressing movements as discussed previously for the dumbbell press. Similarly, the position of the resting dumbbell also can be varied from on the shoulder to overhead.

Coaching Tip

The standing position typically allows more load to be used. The press to the front is generally preferred to the behind-the-neck version, which can be more stressful on athletes' shoulder joints, especially those who do not have sufficient shoulder function to be able to perform the entire motion in this position. Dumbbells allow for a more natural motion range and might be preferred for some athletes.

Figure 7.6 Shoulder press: *(a)* beginning position; *(b)* extended position.

PULLING EXERCISES

BENT-OVER ROW

This is perhaps the primary horizontal pulling exercise.

Primary Muscles Trained

Latissimus dorsi, middle trapezius, rhomboids, teres major, posterior deltoids

Beginning Position

- Position the feet in a jump position, with the knees slightly flexed.
- Use a closed pronated grip, wider than shoulder-width apart.
- Deadlift the bar to an upright position, then flex the torso forward to a point somewhat above parallel, maintaining a neutral spine *(a)*.
- Allow the arms to fully extend

Movement Phases

1. Keeping the torso position rigid, with the knees slightly flexed and the back in a neutral posture, pull the bar toward the torso.
2. Bring the bar to the lower ribs, gently touching the torso and squeezing the shoulder blades together at the top of the movement *(b)*.

3. Lower the bar to the beginning position.

4. Repeat for the required number of repetitions.

5. At the conclusion of the set flex the hips and knees to return the bar to the floor.

Breathing Guidelines

Breathing in rowing-based exercises plays an important role in stabilizing the torso and therefore needs to be considered when performing the exercise. Take a breath in at the start of the movement; this increases intraabdominal pressure, thus providing greater stability. Hold the breath through the sticking point and the rest of the concentric (raising) phase and during the initial eccentric phase. Exhale as the bar continues to be lowered, but ensure that torso stability is not compromised. Repeat the pattern with all repetitions.

Exercise Modifications and Variations

This exercise can also be performed on a T-bar, which allows for a closer grip and, for many, allows a greater load to be lifted.

Coaching Tips

- Many athletes tend to cheat in this exercise in order to lift more weight. Ensure that the torso remains stationary throughout the movement and the repetition remains smooth.
- Focusing the movement on pulling the elbows back can help avoid the tendency to pull excessively with the arms.
- Some athletes might demonstrate a posture similar to that seen in upper crossed syndrome, where the head juts forward during the movement. This can be avoided by emphasizing the correct technique and body position throughout.

Figure 7.7 Bent-over row: (a) beginning position; (b) top of the movement.

ONE-ARM DUMBBELL ROW (HAND AND KNEE SUPPORTED)

Primary Muscles Trained

Latissimus dorsi, middle trapezius, rhomboids, teres major, posterior deltoids

Beginning Position

- Place one hand on a parallel bench or sturdy surface so that the torso is slightly above parallel to the floor, with the knee and shin of the same side on the bench.
- Hold a dumbbell in the opposite hand using a neutral grip, with the arm extended and hanging straight down (a).

Movement Phases

1. Keeping the spine neutral throughout, pull the dumbbell straight up toward the torso. If performed correctly, the elbow will go straight back.
2. At the finish position the hand should be at the same level as the lower ribs (b).
3. Lower the weight to the beginning position and repeat for the required repetitions.

Breathing Guidelines

Take a breath in at the start of the movement and hold it through the sticking point and the rest of the concentric (raising) phase and during the initial eccentric phase. Exhale as the bar continues to be lowered, but ensure that torso stability is not compromised. Repeat the pattern with all repetitions.

Exercise Modifications and Variations

This exercise can be performed in an unsupported position, just as in the bent-over row. Either a single dumbbell or two dumbbells can be used at any time. This position places a greater emphasis on the ability to stabilize the torso when producing pulling forces.

Figure 7.8   One-arm dumbbell row (hand and knee supported): (a) beginning position; (b) row.

ONE-ARM DUMBBELL ROW (THREE POINTS SUPPORTED)

Primary Muscles Trained

Latissimus dorsi, middle trapezius, rhomboids, teres major, posterior deltoids

Beginning Position

- Place one hand on a bench or sturdy surface placed perpendicular to the torso and at a height that allows the torso to be slightly higher than parallel.
- Place the feet in a square or slightly split stance sufficiently away from the bench so that the torso is a bit above parallel and the spine is neutral.
- Hold a dumbbell in the opposite hand using a neutral grip, with the arm extended and hanging straight down (a).

Movement Phases

1. Keeping the spine neutral throughout, pull the dumbbell up and slightly back toward the torso and hips. If performed correctly, the elbow will go straight back.
2. At the finish position, the hand should be at the same level as the oblique muscles (b).
3. Lower the weight to the beginning position, and repeat for the required repetitions.

Breathing Guidelines

Take a breath in at the start of the movement, and hold it through the concentric (raising) phase and the start of the eccentric phase. Exhale as the dumbbell is lowered. Repeat the pattern with all repetitions.

Coaching Tip

Ensure that the torso angle is maintained and that the athlete does not cheat so as to handle more weight.

Figure 7.9 One-arm dumbbell row (three points supported): (a) beginning position; (b) row.

TWO-ARM DUMBBELL ROW (HEAD SUPPORTED)

Primary Muscles Trained

Latissimus dorsi, middle trapezius, rhomboids, teres major, posterior deltoids

Beginning Position

- Set up a bench so that when resting the head on it the torso is slightly higher than parallel.
- Place the feet in a square stance sufficiently away from the bench so that the torso is slightly above parallel and the spine is neutral.
- Hold a dumbbell in each hand using a neutral grip, with the arms extended and hanging straight down *(a)*.

Movement Phases

1. Keeping the spine neutral throughout, pull the dumbbells up toward the torso. If performed correctly, the elbows will go straight back.
2. At the finish position the hands should be at the same level as the lower ribs *(b)*.
3. Lower the weight to the beginning position, and repeat for the required repetitions.

Breathing Guidelines

Take a breath in at the start of the movement, and hold it through the concentric (raising) phase and the start of the eccentric phase. Exhale as the dumbbell is lowered. Repeat the pattern with all repetitions.

Exercise Modifications and Variations

As before, removing the head support focuses to a greater degree on the ability to stabilize the torso.

Coaching Tip

Ensure that the torso angle is maintained, and that the athlete does not cheat so as to handle more weight.

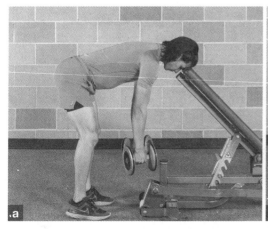

Figure 7.10 Two-arm dumbbell row (head supported): *(a)* beginning position; *(b)* row.

STANDING CABLE ROW

Primary Muscles Trained

Latissimus dorsi, middle trapezius, rhomboids, teres major, posterior deltoids

Beginning Position

- Stand with feet shoulder-width apart in a split stance, with knees slightly flexed.
- Take a one-handed grip on a low cable.
- Hinge at the hips so that the body is in a roughly 45-degree angle. Maintain a neutral spine.
- Step back sufficiently so that the resistance is active in the beginning position (a).

Movement Phases

1. Keeping the spine neutral throughout, pull the cable up toward the torso.
2. At the finish position the hand should be at the same level as the lower ribs (b).
3. Lower the cable to the beginning position, and repeat for the required repetitions.
4. Repeat with the other arm.

Breathing Guidelines

Take a breath in at the start of the movement, and hold it through the concentric (raising) phase. Exhale as the cable is lowered. Repeat the pattern with all repetitions.

Exercise Modifications and Variations

The cable pull has a number of variations that can change the stimulus.

- This exercise can be performed with two arms on the cable so that it is more of a traditional cable row.
- The height of the pulley can be varied from low to horizontal to provide different angles of pull.
- The exercise can incorporate a rotational element. Here, the beginning position involves the arm reaching across the body slightly, toward the opposite foot. During the rowing action the torso rotates in the opposite direction to allow the hand to extend almost behind the body.
- The exercise can also be performed on one leg to provide a more stability-based challenge.

Coaching Tip

Choose the best variation based on the goal of the exercise; with the number of variations, it is easy to lose sight of the goal. The objective of the exercise should dictate the option chosen.

Figure 7.11 Standing cable row: (a) beginning position; (b) row.

PULL-UP (NEUTRAL, PRONATED, AND SUPINATED GRIP)

This is the workhorse of the vertical pulling exercises, and a highly effective strength builder.

Primary Muscles Trained

Latissimus dorsi, teres major, rhomboids, middle trapezius, posterior deltoids

Beginning Position

- Grasp a pull-up bar with the chosen grip (pronated, neutral, or supinated; the photos show a neutral grip).
- With the head positioned between the arms, hang at arm's length (a).

Movement Phases

1. In a controlled motion, pull the body up until the chin is above the bar *(b)*.
2. Lower the body to the beginning position under control.
3. Repeat for the required repetitions.

Breathing Guidelines

Ensure a full breath is taken before starting the exercise. Exhale or hold the breath during the ascent, and inhale during the eccentric (lowering) phase.

Exercise Modifications and Variations

The major modifications to this exercise relate to the grip.

- The supinated grip generally allows the greatest number of repetitions to be achieved by placing the biceps in a stronger position. This version is often called a *chin-up*.
- The pronated grip with hands wider than shoulder width is the classic pull-up grip. It is believed to better activate the lats but has less biceps contribution because they are in a less advantageous position. It tends to result in fewer repetitions than the chin-up.
- The neutral grip is essentially a halfway point between the previous two variations and is a useful addition to a training regime. However, it does require a special attachment or a bar with neutral handles.

Coaching Tips

- Try to ensure that the full range of motion is used wherever possible. When sufficient quality repetitions cannot be performed to achieve the training aims, bands can be used to provide a suitable level of assistance. A series of bands allows resistance to be modified over time until the athlete is able to perform the desired number of repetitions unassisted.
- To provide progression from the standard pull-up, additional resistance can be added by attaching weight via a belt or similar apparatus to the athlete.

Figure 7.12 Pull-up (neutral grip): *(a)* beginning position; *(b)* raised position.

LAT PULLDOWN (NEUTRAL, PRONATED, AND SUPINATED GRIP)

Primary Muscles Trained

Latissimus dorsi, middle trapezius, posterior deltoids, rhomboids, teres major, rhomboids

Beginning Position

- Set the seat at a height that when the arms are fully extended the resistance is active.
- Adjust the pads so that the thighs fit under them and the feet are flat on the floor.
- Take the chosen grip on a pull-down cable attachment.
- Sit down facing the machine, with the thighs under the pads and the feet flat on the floor.

Movement Phases

1. Lean the torso back slightly (a).
2. Pull the bar or attachment toward the upper chest, touching briefly and squeezing the shoulder blades together (b).
3. Reverse the motion, keeping the torso stable and extending the arms back to arm's length.
4. Repeat for the required number of repetitions.
5. At the end of the set, stand up and return the attachment to its original position.

Breathing Guidelines

Ensure a full breath is taken before starting the exercise. Exhale during the concentric (pulling down) phase, and inhale during the eccentric (lowering) phase.

Figure 7.13   Lat pulldown: (a) beginning phase; (b) end phase.

Exercise Modifications and Variations

As with the pull-up, the major modifications to this exercise relate to the grip.

- The supinated grip generally allows the greatest number of repetitions to be achieved by placing the biceps in a stronger position.
- The pronated grip with hands wider than shoulder width is believed to better activate the lats but has less biceps contribution because they are in a less advantageous position.
- The neutral grip is essentially a halfway point between the two and is a useful addition to a training regime. Some athletes prefer this position.

Coaching Tip

As with the pull-up, avoid the temptation to use the torso to generate movement.

INVERTED ROW

Primary Muscles Trained

Latissimus dorsi, teres major, rhomboids, biceps brachii, middle trapezius, posterior deltoids

Beginning Position

- Set up a barbell on a rack at a height that, when gripped from under, the body hangs at arm's length without touching the floor.
- Take a shoulder-width, pronated grip on the bar.
- Keeping the heels on the floor, hang the body in a supine position. The knees can be slightly flexed or fully extended (a).

Movement Phases

1. Pull the body up until the lower chest or sternum gently touches the bar.
2. Ensure the body moves in a single action, maintaining a straight-line posture.
3. At the final position the elbows should be behind the body (b).
4. Lower the body under control to the beginning position.
5. Repeat for the required number of repetitions.

Breathing Guidelines

Inhale when lowering the body, and exhale during the concentric (upward) phase.

Exercise Modifications and Variations

The resistance can be increased or decreased depending on the height of the bar; the higher the bar, the lower the resistance. Elevating the heels onto a box also adds to the resistance by helping achieve a more horizontal body angle.

A major variation is using a suspension trainer rather than a bar. The performance of the exercise is the same, and similarly the resistance will depend on the height of the suspension trainer.

The exercise can be performed with one hand.

Coaching Tip

Make sure the body moves as a single unit. The athlete should keep the torso tight and squeeze the shoulder blades together.

Figure 7.14   Inverted row: *(a)* beginning position; *(b)* finish position.

ACTIVATION EXERCISES

FACE PULL

Primary Muscles Trained

Posterior deltoids, supraspinatus, rhomboids

Beginning Position

- Stand with feet shoulder-width apart in a slightly split stance, with knees slightly flexed.
- Take a two-handed pronated grip on a rope attachment to a cable machine with a pulley set almost parallel to the head.
- Step back so that the resistance is active in the beginning position *(a)*.

Movement Phases

1. Keeping the spine neutral throughout and the elbows high with the hands pronated, squeeze the shoulder blades together and pull the rope backward, separating the hands to each side of the head.
2. At the finish position the center of the rope should be in front of the eyes *(b)*.
3. Slowly and with control, bring the rope back to the beginning position and repeat for the required repetitions.

Breathing Guidelines

Inhale at the start of the exercise, exhale when pulling the cable toward the face, and inhale when returning to the beginning position.

Exercise Modifications and Variations

The exercise can be modified by adjusting the beginning position of the pulley. Bands can be used instead of a cable.

Coaching Tip

This exercise aims to activate key musculature involved in the retraction of the shoulders, so load is not a priority. As a result, ensure that the action is isolated in the target musculature, and try to keep the upper body still.

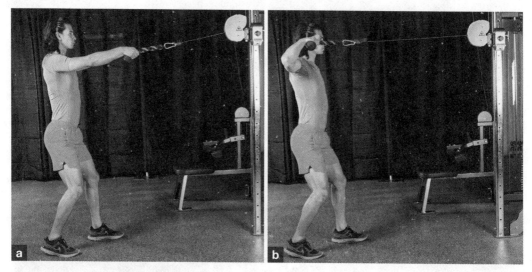

Figure 7.15 Face pull: (a) beginning position; (b) pull.

PRONE Y

Primary Muscles Trained

Upper trapezius, middle trapezius, lower trapezius, supraspinatus, infraspinatus, teres minor and major, mid and low trapezius, rhomboids, posterior deltoids

Beginning Position

- Lie in a prone position, either on a bench or stability ball. If a bench is used, position the body so that the sternum is near the edge of the bench.
- Hang the arms down to the floor with the thumbs facing forward (a).

Movement Phases

1. While keeping the arms straight and head stationary, glide the shoulder blades down and back.
2. Use this shoulder motion to initiate the lifting of the arms into a position parallel to the head and where they form a Y shape (b).

3. Slowly reverse the shoulder motion, and bring the arms under control back to the beginning position.

4. Repeat for the required repetitions.

Breathing Guidelines

Inhale while performing the eccentric (lowering) portion of the exercise, and exhale during the concentric (lifting) portion of the exercise.

Exercise Modifications and Variations

At first, the exercise can be performed prone on the floor, but the range of motion only focuses on the final part of the exercise, essentially just raising the arms off the floor.

The exercise also can be performed in a standing position with the hips flexed so that the upper body is just above parallel. Resistance bands or dumbbells can be used to add additional resistance to the exercise.

A pair of suspension straps that are set to approximately mid-length can be used. Here the athlete needs to lean back until the torso is at a 45-degree angle to the floor with the shoulder blades pulled together. The same arm position and range of motion as the prone version can be used.

Coaching Tip

The focus of this exercise should be on movement quality and not on load.

Figure 7.16   Prone Y: (a) beginning position; (b) Y shape.

PRONE T

Primary Muscles Trained

Upper trapezius, middle trapezius, lower trapezius, supraspinatus, infraspinatus, teres minor and major, mid and low trapezius, rhomboids, posterior deltoids

Beginning Position

- Lie in a prone position, either on a bench or stability ball. If a bench is used, position the body so that the sternum is near the edge of the bench.
- Hang the arms down to the floor with the palms facing forward (a).

Movement Phases

1. While keeping the arms straight and head stationary, pull the shoulder blades in toward the spine.
2. Use this shoulder motion to initiate the lifting of the arms to the side at an angle of 90 degrees to the torso to form a T shape (b).
3. Slowly reverse the shoulder motion, and bring arms under control back to the beginning position.
4. Repeat for the required repetitions.

Breathing Guidelines

Inhale while performing the eccentric (lowering) portion of the exercise, and exhale during the concentric (lifting) portion of the exercise.

Exercise Modifications and Variations

At first the exercise can be performed prone on the floor, but the range of motion only focuses on the final part of the exercise, essentially just raising the arms off the floor. Resistance bands or dumbbells can be used to add resistance to the exercise.

The exercise also can be performed in a standing position with the hips flexed so that the upper body is just above parallel.

A pair of suspension straps that are set to approximately mid-length can be used. Here the athlete needs to lean back until the torso is at a 45-degree angle to the floor with the shoulder blades pulled together. The same arm position and range of motion as the prone version can be used.

Coaching Tip

This exercise should focus on movement quality and not on load.

Figure 7.17 Prone T: *(a)* beginning position; *(b)* T shape.

PRONE W

Primary Muscles Trained

Upper trapezius, middle trapezius, lower trapezius, supraspinatus, infraspinatus, teres minor and major, mid and low trapezius, rhomboids, posterior deltoids

Beginning Position

- Lie in a prone position, either on a bench or stability ball. If a bench is used, position the body so that the sternum is near the edge of the bench.
- Keep the upper arms next to the torso *(a)*.

Movement Phases

1. Squeeze the elbows into the body.
2. Externally rotate the shoulders, bringing the arms into a W position *(b)*.
3. Lower the arms to the beginning position, and repeat for the required repetitions.

Breathing Guidelines

Inhale while performing the eccentric (lowering) portion of the exercise, and exhale during the concentric (lifting) portion of the exercise.

Exercise Modifications and Variations

Resistance bands or dumbbells can be used to add resistance to the exercise. The exercise also can be performed in a standing position with the hips flexed so that the upper body is just above parallel.

A pair of suspension straps that are set to approximately mid-length can be used. Here the athlete needs to lean back until the torso is at a 45-degree angle to the floor with the shoulder blades pulled together. The same arm position and range of motion as the prone version can be used.

Coaching Tip

The focus of this exercise should be on movement quality and not on load.

Figure 7.18   Prone W: *(a)* beginning position; *(b)* W shape.

ANATOMICAL CORE EXERCISE TECHNIQUE

CAT WADE AND KEVIN CRONIN

This chapter reviews the anatomical core and exercises associated with training the anatomical core. In the game of soccer, the core plays a major factor in an athlete's ability to stay on the ball along with battling to maintain possession. It also plays an important role in energy transfer when striking and passing the ball. It has been said that core weakness and poor proprioception is associated with lateral trunk displacement, altered dynamic knee stability, and predicted knee injury risk (2, 3, 4, 5, 6, 13, 14, 15). This injury incidence might be due to a weak link in the athlete's kinetic chain because he or she is exposed to high-force movements.

For this chapter, the core is defined as the lumbar spine, the muscles of the abdominal wall, the back extensors, and quadratus lumborum (7). Also included are the multi-joint muscles, (i.e., latissimus dorsi and psoas) that pass through the core, linking it to the pelvis, legs, shoulders, and arms (7). Given the anatomical and biomechanical synergy with the pelvis, the gluteal muscles also can be considered essential components as primary power generators. (The synergy of these components is outlined elsewhere [8].)

According to McGill (7), most often during human movement the function of the core musculature is to cocontract, stiffen, and prevent motion rather than produce it. Proficient human movement involves the limb muscles generating power that must be transferred through a stiffened core so that the entire body can be moved efficiently during required tasks (7). It is believed that if proper core stabilization is not maintained, when power is developed from the ball and socket joints (hips and shoulders), the spine will flex or lose its neutral alignment (7). This spinal movement is considered an *energy leak*, because the power generated from the limbs is absorbed proximally in the soft tissues of the spine and not transferred distally as efficiently as possible (7).

It is the goal of this chapter to provide anatomical descriptions (1, 11) and properly progressed exercises (9) to help improve stability and function within the core. Additionally, the chapter includes a discussion on proper breathing techniques during each movement. Ideally, as an athlete's core musculature improves (strength and stabilization), his or her performance will improve and the risk of severe injuries will decrease.

Exercise Finder

Bear Crawl 165
Chop and Lift From Low Split Stance 173
Dead Bug (Contralateral and Ipsilateral) 176
Farmer's Walk 161
Farmer's Walk—Double Rack Hold 163
Farmer's Walk—Single-Bell Rack Hold 164
Farmer's Walk With Contralateral Rack Hold 162
Half-Kneeling Chop and Lift 170
Lateral Plank 155
Lateral Plank (Kettlebell Loaded) 156
Lateral Plank (Partner or Bench Supported) 160
Lateral Plank With Arm Extended 157
Lateral Plank With One-Arm Row 158
Pallof Press Kneeling Anti-Rotation Press 177
Partner Bear Crawl 166
Prone Plank (on Slideboard)—Body Saw 152
Prone Plank (Partner or Bench Supported) 154
Prone Plank on Hands 150
Prone Plank With One-Arm Row 151
Quadruped Birddog 146
Reverse Crunch (Floor) 148
Tall Kneeling Chop and Lift 168

QUADRUPED BIRDDOG

Primary Muscles Trained

The primary muscles involved are the stabilizing muscles of the posterior shoulder girdle (supraspinatus, infraspinatus, teres minor and major, triceps) along with the flexors (rectus abdominis, internal and external oblique) and extensors (longissimus, iliocostalis, multifidi, rotators, spinalis) of the vertebral column. During the movement an emphasis is observed on muscles involved in shoulder flexion (deltoids, pectoralis major—upper fibers, biceps brachii) and hip extension (gluteus maximus, biceps femoris, semitendinosus, semimembranosus).

Beginning Position

- Begin on all fours with six points of contact (two hands, two knees, and two feet).
- The hands should be underneath the shoulders, and the knees should be underneath the hips. The knees should be flexed at 90 degrees and the toes pointed to the shins (90-degree angle at the ankle joint).

- The arms and thighs should be perpendicular to the floor *(a)*.
- Prior to any movement, brace the torso, with the rib cage down and the abdominal muscles squeezed.

Movement Phases

1. From the quadruped position, reach out with the right arm (shoulder flexion) and reach back with the left leg (hip extension); this movement results in three points of contact (the hand, knee, and foot).
2. The right arm and left leg maintain a parallel position with the floor *(b)*.
3. Once full flexion (shoulder) and full extension (hip) are achieved, move into right shoulder extension and elbow flexion along with the left leg hip and knee flexion. During this movement the right hand's palm should face the ear and the left toe should be pointed down to the floor.
4. The right elbow meets with the left knee at the umbilicus *(c)*. During this movement the vertebral column should not flex excessively.
5. Once this has been achieved, reverse the movement and complete the required number of repetitions.
6. Once repetitions are finished, return to the beginning quadruped position with six points of contact and complete the same number of repetitions on the other side of the body.

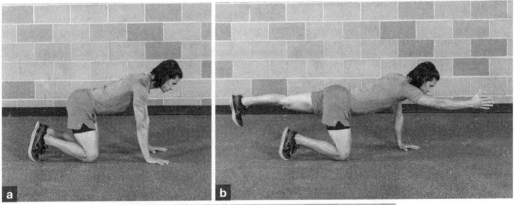

Figure 8.1   Quadruped birddog: *(a)* beginning position; *(b)* shoulder flexion and hip extension; *(c)* elbow and knee meet.

Breathing Guidelines

During the quadruped birddog it is recommended that athletes take in a deep breath prior to beginning the movement and to create intra-abdominal pressure (brace), which should be maintained throughout the movement. During the movement athletes should be able to maintain pressure while holding a conversation along with contracting the involved musculature to keep proper posture. Athletes also should keep their rib cage down and not move into excessive vertebral flexion or extension during the movement.

Exercise Modifications and Variations

If athletes exhibit a great deal of instability or excessive flexion and extension of the vertebral column during the movement, they should break up the movement. That is, the athlete can start by only moving one arm (maintaining five points of contact) and then completing repetitions with only one leg (maintaining four points of contact). This allows the strength and conditioning professional to see the movement in segments and potentially allow for a further dissection of the movement. Once the athlete exhibits better movement patterns, he or she can move back to the standard quadruped birddog.

During this movement, the strength and conditioning professional should focus on flexion and extension of the vertebral column. If excessive flexion or extension is observed, he or she can add a few coaching points to combat these errors. For excessive flexion, the athlete can focus on pinching the shoulder blades (scapulae) together and on maintaining a "proud chest." For excessive extension, the athlete can focus on contracting the abdominals along with maintaining a straight line from the ear to the foot.

REVERSE CRUNCH (FLOOR)

Primary Muscles Trained

The reverse crunch is considered a low-intensity fundamental core exercise with a focus on the musculature of the anterior torso and hip flexors. The primary muscles involved are the flexors (rectus abdominis, external oblique, internal oblique) of the vertebral column and flexors (psoas major, iliacus, tensor fascia latae, sartorius, rectus femoris) of the hip.

Beginning Position

- Lie in a supine position on the floor with knees flexed at 90 degrees, feet flat on the floor, and hands at the side (a).
- The back should be flat on the floor; no space should be observed between the low back and the floor.

Movement Phases

1. From a supine position, begin the reverse crunch (floor) by initiating the activation of the anterior abdominal muscles.
2. This initiation is also associated with a rise of the feet from the floor.
3. As the knees rise toward the chest, maintain pressure with the lower back, keep the rib cage down, and focus on driving the belly button down into the floor. Maintain a position with no space observed between the floor and the low back (b).

4. Once the knees are close enough to the chest where the hips are flexed at 90 degrees, reverse the movement, maintaining pressure with the floor through the lumbar spine region.

5. Complete the required number of repetitions.

Breathing Guidelines

During the reverse crunch (floor) it is recommended athletes take in a deep breath prior to the start of the movement and to create intra-abdominal pressure (brace), which should be maintained throughout the movement. During the movement athletes should be able to maintain pressure while holding a conversation along with contracting the involved musculature to keep proper posture. Athletes also should keep their rib cage down and minimize rib cage flair during the eccentric portion of the movement (hips going into extension).

Exercise Modifications and Variations

The reverse crunch (floor) can be used early in the athlete's training program to train him or her how to brace during lower extremity movement.

If athletes exhibit a lack of control during this exercise, the strength and conditioning professional can use dead bug variations (see pages 176-177) to improve stability and control.

A progression to the reverse crunch (floor) is the hanging reverse crunch. The hanging reverse crunch is a low-intensity fundamental core exercise with a focus on the musculature of the anterior torso and hip flexors along with the stabilizing muscles of the shoulder girdle. For the hanging reverse crunch the athlete begins from a hanging position above the floor with hands shoulder-width apart, grasping a bar with a pronated grip. This position involves full shoulder flexion and full elbow extension. The athlete's hips and knees are extended, and no extra flexion or extension should be observed in the vertebral column; a normal lordotic curve should be observed. The athlete then brings the knees up to a point where the hip is flexed at 90 degrees. As the knees move upward, the rib cage should not, and minimal torso flexion or extension should be observed.

Coaching Tip

During this movement it is imperative that strength and conditioning professionals notice potential rib cage flair along with excessive thoracic and lumbar extension. This is a great exercise to teach athletes to brace into the floor and maintain proper posture.

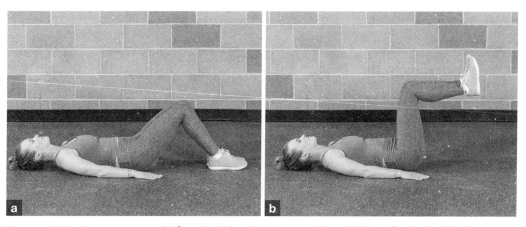

Figure 8.2   Reverse crunch (floor): (a) beginning position; (b) hips flexed at 90 degrees.

PRONE PLANK ON HANDS

Primary Muscles Trained

The prone plank on hands is a total body core exercise. Based on the position achieved, the primary muscles trained during this exercise are the stabilizing muscles of the posterior shoulder girdle (supraspinatus, infraspinatus, teres minor and major, triceps); iliocostalis group; multifidi; gluteus maximus; rectus abdominis; and internal, external, and transverse oblique.

Figure 8.3 Prone plank on hands.

Beginning Position

- Assume a prone position flat on the floor.
- Dig the toes into the floor, and keep the thumbs directly underneath the armpits. The elbows are fully flexed, and the knees and hips are extended.

Movement Phases

1. With the entire body engaged, fully extend (straighten) the elbows.
2. Throughout this movement, maintain a rigid torso while engaging the muscles previously stated along with extended knees and hips. Keep the rib cage down and gluteal muscles squeezed.
3. Avoid any major break in posture or sag throughout the body. If this occurs, regress to the one of the modification movements.
4. Once in the position of fully extended elbows, maintain this position for the required amount of time.

Breathing Guidelines

It is recommended that athletes take in a deep breath prior to beginning the movement and to create intra-abdominal pressure, which should be maintained throughout the movement. During the movement athletes should be able to maintain pressure while holding a conversation along with contracting the abdominal, latissimus dorsi, erector spinae, and gluteal muscles isometrically.

Exercise Modifications and Variations

If athletes struggle to maintain adequate posture and a sag is observed during the movement, they can raise feet off the floor and flex the knee joint to 90 degrees so that the two points of contact are now the knees and the hands. This will improve support and allow for progressing back to the feet and the hands being the two points of contact.

Coaching Tip

During this movement make sure that the athlete maintains proper position and the entire body stays engaged.

PRONE PLANK WITH ONE-ARM ROW

Primary Muscles Trained

The prone plank with one-arm row is a total body core exercise with an increased focus on the elevator and depressor muscles of the scapula or scapulothoracic joint (upper trapezius, levator scapulae, rhomboids—lower trapezius, latissimus dorsi, pectoralis minor, subclavius) along with the biceps brachii. The iliocostalis group; multifidi; gluteus maximus; rectus abdominis; and internal, external, and transverse oblique are also trained during the prone plank with one-arm row.

Beginning Position

- Assume a prone position flat on the floor, with one hand grasping a resistive mechanism (e.g., band or cable column handle).
- Dig the toes and elbows into the floor. The elbows should be flexed at 90 degrees directly below the shoulders.
- The knees and hips should be extended, and the grip should be neutral.

Movement Phases

1. With the entire body engaged, lift the hips off the floor until a neutral spine position has been achieved. In this position focus on maintaining solid posture and avoiding a sag in the torso (a).
2. Reach out in front, flexing the shoulder joint, allowing the scapula to elevate. Continue this movement until the elbow is fully extended and the arm is parallel with the floor.
3. Flex the elbow, and move into a depression of the scapula and extension of the shoulder (b). The palm of the involved arm will stay facing the head. Perform the required number of repetitions on each arm.
4. If proper posture cannot be maintained, move to a regressed version of the prone plank.

Breathing Guidelines

During the prone plank with one-arm row it is recommended athletes take in a deep breath prior to beginning the movement and to create intra-abdominal pressure, which should be maintained throughout the movement. During the movement athletes should be able to maintain pressure while holding a conversation along with contracting the abdominal, latissimus dorsi, erector spinae, and gluteal muscles isometrically. Athletes also should keep their rib cage down and gluteal muscles squeezed during the movement.

Exercise Modifications and Variations

If athletes struggle to maintain adequate posture and a sag is observed during the movement, they can raise their feet off the floor and flex the knee joint to 90 degrees so that the two points of contact are now the knees and the hands. This will improve support and allow for progressing back to the feet and the hands being the two points of contact.

If this modification is too easy, the athlete can take a larger base of support by moving the feet further away from each other. The point of contact is still one elbow and two feet.

Coaching Tip

During this movement make sure that as the athlete rows, the hips and torso stay rigid. The resistance used should not be so much that it compromises the athlete's posture or positioning.

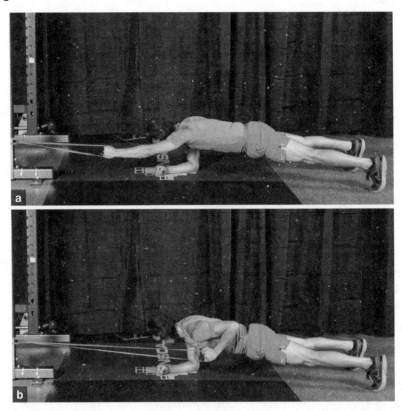

Figure 8.4 Prone plank with one-arm row: *(a)* beginning position; *(b)* row.

PRONE PLANK (ON SLIDEBOARD)— BODY SAW

Primary Muscles Trained

The prone plank on slideboard (body saw) is a total body core exercise. Based on the position achieved, this exercise targets the stabilizing muscles of the posterior shoulder with a major focus on the latissimus dorsi and teres major during shoulder flexion (above 90 degrees). The iliocostalis group; gluteus maximus; rectus abdominis; and internal, external, and transverse oblique are also primary muscles trained during this exercise.

Beginning Position

- Assume a prone position flat on the floor.
- Dig the toes and elbows into the floor. The elbows should be flexed at 90 degrees directly below the shoulders. The toes should also be dug into the slideboard.
- The knees and hips should be extended.

Movement Phases

1. With the entire body engaged, lift the hips off the floor. The elbows are fixed directly under the shoulders, and the hips and knees are extended *(a)*.

2. Once this position is achieved, push back, allowing the toes to move away from the body and the shoulders to go into forward shoulder flexion *(b)*. Pressure should be maintained from the toes and elbows into the floor through the duration of the movement.

3. Move into forward shoulder flexion to a point of feeling comfortable while maintaining proper posture. Once this distance has been reached, move the toes back toward the beginning position by engaging the torso and moving into shoulder flexion.

4. The movement is complete once the elbows return to directly under the shoulders.

5. Complete the required number of repetitions.

Exercise Modifications and Variations

During this movement, if athletes cannot maintain proper position (rigid torso and no break in posture), they should regress back to a prone plank or prone plank on hands.

Breathing Guidelines

During the prone plank on slideboard it is recommended athletes take in a deep breath prior to beginning the movement and to create intra-abdominal pressure, which should be maintained throughout the movement. During the movement athletes should be able to maintain pressure while holding a conversation along with contracting the abdominal, latissimus dorsi, erector spinae, and gluteal muscles isometrically. Athletes also should keep their rib cage down and gluteal muscles squeezed during the movement.

Coaching Tip

If slideboards are not available, use any surface that has a low coefficient of friction.

Figure 8.5 Prone plank (on slideboard)—body saw: *(a)* beginning position; *(b)* pushed back position.

PRONE PLANK (PARTNER OR BENCH SUPPORTED)

Primary Muscles Trained

The prone plank with the feet elevated by a bench or partner is a total body core exercise. Based on the position achieved, the primary muscles trained during this exercise are the stabilizing muscles of the posterior shoulder girdle (posterior deltoid, infraspinatus, teres minor and major, latissimus dorsi); iliocostalis group; gluteus maximus; rectus abdominis; and internal, external, and transverse oblique.

Figure 8.6   Prone plank (partner or bench supported).

Beginning Position

- Assume a prone position flat on the floor with the feet held by a partner or up on a bench.
- Dig the toes into the bench, and place the thumbs directly underneath the arm pits. The elbows are fully flexed, and the knees and hips are extended.

Movement Phases

1. With the entire body engaged, fully extend (straighten) the elbows.
2. Throughout this movement maintain a rigid torso while engaging the muscles previously stated, keep the knees and hips extended, and keep the rib cage down and gluteal muscles squeezed.
3. Once in the position of fully extended elbows, hold this position for the required amount of time.

Breathing Guidelines

During the prone plank (partner or bench supported) it is recommended athletes take in a deep breath prior to beginning the movement and to create intra-abdominal pressure, which should be maintained throughout the movement. During the movement athletes should be able to maintain pressure while holding a conversations along with contracting the abdominal, latissimus dorsi, erector spinae, and gluteal muscles isometrically. Athletes also should keep their rib cage down and gluteal muscles squeezed during the movement.

Exercise Modifications and Variations

If athletes struggle to maintain adequate posture and a sag is observed during the movement, athletes can move their feet down to the floor. If athletes use poor posture, regress their feet back to the floor (the prone plank from hands); this will improve support and allow for progressing back to the elevated level.

Coaching Tip

Throughout this movement the athletes should maintain a rigid torso while engaging the muscles previously stated and maintaining extended knees and hips. During the movement athletes also should keep their rib cage down and gluteal muscles squeezed.

LATERAL PLANK

Primary Muscles Trained

The lateral plank is a total body core exercise. Based on the position achieved, this exercise targets the stabilizing muscles of the shoulder (infraspinatus, teres major and minor, trapezius) with a major focus on the external obliques and quadratus lumborum. The iliocostalis group, gluteus maximus, rectus abdominis, and internal and transverse oblique are also primary muscles trained during this exercise.

Figure 8.7   Lateral plank.

Beginning Position

- Assume a side-lying position flat on the floor with the feet stacked on top of each other.
- The elbow should be flexed at 90 degrees directly under the shoulder.
- Extend the hips and knees.

Movement Phases

1. With the athlete's entire body engaged, lift the hips off the floor while digging the elbow and side of the foot into the floor and maintaining a good posture.
2. Once the hips are off the floor, raise the body so that a straight line is maintained from the feet to the head.
3. Hold this position for the required amount of time, then switch to the other side.

Breathing Guidelines

During the lateral plank it is recommended athletes take in a deep breath prior to beginning the movement and to create intra-abdominal pressure, which should be maintained throughout the movement. During the movement athletes should be able to maintain pressure while holding a conversations along with contracting the abdominal, latissimus dorsi, erector spinae, and gluteal muscles isometrically.

Exercise Modifications and Variations

If athletes struggle to maintain adequate posture and a sag is observed, athletes can flex their knees to 90 degrees and maintain the same position. This will provide more stability. As stability improves, athletes can progress back to the lateral plank.

Coaching Tip

During this movement make sure that the athlete maintains proper position, the entire body stays engaged, and a straight line is maintained from the feet to the head.

LATERAL PLANK (KETTLEBELL LOADED)

Primary Muscles Trained

The lateral plank (kettlebell loaded) is a total body core exercise. Based on the position achieved, this exercise targets the stabilizing muscles of the shoulder (infraspinatus, teres major and minor, trapezius) with a major focus on the external obliques and quadratus lumborum. The iliocostalis group, gluteus maximus, rectus abdominis, and internal and transverse oblique are also primary muscles trained during this exercise.

Figure 8.8 Lateral plank (kettlebell loaded).

Beginning Position

- Assume a side-lying position flat on the floor with the feet stacked on top of each other.
- The elbow should be flexed at 90 degrees directly under the shoulder. The opposite hand grasps a kettlebell with the knuckles facing up and a firm grip.
- The kettlebell should rest comfortably on the shoulder prior to the start of the movement.
- Extend the hips and knees.

Movement Phases

1. With the entire body engaged, lift the hips off the floor while digging the elbow and side of the foot into the floor. During this phase, it is important to focus the eyes on the kettlebell.
2. Maintain a good posture while hips move off the floor.
3. Once the hips are off the floor, the body should raise so that a straight line is maintained from the feet to the head.
4. Once this position is achieved, extend the elbow and press the kettlebell up toward the ceiling in line with the down elbow, maintaining good posture. The arm that is pressing the kettlebell should remain perpendicular to the floor.
5. Hold this position for the required amount of time, then switch to the other side. In between each side, reset the kettlebell by bringing it back to the floor to allow proper transition between each side of the body.

Exercise Modifications and Variations

If athletes struggle to maintain adequate posture, sag, or are unable to maintain a stable overhead, they can flex their knees to 90 degrees and maintain the same position. This keeps the athletes safe and allows a proper stimulus to be applied while not being too difficult. This gives athletes more stability. As stability improves, athletes can progress back to the lateral plank (kettlebell loaded).

Breathing Guidelines

During the lateral plank (kettlebell loaded) it is recommended athletes take in a deep breath prior to beginning the movement and to create intra-abdominal pressure, which should be maintained throughout the movement. During the movement athletes should be able to maintain pressure while holding a conversation along with contracting the abdominal, latissimus dorsi, erector spinae, and gluteal muscles isometrically.

Coaching Tip

During this movement make sure that athletes maintain proper position, the entire body stays engaged, and a straight line is maintained from the feet to the head. During the pressing movement of the kettlebell, emphasize a proper pressing pattern and suggest keeping the weight very light to start.

LATERAL PLANK WITH ARM EXTENDED

Primary Muscles Trained

The lateral plank with arm extended is a total body core exercise. Based on the position achieved, this exercise targets the stabilizing muscles of the shoulder (infraspinatus, teres major and minor, trapezius) with a major focus on the external obliques and quadratus lumborum. The iliocostalis group, gluteus maximus, rectus abdominis, and internal and transverse oblique are also primary muscles trained during this exercise.

Figure 8.9   Lateral plank with arm extended.

Beginning Position

- Assume a side-lying position flat on the floor. If the exercise will be loaded, place a dumbbell or kettlebell on the floor in front of the torso.
- Stack the feet, knees, hips, and shoulders on top of each other and in vertical alignment.
- Position the elbow of the bottom arm at 90 degrees and directly under the bottom shoulder so that the upper arm is perpendicular to the floor.
- If the exercise will be loaded, grasp the dumbbell or kettlebell with the top hand.
- Reach the top arm up so that it is perpendicular to the floor. If the exercise is loaded, tightly hold the dumbbell or kettlebell in the hand of the extended arm.

Movement Phases

1. Begin by driving the bottom elbow and bottom side of the feet into the floor to lift the hips up until the feet, knees, hips, and spine are in a line.
2. Keep the entire body engaged with the hips off the floor while maintaining the same 90-degree flexed elbow position of the bottom arm. The upper arm of the bottom arm should be perpendicular to the floor.

3. Keep the top arm perpendicular to the floor and fully extended. If the exercise is loaded, keep the dumbbell or kettlebell stationary.

4. Hold the lateral plank with arm extended position for the required time then place the dumbbell or kettlebell on the floor (if applicable) before switching to the other side.

Exercise Modifications and Variations

If athletes struggle to maintain adequate posture, sag, or are unable to maintain a stable overhead position, athletes can flex their knees to 90 degrees and maintain the same position. If instability is still observed with the involved shoulder, it is recommended to bring the arm back down to the athlete's side as in the lateral plank.

Breathing Guidelines

During the lateral plank with arm extended it is recommended athletes take in a deep breath prior to beginning the movement and to create intra-abdominal pressure, which should be maintained throughout the movement. During the movement athletes should be able to maintain pressure while holding a conversation along with contracting the abdominal, latissimus dorsi, erector spinae, and gluteal muscles isometrically.

Coaching Tip

During this movement make sure the athlete maintains proper position, with the entire body staying engaged and a straight line maintained from the feet to the head and with a perpendicular arm position.

LATERAL PLANK WITH ONE-ARM ROW

Primary Muscles Trained

The lateral plank with one-arm row is a total body core exercise. Based on the position achieved, this exercise targets the stabilizing muscles of the shoulder (infraspinatus, teres major and minor, trapezius) with a major focus on the external obliques, quadratus lumborum, as well as the retractors (trapezius, rhomboid major and minor) and the protractors (serratus anterior and pectoralis minor) of the scapula. The iliocostalis group, gluteus maximus, rectus abdominis, and internal and transverse oblique are also primary muscles trained during this exercise.

Beginning Position

- Assume a side-lying position flat on the floor with the feet stacked on top of each other.
- The elbow should be flexed at 90 degrees directly under the shoulder.
- With the body far enough away from the resistive mechanism (e.g., band or cable column handle) that the opposite arm is extended and relaxed, the opposite hand should grasp the resistive mechanism.
- Extend the hips and knees.

Movement Phases

1. With the entire body engaged, lift the hips off the floor while digging the elbow and side of the foot into the floor (a).

2. Maintain a good posture while hips move off the floor, with the involved arm staying extended while grasping the resistive mechanism.

3. Once the hips are off the floor, raise the body so that a straight line is maintained from the feet to the head.

4. Once this position is achieved, flex the elbow and pull the resistive mechanism toward the rib cage (b). The torso should stay rigid, and the shoulder should stay perpendicular to the floor.

5. Continue to flex and extend the elbow until the required number of repetitions have been performed.

6. Switch sides. In between each side reset by releasing the resistive mechanism and switching hands.

Exercise Modifications and Variations

If athletes struggle to maintain adequate posture or they sag, they can flex their knees to 90 degrees and maintain the same position. If instability is still observed with the involved shoulder, arm, or torso during the rowing movement, remove the resistive mechanism.

These modifications provide more stability, allowing the athletes to stay safe, providing a proper stimulus to be applied, and decreasing the exercise's level of difficulty. As stability improves, athletes can progress back to the lateral plank with one-arm row.

Breathing Guidelines

During the lateral plank with one-arm row it is recommended athletes take in a deep breath prior to beginning the movement and to create intra-abdominal pressure, which should be maintained throughout the movement. During the movement athletes should be able to maintain pressure while holding a conversation along with contracting the abdominal, latissimus dorsi, erector spinae, and gluteal muscles isometrically.

Coaching Tip

During this movement make sure that athlete maintains proper position, with the entire body staying engaged and a straight line maintained from the feet to the head.

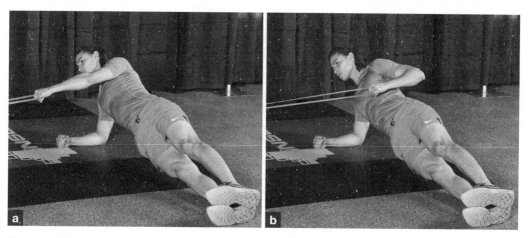

Figure 8.10   Lateral plank with one-arm row: (a) beginning position; (b) row.

LATERAL PLANK (PARTNER OR BENCH SUPPORTED)

Primary Muscles Trained

The lateral plank (partner or bench supported) is a total body core exercise. Based on the position achieved, the primary muscles trained are the stabilizing muscles of the posterior shoulder girdle (posterior deltoid, infraspinatus, teres minor and major, latissimus dorsi); iliocostalis group; gluteus maximus; rectus abdominis and internal, external, and transverse oblique.

Figure 8.11 Lateral plank (partner or bench supported).

Beginning Position

- Assume a side-lying position flat on the floor with the feet held by a partner or up on a bench. The feet should not be too high, and the body should stay parallel to the floor, nothing higher.
- Dig the elbow and side of the foot into the bench with the elbow flexed at 90 degrees directly underneath the shoulder.
- Extend the knees and hips.

Movement Phases

1. With the entire body engaged, raise the hips off the floor.
2. Through this movement maintain a rigid torso, engage the involved muscles, keep the knees and hips extended, and keep the rib cage down and gluteal muscles squeezed.
3. Once the body is parallel with the floor, hold this position for the required amount of time.

Breathing Guidelines

During the lateral plank (partner or bench supported) it is recommended athletes take in a deep breath prior to beginning the movement and to create intra-abdominal pressure, which should be maintained throughout the movement. During the movement athletes should be able to maintain pressure while holding a conversation along with contracting the abdominal, latissimus dorsi, erector spinae, and gluteal muscles isometrically. Athletes also should keep their rib cage down and gluteal muscles squeezed during the movement.

Exercise Modifications and Variations

If athletes struggle to maintain adequate posture, sag, or exhibit poor posture, they can move feet down to the floor for the lateral plank. This will improve support and allow for progressing back to the elevated level.

If athletes experience a great deal of pain in their shoulder during this exercise, lower the support height. If they still experience pain, move their feet back down to the floor.

Coaching Tip

Through this movement, the athletes should maintain a rigid torso, keep the knees and hips extended, and keep the elbow directly under the shoulder.

FARMER'S WALK

Primary Muscles Trained

The farmer's walk is a total body core exercise. Based on the activity, the primary muscles trained are the flexor muscles of the hand (flexor carpi radialis, flexor carpi ulnaris, palmaris longus, flexor digitorum super- ficialis, and flexor digitorum profundus); the stabilizing muscles of the posterior shoulder girdle (supraspi- natus, infraspinatus, teres minor and major, serratus anterior, triceps); iliocostalis group; multifidi; gluteus maximus; rectus abdominis; and internal, external, and transverse oblique.

Figure 8.12   Farmer's walk.

Beginning Position

- Prepare any of the following: trap bar or hex bar, a pair of equal-weight kettlebells, or a pair of equal-weight dumbbells.

- Hinge over to deadlift the implement up to a tall standing position, fully braced. (If using a pair of kettlebells or dumbbells, stand between them, with the bells at the ankle.) Engage the shoulders and abdominals before lifting the implement.

Movement Phases

1. With the entire core engaged, begin to walk a predetermined distance or time and at a predetermined pace while maintaining control over the implement, not allowing it to swing.
2. Throughout this movement, avoid any major break in posture (e.g., slumping, extension, or leaning forward). If a break in posture is observed, decrease the load.

Breathing Guidelines

During the farmer's walk it is recommended athletes take in a deep breath prior to begin- ning the deadlift portion of the movement and to create intra-abdominal pressure, which should be maintained throughout the movement. During the movement athletes should be able to maintain pressure, create as much tension as possible throughout their core, and breathe behind the shield they have created, contracting the abdominal, latissimus dorsi, erector spinae, and gluteal muscles isometrically.

Exercise Modifications and Variations

As athletes progress in this movement they can increase the load carried or the time for which the load is carried, or they can hold different loads in each hand.

Coaching Tip

During this movement make sure the athlete maintains proper position and the spine never flexes or goes into extension, and that the athlete does not sway laterally when walking.

FARMER'S WALK WITH CONTRALATERAL RACK HOLD

Primary Muscles Trained

The farmer's walk with contralateral rack hold is a total body core exercise. Based on the activity, the primary muscles trained are the flexor muscles of the hand (flexor carpi radialis, flexor carpi ulnaris, palmaris longus, flexor digitorum superficialis, and flexor digitorum profundus); the stabilizing muscles of the posterior shoulder girdle (supraspinatus, infraspinatus, teres minor and major, serratus anterior, triceps); iliocostalis group; multifidi; gluteus maximus; rectus abdominis; and internal, external, and transverse oblique.

Figure 8.13 Farmer's walk with contralateral rack hold.

Beginning Position

- Prepare a pair of equal-weight kettlebells or dumbbells.
- Bring the bell into the rack position, ideally done by performing a kettlebell or dumbbell clean with the bell resting at the shoulder. Maintain a vertical forearm so the wrist is stacked directly over the elbow.
- Perform a suitcase deadlift for the bell that will be carried down at the waist.

Movement Phases

1. With the entire core engaged, begin to walk a predetermined distance or time and at a predetermined pace while maintaining control over the implement, not allowing it to swing.
2. Throughout this movement, avoid any major break in posture (e.g., slumping, extension, or leaning forward). If a break in posture is observed, decrease the load.

Breathing Guidelines

During the farmer's walk it is recommended athletes take in a deep breath prior to beginning the deadlift portion of the movement and to create intra-abdominal pressure, which should be maintained throughout the movement. During the movement athletes should be able to maintain pressure, create as much tension as possible throughout their core, and breathe behind the shield they have created, contracting the abdominal, latissimus dorsi, erector spinae, and gluteal muscles isometrically.

Exercise Modifications and Variations

As athletes progress in this movement they can increase the load carried or the time for which the load is carried, or they can hold different loads in each hand or extend the bell from the rack position to the overhead position.

Coaching Tip

During this movement make sure the athlete maintains proper position and the spine never flexes or goes into extension, and that the athlete does not sway laterally when walking.

FARMER'S WALK—DOUBLE RACK HOLD

Primary Muscles Trained

The farmer's walk with double rack hold is a total body core exercise. Based on the activity, the primary muscles trained are the flexor muscles of the hand (flexor carpi radialis, flexor carpi ulnaris, palmaris longus, flexor digitorum superficialis, and flexor digitorum profundus); the stabilizing muscles of the posterior shoulder girdle (supraspinatus, infraspinatus, teres minor and major, serratus anterior, triceps); iliocostalis group; multifidi; gluteus maximus; rectus abdominis; and internal, external, and transverse oblique.

Beginning Position

- Prepare a pair of equal-weight kettlebells or dumbbells.

Figure 8.14   Farmer's walk—double rack hold.

- Bring the bells into the rack position, ideally by performing a kettlebell or dumbbell clean with the bells resting at the shoulder. Maintain a vertical forearm so the wrist is stacked directly over the elbow.

Movement Phases

1. With the entire core engaged, begin to walk a predetermined distance or time and at a predetermined pace while maintaining control over the implement, not allowing it to pull the wrist end elbow out of vertical alignment.
2. Throughout this movement, avoid any major break in posture (e.g., slumping or extension). If a break in posture is observed, decrease the load. An increased effort must be given to maintain lat engagement while not winging the scapula.

Breathing Guidelines

During the farmer's walk—double rack hold it is recommended athletes take in a deep breath prior to cleaning the bells and that they create intra-abdominal pressure, which should be maintained throughout the movement. During the movement athletes should be able to maintain pressure, create as much tension as possible throughout their core, and breathe behind the shield they have created, contracting the abdominal, latissimus dorsi, erector spinae, and gluteal muscles isometrically.

Exercise Modifications and Variations

As athletes progress in this movement they can increase the load carried or the time for which the load is carried, or they can use more difficult versions of carries such as the double-bell rack march.

Coaching Tip

During this movement make sure the athlete maintains proper position and the spine never flexes or goes into extension, and that the athlete does not sway laterally when walking. Be sure the forearm remains vertical, with the wrist stacked over the elbow.

FARMER'S WALK—SINGLE-BELL RACK HOLD

Primary Muscles Trained

The farmer's walk with single-bell rack hold is a total body core exercise. Based on the activity, the primary muscles trained are the flexor muscles of the hand (flexor carpi radialis, flexor carpi ulnaris, palmaris longus, flexor digitorum superficialis, and flexor digitorum profundus); the stabilizing muscles of the posterior shoulder girdle (supraspinatus, infraspinatus, teres minor and major, serratus anterior, triceps); iliocostalis group; multifidi; gluteus maximus; rectus abdominis; and internal, external, and transverse oblique.

Figure 8.15 Farmer's walk—single-bell rack hold.

Beginning Position

- Prepare a single kettlebell or dumbbell.
- Bring the bell into the rack position, ideally by performing a kettlebell or dumbbell clean with the bell resting at the shoulder. Maintain a vertical forearm so the wrist is stacked directly over the elbow.

Movement Phases

1. With the entire core engaged, begin to walk a predetermined distance or time and at a predetermined pace while maintaining control over the implement, not allowing it to pull the wrist end elbow out of vertical alignment.
2. Throughout this movement, avoid any major break in posture (e.g., slumping or extension). If a break in posture is observed, decrease the load. An increased effort must be given to maintain lat engagement while not winging the scapula.

Breathing Guidelines

During the farmer's walk with single-bell rack hold it is recommended athletes take in a deep breath prior to cleaning the bells and that they create intra-abdominal pressure, which should be maintained throughout the movement. During the movement athletes should be able to maintain pressure, create as much tension as possible throughout their core, and breathe behind the shield they have created, contracting the abdominal, latissimus dorsi, and erector spinae isometrically.

Exercise Modifications and Variations

As athletes progress in this movement they can increase the load carried or the time for which the load is carried.

Coaching Tip

During this movement make sure the athlete maintains proper position and the spine never flexes or goes into extension, and that the athlete does not sway laterally when walking. Be sure the forearm remains vertical, with the wrist stacked over the elbow, and that the opposite lat remains engaged.

BEAR CRAWL

Primary Muscles Trained

The bear crawl is considered a total body core exercise. Based on the activity, the primary muscles trained are the triceps; the stabilizing muscles of the posterior shoulder girdle (supraspinatus, infraspinatus, teres minor and major, serratus anterior); iliocostalis group; multifidi; rectus abdominis; internal, external, and transverse oblique; and quadriceps.

Beginning Position

- Assume a quadruped position, where the hands help to support the body and are directly under the shoulders, the knees support the weight of the body and are directly under the hips, and the toes are dorsiflexed and in alignment with the knees.
- Begin by taking a deep breath to create intra-abdominal pressure, then press the hands and toes into the floor so the knees lift off of the floor about 2 inches (5.1 cm) (a).

Movement Phases

1. With the entire core engaged, begin the movement by crawling, with the knees never touching the floor (b). Crawl a predetermined distance or time while maintaining control over the lumbar spine and hips. Ideally, an item placed on the lower back just above the waistline would not move throughout the movement.
2. Throughout this movement, avoid any major break in posture (e.g., slumping or extension). If a break in posture is observed, decrease the distance or time held in this posture.

Breathing Guidelines

During the bear crawl it is recommended athletes take in a deep breath prior to the lift of the knees and that they create intra-abdominal pressure and tighten the abs before beginning to crawl. This pressure should be maintained throughout the movement. During the movement athletes should be able to maintain pressure, create as much tension as possible throughout their core, and breathe behind the shield they have created, contracting the abdominal, triceps, and erector spinae isometrically.

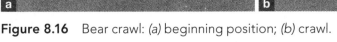

Figure 8.16   Bear crawl: (a) beginning position; (b) crawl.

Exercise Modifications and Variations

If athletes are unable to crawl, they can begin by holding the static position with the knees off the floor for increasing amounts of time. They can progress to picking up one hand or one foot, leaving only three points of contact, then to picking up one arm and the foot, leaving only two points of contact.

As athletes progress they can try multidirectional crawling laterally and reverse. If large gymnastic mats are available, set varying heights for the athletes to crawl up and over. Another progression is to have athletes drag a kettlebell while they are crawling either forward or backward. For this, a nylon strap or several monster bands long enough to hook over the athletes' shoulders are needed. The strap should extend about 2 feet (0.6 m) beyond the athletes' heels to give enough space for external load.

Coaching Tip

During this movement make sure the athlete maintains proper position and the spine never flexes or goes into extension and that the athlete does not lose spinal or pelvic control when crawling. The athlete should demonstrate such control that an item placed on his or her lower back would not fall off.

PARTNER BEAR CRAWL

Primary Muscles Trained

The partner bear crawl is considered a total body core exercise. Based on the activity, the primary muscles trained are the triceps; the stabilizing muscles of the posterior shoulder girdle (supraspinatus, infraspinatus, teres minor and major, serratus anterior); iliocostalis group; multifidi; rectus abdominis; internal, external, and transverse oblique; and quadriceps.

Beginning Position (for the pair of athletes)

- Assume a quadruped position facing each other, where the hands help to support the body and are directly under the shoulders, the knees support the weight of the body and are directly under the hips, and the toes are dorsiflexed and in alignment with the knees.

- Position a 36-inch (91 cm) foam roller between both foreheads and press just enough to hold the foam roller in place.

- Take a deep breath to create intra-abdominal pressure, then press the hands and toes into the floor so the knees lift off of the floor about 2 inches (5.1 cm) (a). Once in the crawling position, the foam roller should be held between their foreheads.

Movement Phases (for the pair of athletes)

1. With the entire core engaged, begin the movement by crawling in the direction called by the strength and conditioning professional, not letting the knees touch the floor or the foam roller drop (b). Ideally, an item placed on the lower back just above the waistline on both athletes would not move throughout the movement.

2. Throughout this movement, avoid any major break in posture (e.g., slumping or extension). If a break in posture is observed, decrease the distance or time held in this posture.

Breathing Guidelines

During bear crawls it is recommended athletes take in a deep breath prior to lifting the knees and that they create intra-abdominal pressure and tighten the abs before beginning to crawl. This pressure should be maintained throughout the movement. During the movement athletes should be able to maintain pressure, create as much tension as possible throughout their core, and breathe behind the shield they have created, contracting the abdominal, triceps, and erector spinae isometrically.

Exercise Modifications and Variations

If athletes are unable to crawl while keeping the foam roller in place, they can begin by holding the static position with the knees off the floor for increasing amounts of time. They can progress to picking up one hand or one foot, leaving only three points of contact, then to picking up one arm and the foot, leaving only two points of contact.

Once athletes are proficient, progressions can be made by adding an external load using a weighted vest or plates on their backs. Again, the goal is to maintain control of the shoulder blades, spine, and pelvis. It is not encouraged to let quality fall by the wayside for the sake of progression. If athletes are not proficient at crawling on their own, this version is not encouraged.

Coaching Tip

When calling out directions choose landmarks (e.g., windows, door, racks, foam rollers) as opposed to simply left and right. During this movement make sure the athlete maintains proper position and the spine never flexes or goes into extension and that the athlete does not lose spinal or pelvic control when crawling. The athlete should demonstrate such control that an item placed on his or her lower back would not fall off.

Figure 8.17   Partner bear crawl: *(a)* beginning position; *(b)* crawl.

TALL KNEELING CHOP AND LIFT

Primary Muscles Trained

The tall kneeling chop and lift is a staple of anti-rotation core exercises and involves a great deal of musculature along with the fascial spiral line of the upper body and hips. The spiral line loops around the body in a helix, joining one side of the skull across the back and the opposite shoulder, then across the front to the same hip, knee, and foot arch, running up the back of the body to rejoin the fascia on the skull (10).

Based on the position achieved and the muscle actions, this exercise targets the rotators of the torso (internal and external oblique, multifidi, and rotators), which act isometrically to limit rotation. During the chop and lift the major muscles trained are the retractors (trapezius and rhomboid major and minor) and protractors (serratus anterior and pectoralis minor) of the scapula along with the flexors and extensors of the elbow. During the chop, the major muscles trained are the latissimus dorsi, and during the lift, the pectoralis major and minor along with the deltoids.

Beginning Positions

Chop

- Assume a tall kneeling position with the knees flexed at 90 degrees and the hips fully extended, and line up perpendicular to the resistive mechanism (e.g., band or cable column handle) with both knees on the floor.
- Extend the shoulder and elbow. The torso should remain upright in a good posture with the shoulders back.
- Grasp the resistive mechanism with both hands by reaching up diagonally. The resistive mechanism should be high enough that the angle of pull is 45 degrees (a).

Lift

- Assume a tall kneeling position with the knees flexed at 90 degrees and the hips fully extended, and line up perpendicular to the resistive mechanism with both knees on the floor.
- Fully flex the shoulders and extend the elbow. The torso should remain upright in a good posture with the shoulders back.
- Grasp the resistive mechanism with both hands by reaching down diagonally. The resistive mechanism should be low enough that the angle of pull is 45 degrees (c).

Movement Phases

Tall Kneeling Chop

1. Start to pull the handle of the resistive mechanism to the logo on the shirt (i.e., in line with the sternum). This pull is a top-down movement.
2. As the handle moves toward the shirt's logo, flex the elbows and move the shoulders into slight extension.
3. Once the handle has reached the logo, move into elbow extension and punch the hands toward the floor. Maintain control and good posture during this punch.
4. At the end of the movement the arms should be at a 45-degree angle to the floor (b).

5. Reverse the movement to get back to the beginning position.

6. Perform the required number of repetitions, then switch sides.

Tall Kneeling Lift

1. Start to pull the handle of the resistive mechanism to the logo on the shirt (i.e., in line with the sternum). This pull is a bottom-up movement.

2. As the handle moves toward the shirt's logo, flex the elbows.

3. Once the handle has reached the logo, move into elbow extension and punch the hands toward the ceiling. Maintain control and good posture during this punch.

4. At the end of the movement the arms should be at a 45-degree angle to the floor (d).

5. Reverse the movement to get back to the beginning position.

6. Perform the required number of repetitions, then switch sides.

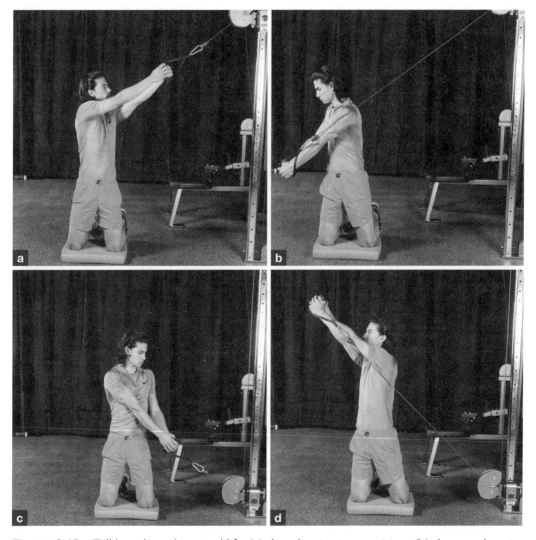

Figure 8.18   Tall kneeling chop and lift: (a) chop beginning position; (b) chop end position; (c) lift beginning position; (d) lift end position.

Breathing Guidelines

During the tall kneeling chop and lift it is recommended athletes take in a deep breath prior to beginning the movement and to create intra-abdominal pressure, which should be maintained throughout the movement. During the movement athletes should be able to maintain pressure while holding a conversation along with contracting the involved musculature to keep proper posture. It also is recommended that athletes keep their rib cage down and gluteal muscles squeezed during the movement.

Exercise Modifications and Variations

If athletes struggle to maintain adequate posture during the movement, regress the intensity (weight or resistance used) or move the angle of pull to a lower position, closer to the height of the hips. This allows athletes to not have to reach as much, which will improve posture and make the exercise easier.

As athletes become more efficient with this movement, they can speed up the movement to target power adaptations. This can be very beneficial with regards to energy transfer through the torso.

Coaching Tip

During this movement it is imperative to coach control and make sure the athlete maintains great posture throughout. If poor posture is observed, either provide a high level of feedback to improve the movement or regress the exercise.

HALF-KNEELING CHOP AND LIFT

Primary Muscles Trained

The half-kneeling chop and lift is a staple of anti-rotation core exercises (progression from the tall kneeling chop and lift) and involves a great deal of musculature along with the fascial spiral line of the upper body and hips. The spiral line loops around the body in a helix, joining one side of the skull across the back and the opposite shoulder, then across the front to the same hip, knee, and foot arch, running up the back of the body to rejoin the fascia on the skull (10).

Based on the position achieved and the muscle actions, this exercise targets the rotators of the torso (internal and external oblique, multifidi, and rotators), which act isometrically to limit rotation. During the chop and lift the major muscles trained are the retractors (trapezius and rhomboid major and minor) and protractors (serratus anterior and pectoralis minor) of the scapula along with the flexors and extensors of the elbow. During the chop the major muscles trained are the latissimus dorsi, and during the lift, the pectoralis major and minor and the deltoids.

Beginning Positions

Half-Kneeling Chop

- Assume a half-kneeling position with one knee on the floor and the opposite hip flexed at 90 degrees. In this position there should be three points of contact with the floor: toe, back knee, and front foot. Line up perpendicular to the resistive mechanism (e.g., band or cable column handle) with the inside knee up; this is a *closed position* relative to the resistive mechanism.

- The front foot, back knee, and toe should be in line to create a narrow base of support.
- The torso should remain upright in a good posture with the shoulders back.
- Grasp the resistive mechanism with both hands by reaching up diagonally. The resistive mechanism should be high that the angle of pull is 45 degrees *(a)*.

Half-Kneeling Lift

- Assume a half-kneeling position with one knee on the floor and the opposite hip flexed at 90 degrees. In this position there should be three points of contact with the floor: toe, back knee, and front foot. Line up perpendicular to the resistive mechanism with the inside knee up; this is an *open position* relative to the resistive mechanism.
- The front foot, back knee, and toe should be in line to create a narrow base of support.
- The torso should remain upright in a good posture with the shoulders back.
- Grasp the resistive mechanism with both hands by reaching down diagonally. The resistive mechanism should be low enough that the angle of pull is 45 degrees *(c)*.

Movement Phases

Half-Kneeling Chop

1. Start to pull the handle of the resistive mechanism to the logo on the shirt (i.e., in line with the sternum). This pull is a top-down movement.
2. As the handle moves toward the shirt's logo, flex the elbows and move the shoulders into slight extension.
3. Once the handle has reached the logo, move into elbow extension and punch the hands toward the floor. Maintain control and good posture during this punch.
4. At the end of the movement the arms should be at a 45-degree angle to the floor *(b)*.
5. Reverse the movement to get back to the beginning position.
6. Perform the required number of repetitions, then switch sides.

Half-Kneeling Lift

1. Start to pull the handle of the resistive mechanism to the logo on the shirt (i.e., in line with the sternum). This pull is a bottom-up movement.
2. As the handle moves toward the shirt's logo, flex the elbows.
3. Once the handle has reached the logo, move into elbow extension and punch the hands toward the ceiling. Maintain control and good posture during this punch.
4. At the end of the movement the arms should be at a 45-degree angle to the floor *(d)*.
5. Reverse the movement to get back to the beginning position.
6. Perform the required number of repetitions, then switch sides.

Breathing Guidelines

During the half-kneeling chop and lift it is recommended athletes take in a deep breath prior to beginning the movement and to create intra-abdominal pressure, which should be maintained throughout the movement. During the movement athletes should be able to maintain pressure while holding a conversation along with contracting the involved musculature to keep proper posture. It is also be recommended that athletes keep their rib cage down and gluteal muscles squeezed during the movement.

Exercise Modifications and Variations

If athletes struggle to maintain adequate posture during the movement, regress the intensity (weight or resistance used) or move the angle of pull to a lower position, closer to the height of the hips. This allows athletes to not have to reach as much, which will improve posture and make the exercise easier. Another modification is to widen the base of support for the athletes (i.e., moving the front foot out and away from the resistive mechanism). This provides additional stability.

As athletes improve, they can speed up the movement to target power adaptations. This can be very beneficial with regards to energy transfer through the torso.

Coaching Tip

During this movement it is imperative to coach control and make sure athletes maintain great posture throughout. If poor posture is observed, either provide a high level of feedback to improve the movement or regress the exercise.

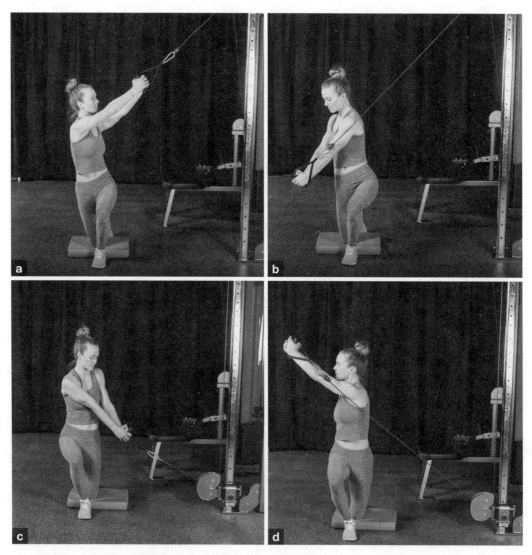

Figure 8.19   Half-kneeling chop and lift: *(a)* chop beginning position; *(b)* chop end position; *(c)* lift beginning position; *(d)* lift end position.

CHOP AND LIFT FROM LOW SPLIT STANCE

Primary Muscles Trained

The chop and lift from low split stance is considered a staple of anti-rotation core exercises and involves a great deal of musculature along with the fascial spiral line of the upper body and hips. The spiral line loops around the body in a helix, joining one side of the skull across the back and the opposite shoulder, then across the front to the same hip, knee, and foot arch, running up the back of the body to rejoin the fascia on the skull (10).

Based on the position achieved and the muscle actions, this exercise targets the rotators of the torso (internal and external oblique, multifidi, and rotators), which act isometrically to limit rotation. During the chop and lift the major muscles trained are the retractors (trapezius and rhomboid major and minor) and protractors (serratus anterior and pectoralis minor) of the scapula along with the flexors and extensors of the elbow. During the chop, the major muscles trained are the latissimus dorsi and during the lift, the pectoralis major and minor and the deltoids.

This variation also trains the lower body musculature isometrically. This includes the hip flexors (psoas major, iliacus, tensor fasciae latae, sartorius, rectus femoris, gluteus medius and minimus) and extensors (gluteus maximus, biceps femoris, semitendinosus, semimembranosus) along with the knee flexors (biceps femoris, semitendinosus, semimembranosus, gastrocnemius) and extensors (rectus femoris, vastus lateralis, vastus medialis).

Beginning Positions

Chop From Low Split Stance

- Assume a low split stance position with one knee hovering just above the floor and the opposite hip flexed at 90 degrees. In this position there should be two points of contact with the floor (i.e., back toe and front foot). Line up perpendicular to the resistive mechanism (e.g., band or cable column handle) with the inside knee up; this is a *closed position* relative to the resistive mechanism.
- The front foot and back knee should be in line to create a narrow base of support.
- The torso should remain upright in a good posture with the shoulders back. A straight line is formed from the shoulders to the hips.
- Grasp the resistive mechanism with both hands by reaching up diagonally. The resistive mechanism should be high enough that angle of pull is 45 degrees (a).

Lift From Low Split Stance

- Assume a low split stance position with one knee hovering just above the floor and the opposite hip flexed at 90 degrees. In this position there should be two points of contact with the floor (i.e., back toe and front foot). Line up perpendicular to the resistive mechanism with the outside knee up; this is an *open position* relative to the resistive mechanism.
- The front foot and back knee should be in line to create a narrow base of support.
- The torso should remain upright in a good posture with the shoulders back. A straight line is formed from the shoulders to the hips.
- Grasp the resistive mechanism with both hands by reaching down diagonally. The resistive mechanism should be low enough that the angle of pull is 45 degrees from the floor (c).

Movement Phases

Chop From Low Split Stance

1. Start to pull the handle of the resistive mechanism to the logo on the shirt (i.e., in line with the sternum). This pulling action is a top-down movement.
2. As the handle moves toward the shirt's logo, flex the elbows and move the shoulders into slight extension.
3. Once the handle has reached the logo, move into elbow extension and punch the hands toward the floor. Maintain control and good posture during this punch.
4. At the end of the movement the arms should be at a 45-degree angle to the floor *(b)*.
5. Reverse the movement to get back to the beginning position.
6. Perform the required number of repetitions, then switch sides.

Lift From Low Split Stance

1. Start to pull the handle of the resistive mechanism to the logo on the shirt (i.e., in line with the sternum). This pulling action is a bottom-up movement.
2. As the handle moves toward the shirt's logo, flex the elbows.
3. Once the handle has reached the logo, move into elbow extension and punch the hands toward the ceiling. Maintain control and good posture during this punch.
4. At the end of the movement the arms should be at a 45-degree angle to the floor *(d)*.
5. Reverse the movement to get back to the beginning position.
6. Perform the required number of repetitions, then switch sides.

Breathing Guidelines

During the chop and lift from low split stance it is recommended athletes take in a deep breath prior to beginning the movement and to create intra-abdominal pressure, which should be maintained throughout the movement. During the movement athletes should be able to maintain pressure while holding a conversation along with contracting the involved musculature to keep proper posture. It also is recommended that athletes keep their rib cage down and gluteal muscles squeezed during the movement.

Exercise Modifications and Variations

If athletes struggle to maintain adequate posture during the movement, regress the intensity (weight or resistance used) or move the angle of pull to a lower position, closer to the height of the hips. This allows athletes to not have to reach as much, which will improve the posture and make the exercise easier. Another modification is to widen the base of support for the athlete (i.e., moving the front foot out and away from the resistive mechanism). This provides additional stability. If these modifications do not create a better environment, it is recommended that athletes drop the knee down to the floor for more stability.

As athletes improve with this movement, they can speed up the movement to target power adaptations. This can be very beneficial with regards to energy transfer through the torso.

Coaching Tips

During this movement it is imperative to coach control and make sure athletes maintain great posture throughout. If poor posture is observed the strength and conditioning professional either needs to provide a high level of feedback to improve the movement or regress to variations suggested above.

Cue athletes to dig their points of contact into the floor. This will allow for a better connection to be built from the floor through the entire kinetic chain.

Figure 8.20 Chop and lift from low split stance: *(a)* chop beginning position; *(b)* chop end position; *(c)* lift beginning position; *(d)* lift end position.

DEAD BUG (CONTRALATERAL AND IPSILATERAL)

Primary Muscles Trained

The dead bug is a developmental stability exercise. It is considered developmental because in the teachings of dynamic neuromuscular stabilization, humans first gain stability during infancy when lying on their backs (12). Based on the activity, the primary muscles trained during this exercise are the stabilizing muscles of the spinal column (transversus abdominus; quadratus lumborum; internal, external, and transverse oblique; multifidus; and erector spinae).

Beginning Position

- Assume a supine position with the feet flat on the floor and the knees flexed at 90 degrees. Reach the arms up toward the ceiling, and focus the gaze there.
- Place a band under the body near region of the thoracic spine so as to have some tactile cueing and something to fight to hold down.
- Take a deep breath to create intra-abdominal pressure, then press down on the band underneath the thoracic spine while reaching the hands to the ceiling. The strength and conditioning professional will apply slight pressure to the band, trying to pull it out from under the athlete (a).

Movement Phases

1. With the core engaged, begin to reach the thumbs to the floor, taking the biceps toward the ears (b).
2. Throughout this movement focus on a hard reach as if trying to reach for the ceiling. Continue this as the arms move. During the movement, maintain pressure on the band and do not allow the strength and conditioning professional to pull it out from under the body.

Breathing Guidelines

During the dead bug the athlete needs to be able to fill low in the intra-abdominal cavity, which will allow the athlete to maintain pressure on the band. This is an excellent teaching tool for breathing mechanics for all movements in which intra-abdominal pressure is needed.

Exercise Modifications and Variations

Once athletes are proficient at moving both hands to the floor allowing the thumbs to touch the floor and returning back to the beginning position, progressions can be made by moving the feet closer together until they touch, reducing the base of stability. Alternatively, athletes can flex 90 degrees at the hip so one leg is held off the floor statically, then alternate the legs that are flexed at the hip while simultaneously moving the arms and reaching the thumbs to the floor. Another option is to lie on a 36-inch (91 cm) foam roller, with both the head and tailbone supported, and repeat the above progressions.

Coaching Tip

During this movement make sure the athlete is successful in holding down the band before moving on to a more challenging version. Look for a hard reach of the arms achieving as much distance as possible between the fingers and the face. Be sure the neck is relaxed. Once an athlete has progressed to lying supine on a foam roller, it might be necessary to adjust the pressure on the band so as not to pull the foam roller out from under the athlete.

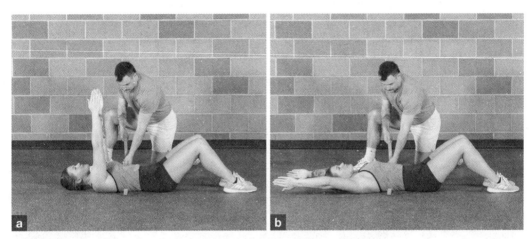

Figure 8.21   Dead bug (contralateral and ipsilateral): *(a)* beginning position; *(b)* reach.

PALLOF PRESS KNEELING ANTI-ROTATION PRESS

Primary Muscles Trained

The Pallof press is an anti-rotational stability exercise that targets the rotators of the torso (internal and external oblique, multifidi, and rotators), which act isometrically to limit rotation.

Beginning Position

- Assume a tall kneeling position with the knees flexed at 90 degrees and the hips fully extended, and line up perpendicular to the resistive mechanism (e.g., band or cable column handle) with both knees on the floor.
- Grasp the handle at the abdominal level, which allows the elbows to be flexed at 90 degrees when returning to the rest position *(a)*.

Movement Phases

1. Press both hands straight out in front of the body *(b)*.
2. Throughout this movement remain static everywhere but the arms. When the arms are fully extended it will feel as though the cable is rotating and pulling on the body. Resisting this movement is most of the exercise's work.

Breathing Guidelines

During the Pallof press kneeling anti-rotation press it is recommended to create intra-abdominal pressure and to breathe behind the shield to create stability.

Exercise Modifications and Variations

The modifications of this exercise are almost limitless. Some of the most common include variations in the stance such as standing, a half-kneeling stance with the inside leg down, a split stance, or lunge stance. Other variations include a walk out, where athletes maintain the athletic stance and laterally walks away from the cable machine or attachment where the band is placed. As athletes progress in stability, the difficulty can be increased by raising the band overhead.

Coaching Tip

During this movement make sure that the athlete is not pulled into rotation during any of the variations and that spinal alignment is not lost. One of the main purposes of the core is to resist movement of the trunk.

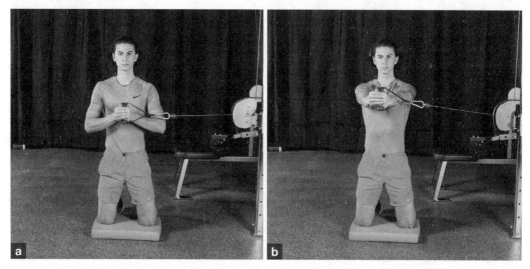

Figure 8.22 Pallof press kneeling anti-rotational press: *(a)* beginning position; *(b)* press.

PART III

PROGRAM DESIGN GUIDELINES AND SAMPLE PROGRAMS

OFF-SEASON PROGRAMMING

JULIA EYRE AND IVI CASAGRANDE

The soccer off-season, also known as the *transition* or *preparatory period*, is a crucial part of the annual training cycle in which athletes recover from the fatigue of the competitive season and focus on improving their own athleticism. Specifically, resistance training programs should focus on addressing weaknesses, potential injury risks, and movement dysfunctions through the development of strength and power qualities. This should be planned by the strength and conditioning professional on the basis of individual athlete needs such as time constraints, preseason start date, demands of the game and athlete's position, training age, postseason performance assessment data, and injury history. Some athletes might demonstrate a need for increased baseline fitness due to a lack of foundational strength and the increasingly high athletic demands of the sport. However, it is critical to build sufficient chronic load in this phase, avoid detraining, and ensure that athletes are building their foundational strength enough that they are equipped for when the preseason cycle begins (including team training and scrimmages).

GOALS AND OBJECTIVES

Contrary to other phases within the annual plan, the off-season is heavily focused on implementing resistance training and on developing strength, resilience, and power. These qualities are generated through periodized training plans as opposed to randomized resistance training protocols or a primary emphasis on conditioning (11a). Although improving maximal strength can lead to increased running economy and time to exhaustion (25), it is important to strike a balance between conditioning protocols and resistance training in the off-season. Aerobic endurance will not be discussed in further detail in this chapter.

Key performance indicators (KPIs) for the sport and specific athlete-positional demands such as jumping and sprinting should contribute to how programs are structured. It is important, however, to not only progressively develop these neuromuscular abilities in the weight room but also understand the challenge of improving these abilities during periods of high exposure to aerobic endurance training (i.e., preseason), whereby the interference effect might reduce power and speed performance adaptations (16). Thus, emphasis on strength endurance, maximal strength, rate of force development, and reactive strength qualities should be implemented across mesocycles appropriately, allowing for calculated development of all four components across the off-season phase and potential carryover to the precompetitive period.

Training compliance, or the actual and appropriate execution of the program by the athletes, during the off-season is extremely important. Proper periodized resistance training serves not only to improve athlete fitness and ability to withstand match demands, but also reduces the risk of injury (5). Athletes might be more likely to experience non-contact time-loss injuries if resistance training is neglected in the off-season (4). Strength and conditioning professionals can influence compliance and establish consistent communication throughout that period in a variety of ways so that best results can be attained when athletes come back from the off-season period. This might include weekly logs through online questionnaires, using remote training program software, readiness questionnaires and submission of training loads, interacting with athletes on a consistent basis, and adding in elements of challenge or competition.

Additionally, the development of a healthy working relationship should be prioritized between the strength and conditioning professional and athletes, because this enhances communication and creates productive interactions, allowing both sides to better measure progress throughout the off-season program. Strength and conditioning professionals might request that athletes, especially when training remotely, submit videos of drills or exercises, which allows for more athlete-specific feedback and the tracking of improvement via film or other objective measures such as new personal records. Providing education to athletes about the value of resistance training in the off-season is also critical to securing training compliance, even at the youth level. Through reports from strength and conditioning professionals and medical staff at the end of the competitive season and by providing scientific research using simple language and visuals, athletes can learn about the value of developing strength capabilities, the importance of avoiding detraining, and the impacts on their performance and success of the team during the preseason. Anecdotal evidence, such as having more experienced athletes or leaders from teams share with their teammates about how compliance and buy-in to off-season training positively affected their game, is another productive, persuasive way to educate.

LENGTH, STRUCTURE, AND ORGANIZATION

The duration of each training phase in the off-season depends on the competitive schedule, training age, proficiency in and necessary improvement of certain skills, and the athletes' individual neural attributes (3). Length of the off-season is based on league structures, tournament schedules, and international friendlies and competitions. Although this phase ranges from 6 weeks in European leagues to 16 weeks in some North American leagues, for the purpose of this chapter, a 12-week off-season cycle is proposed.

Recovery blocks must be purposefully scheduled following the competitive phase and before starting the 12-week off-season. This is vital for athletes' physiological and psychological regeneration. A two-week break can allow athletes to regenerate from the season with little detrimental effects on fat-free mass and physical performance, with preserved or even potential increased levels of strength and cardiorespiratory fitness (6). The efficacy of the regeneration block depends on providing a well-balanced training protocol, decreasing overall volume and intensity of sessions without initiating detraining (6). Regeneration blocks can be used all year as needed.

While athletes are tired and not in peak form immediately after the competitive season, postcompetition assessments should be taken before athletes are released for recovery blocks prior to the first training phase of the off-season. However, because athletes are not in peak physiological or psychological condition in the first weeks of the postseason, with motivation and concentration potentially dropping off, testing should be held to an absolute minimum and athletes only should be required to take part in assessments necessary for off-season planning, such as strength and speed testing. Postseason data provide valuable information in the long term and equip strength and conditioning professionals to build the most efficient and productive off-season possible, which is crucial because time is often limited. Pretesting before the off-season offers the added bonus of recording each athlete's general and specific fitness level before the off-season and, compared to only posttesting before the preseason, offers insight into the long-term athletic development of each individual. This feedback can be used to influence additional parts of the cycle and injury reduction programs or simply to keep a timeline on athletes' athleticism and progress.

The off-season phase can be divided into two periods: (1) the preparatory period, which is composed of the general physical preparation (GPP), hypertrophy/strength endurance, and basic or maximal strength phases, and (2) the specific preparatory period, which contains the strength and power phase (11a).

An optimal protocol during the off-season should be highly individual, with the exercise selection and progression through each phase based on each athlete's capabilities as closely as possible. It is important to consider the training age, physical maturity, and rate of physiological adaptation of each athlete when structuring the off-season plan, because these factors help determine the length of and individual progressions through each micro- and mesocycle. Some athletes might start in different phases or spend different amounts of time in a phase based on individual needs and the calendar of training and competitions. Strength and conditioning professionals need to approach their programs with flexibility to account for the many factors out of their control, such as injuries, postponement of competitions, or calendar congestion (e.g., international or club duties).

Not only should the baseline of strength and power be improved regardless of athlete training age and physical maturity, but biomechanical or movement deficiencies should also be addressed in each cycle. Creating specific warm-up routines and athlete-specific movement protocols based on postcompetition phase assessments should be considered. Athletes should execute their individual activation routine prior to the start of resistance training sessions.

General Physical Preparation

Following the end of the competitive phase, the primary objective of the first microcycle of the off-season involves regeneration and restoration of movement while maintaining athletes' strength-endurance. Most notably, the start of the GPP phase shifts athletes' focus from performance on the pitch onto athletes' well-roundedness and baseline fitness level by increasing strength-endurance, improving mobility, and increasing work capacity. While the plan to achieving these goals is different for every athlete based on his or her peripheral fatigue (especially the lower body), injury status and history, training age, and length of the post- and off-season, GPP is characterized by developing the foundation of total-body athleticism and preparing athletes for an increased load and intensity in the following microcycles.

The length of this microcycle depends largely on whether the athletes' annual schedule already includes a postseason phase and their individual training experience. For athletes with a complete postseason phase that includes high-volume resistance training or those with a high training age, this microcycle might be shortened significantly or eliminated completely before moving onto the hypertrophy/strength endurance microcycle. Athletes with a short postseason or no postseason at all and a 12-week off-season schedule might spend two to six weeks in this phase before transitioning to the next cycle (3).

Because this foundational strength period of the off-season directly follows the end of the season, recovery is emphasized by decreasing the intensity and managing the volume of training compared to the training load of the regular season. This is accomplished, in part, by the absence of or decreased number of team training sessions in a week and by varying the forms of training typically used in the season. Training sessions should take place two to four times weekly, each one beginning with a thorough, total-body warm-up with a high emphasis on regaining mobility, especially of the lower body joints. Although this can be accomplished in part by resistance training at the athletes' full range of motion, a dynamic warm-up, targeted at improving active flexibility and developing ligament and tendon strength, is integral to improving baseline fitness and, thus, the GPP cycle (11a).

The training week might also include sport training sessions on the pitch, because athletes can still practice their sport in the off-season. Because there is wide variation in athletes' schedules and environments during the off-season, strength and conditioning professionals must remain flexible with their planning. An understanding of not only the volume and intensity of sport sessions but also the content of the technical drills can better guide strength and conditioning professionals to design the best program while taking these external factors into consideration. Communication between the strength and conditioning professional and head coaches and other team support staff members is critical to creating the optimal protocol and training environment for athletes.

A thorough warm-up period should be followed by high-volume resistance training with low to moderate loads (3-5 sets of 8-12 repetitions at 70%-75%) (11a). Not all exercises in this microcycle must have obvious or specific application to the pitch, but should generally improve total-body fitness and multidimensionality. Exercise selection ranges from barbell strength and power exercises, such as Olympic lifts and other technical exercises, to bodyweight or minimal-equipment training.

Hypertrophy/Strength Endurance Phase

As part of the GPP and following the postseason microcycle, the focus of the hypertrophy/strength endurance phase is to increase lean body mass and develop a muscular and metabolic endurance base (11a). The time spent in this phase will depend largely on the individual athlete's needs and training age, but for the purpose of this chapter six weeks in length is proposed. Strong athletes can spend less time during this phase because they should emphasize power while maintaining or improving strength at the same time. Weaker athletes should spend more time in this phase to develop a better foundation of strength before emphasizing power-type training (25). Understanding and analyzing the importance of the relative strength standards values for the sport of soccer is critical for strength and conditioning professionals to see where on the spectrum their athletes are and what should be prioritized. Strength and conditioning professionals might create a baseline for athletes' strength by, for example, laying out the expectation that athletes should be able to squat or deadlift at least 1.2 times their body weight after the off-season. This gives athletes an objective measure and goal to work toward in their off-season period.

During this phase, training intensity should be low to moderate (60%-80% of the 1RM) while overall volume remains high (3-6 sets of 8-20 repetitions) (11a). Intensity, volume, and exercise selection determine the length and frequency of training sessions, and athletes should be allowed to sufficiently recover between sessions to reduce unnecessary fatigue and maximize adaptations. Time between sessions is largely dependent on each athlete's condition and the ability of their neuromuscular system to recover; better-conditioned athletes recover faster than less-conditioned athletes (3). However, the strength and conditioning professional might decide to manipulate these training variables under some circumstances to promote super-compensation, in which the athlete is pushed excessively in training and, just as performance begins to decrease, enters a period of prescribed rest, usually of a few days. If this method is not practiced carefully and athlete monitoring is insufficient, it can lead to significant decrements in performance and even overtraining in the long term (9, 11a).

Basic Strength Phase

The **basic strength phase**, also known as maximal strength, follows the hypertrophy/strength endurance phase and can begin as soon as the athlete has achieved the essential movement and strength endurance goals of the previous phase. The objective of resistance training within this microcycle is to increase the maximal force production of the body's prime movers. These muscles are essential to the demands of the sport, especially the quadriceps, hamstrings, gluteal muscles, and latissimus dorsi, although the total body should be trained appropriately throughout the microcycle.

Maximal strength, or the highest possible amount of strength an athlete possesses, plays a vital role in soccer performance; relative strength, the ratio of an athlete's strength to his or her body size, is critical to success in the sport. This is achieved by creating high amounts of tension in muscles by performing contractions under high load with proper technique, which, when performed over time, increase the athlete's ability to produce force through enhanced neuromuscular activation.

In this phase, training sessions should occur three times per week, depending on the athlete's tolerance and whether sessions are total-body or split routines. Training volume should decrease while training intensity increases; that is, heavier loads are used in the lower-repetition ranges (2-6 sets of 2-6 repetitions at 80%-95% of 1RM for core exercises) and feature appropriate accessory exercises, commonly called *assistance exercises* (11a). Where appropriate, loads might sometimes range from 1-3 repetitions at 90%-100% of 1RM (3). Athletes should be allowed adequate rest between sets, usually between two to five minutes, to allow for full regeneration of the primary energy source, **adenosine triphosphate** (ATP), and the **central nervous system** (CNS) to maximize output and intensity of each repetition (3). As intensity increases, allocated rest times between sets should also increase.

An important facet of planning the maximal strength phase is exercise selection. The focus should remain on proper technique at the desired intensity, as opposed to executing unmastered technical exercises, such as Olympic lifts, for the sake of complexity or using a wide variety of exercises instead of training specific muscles and movements (3). Fundamental exercises, commonly called *core exercises*, should take priority in each session and directly follow the warm-up, because these movements require the highest intensity and intention with fewer repetitions and higher loads. This primary block of the training session is then complemented with assistance exercises, which attack specific weaknesses by isolating particular muscle groups. Assistance exercises are always performed after the core exercises. For example, the trap bar deadlift, pull-up, and front squat might be featured in a session as core exercises, while the dumbbell shoulder press, single-leg deadlift, and split squat serve as assistance exercises. Unilateral exercises are also beneficial for increasing maximal strength.

Two additional methods can be used in the development of maximal strength: isometric and eccentric training. Isometric strength can be useful in this phase because it produces high tension in the muscle and is realized through either applying force against an immobile object or attempting to lift heavier weight than one's potential (3). Tendons and ligaments also benefit from isometric training because this method can increase structural stiffness. It is important to ensure that the contraction is near maximum (80%-100%), with a single contraction ranging from 6 to 8 seconds for a total of 30 to 50 seconds per muscle per training session for maximum strength at sport-specific angles (3, 20). Also important is that the progression to increase load should be done by increasing either the load or number of sets, contrary to increasing the duration of contraction. Isometric hamstring exercises can be useful, especially with the high-speed running demands of soccer, because a deficit in hamstring strength endurance is linked to an increase in the risk of hamstring injuries (16). Macdonald and colleagues demonstrated that the single-leg Roman chair hold, an isometric hamstring exercise, might be more effective for improving single-leg hamstring bridge performance than the Nordic hamstring curl, which is primarily an eccentric exercise. Another benefit of using the isometric method is that it does not cause delayed-onset muscle soreness like the eccentric method might in athletes who are not adapted to this training style (16). Isometric exercises can also induce a maximal recruitment in a similar position and range to where maximal hamstring force is generated. A single-leg hamstring bridge hold with a lower-limb position, for example, can reflect the midstance phase of fast running (13).

The eccentric method of resistance training creates high tension in the muscles and minimizes energy cost, allowing eccentric work to be heavier and slower but performed longer than concentric motions (3). Eccentric loads thus can be prescribed at 1 to 5 sets of 2 to 4 repetitions of supramaximal loads. Depending on the muscle group trained, rest between sets should last two to six minutes, and frequency of eccentric training should not exceed two sessions per week.

It should be mentioned that strength gains do not and should not always result in an increase in muscle mass, although it is normal for the untrained athlete to see an initial increase in muscle size in the early phases of strength development. Additionally, because of the CNS-taxing nature of true maximal resistance training, it should not occur when athletes are exhausted (3, 19). Rather, the focus should be on progressive loading, proper recovery, and strength increases over time in a long-term development model.

Power Phase

Given the foundational competencies built throughout the GPP, hypertrophy/strength endurance, and basic strength microcycles, the process of increasing the athlete's baseline of strength for sport performance peaks with the power phase, when explosive strength and skill enhancement become primary objectives. Although maximal strength and movement competency should be maintained throughout the preparatory and competitive phase to keep up peak power qualities, the objective shifts from maximal force production to rapid force production (24). During this microcycle, athletes should become more coordinated and skill execution should occur more quickly and precisely (3).

Power is the product of muscle force and movement velocity ($P = F \times V$) and occurs via rapid muscle contractions. The **rate of force development** (RFD) is a measure of how quickly an athlete can develop force and is a primary KPI in many sports; it is associated with jumping, sprinting, and other performance factors (1, 11a). Training power itself, also termed *explosive strength*, requires rapid force production and implementing exercises at lower volumes and loads while maintaining high velocity. Because high-velocity training stresses the CNS, it is necessary to implement longer rest periods between sets of explosive strength movements to carefully regulate this training, stopping sets when repetition velocity slows significantly from fatigue. High-velocity power training can take place two to three times weekly in the late off-season phase (3, 24).

Isotonic movements, or accelerating weight through the full range of motion as quickly as possible such as during a speed squat or bench press throw, are helpful in the transition from maximal strength to dynamic power. Olympic lifts and barbell and dumbbell exercises are now appropriate and should take place directly after warm-ups for optimal performance (3). Especially for athletes with a lower training age, barbell exercises should be scaled to 40% to 50% of the individual's 1RM to maximize power production. A protocol of 3 to 5 sets of 1 to 5 repetitions is appropriate for this training method, with appropriate rest intervals of 2 to 5 minutes (11a). Accommodating resistance in the form of bands and chains also can be used for more trained athletes using isotonic methods, although rest times should be increased and overall volume of sets and repetitions decreased (3).

Ballistic training is also an effective method of training power, such as with kettlebell swings and medicine ball throwing. Athletes must overcome resistance to project the weight, accelerating it through the entire motion. Training should not take part under significant fatigue; repetitions should be halted as soon as the velocity decreases due to fatigue, only continuing if and when the athlete can maintain speed. However, it has been found that intent, rather than speed of movement, plays a critical role in high-velocity ballistic training; thus, athletes should be physically and mentally alert and prepared to execute power training (2).

Plyometric training, although outside the realm of this book, is also a suitable form of explosive training for soccer athletes, because jumping and sprinting are common demands of the sport. This might involve various jumps, sprint starts, and internal agility-type training sessions (3). High volume is not required in plyometrics; they should be used as a power training tool rather than for conditioning. This method can complement an explosive strength program up to three times weekly in the late off-season and leading into the preseason cycle.

High School

Off-season programming for high school–level athletes should differ when compared to collegiate and professional programming. Movement competency, an individual's ability to perform a movement in an optimal manner, should be the priority for most high school athletes (18). Thus, an off-season program for athletes with a lower training age, including lowerclassmen and any athletes requiring better foundational strength and movement qualities, should feature a significantly longer GPP, geared toward maximizing baseline fitness with hypertrophy/strength endurance and strength, before entering the specific preparatory period to focus on gaining strength and power. Upperclassmen and individuals with higher training ages and well-rounded athletic development can spend less time in the hypertrophy/strength endurance microcycle before proceeding to the strength and power phases.

A 12-week high school off-season program might have an 8-week GPP microcycle and a 4-week strength and power microcycle. This can be accomplished with a four-week GPP or postseason phase, a four-week hypertrophy/strength endurance phase, a two-week basic strength phase, and a two-week power phase (10).

Especially at the high school level, where athletes almost always are adolescents and have a low training age, it is vital that strength and conditioning professionals understand the process of growth and maturation and their effects on not only athletes' performance on the field but also in the weight room (18). Reinforcing movement competency during puberty and beyond is crucial, because a temporary loss of coordination occurs during periods of rapid growth, most commonly known as *adolescent awkwardness* (18). Movement competency can be analyzed through assessments of muscle flexibility, strength imbalances, and general movement proficiency (23). Understanding and tracking when athletes are going through their most rapid rate of growth, called *peak height velocity* (PHV), can help strength and conditioning professionals understand when to apply the most appropriate strategies in the weight room to improve motor control and coordination, which are predominantly affected during this phase (14). Current research into adolescent resistance training emphasizes the development of relative strength and movement skills, particularly around PHV, as important factors in differentiating sprint and jump performance. Special attention needs to be paid to landing mechanics and unilateral strength and stability, specifically with adolescent girls. The modifiable risk factors studied in female high school soccer athletes who experienced noncontact ACL injuries are increased knee abduction, reduced knee flexion angles, higher ground reaction force, and an uneven landing pattern in comparison to females who did not sustain an ACL injury (11b). Further, adolescent girls may show an increase in knee valgus and landing forces as well as a decrease in jump performance compared to male adolescents (12a). Thus, movement competency should be revisited and reinforced continually in high school athletes.

College

The start of the collegiate off-season largely depends on how far teams play into postseason tournaments; in some cases, this training phase might begin in December and last until the end of July. College programs usually organize and require athletes to adhere to off-season strength programs unattended from December until May, at which time athletes either do their summer off-season programs on their own or with their school (8).

The collegiate season is unique from professional league play in that athletes experience multiple stressors at once, including academic and competitive sport demands (8). Time conflicts abound, such as conflicting class and training or game schedules and finding time to study while also prioritizing recovery, sleep, and nutrition in order to optimize performance in the classroom and on the pitch.

The United States collegiate system has two off-season periods, which usually take place from December to February and then over the summer months (May to August). The latter period includes a more fitness-based emphasis compared to the first period, which is more geared toward recovery from the autumn competitive period. In summer, strength and conditioning professionals must balance the strength programs, keeping in mind external factors such as athletes' summer courses, timing, and weather concerns like heat. Load should still be carefully monitored for individual athletes during this time, either via questionnaires or verbal feedback (8, 9.

It is to be expected that some athletes, even at the college level, will lack foundational strength and movement competency; that is, some athletes might still have a low training age. Athletes with less training experience, often lowerclassmen, should take part in an extended GPP phase, concentrated on raising their strength endurance baseline and improving movement competency. More trained athletes might proceed into the strength and power phases more quickly, using GPP-like protocols in their warm-ups and focusing workouts on increasing maximal strength and power.

Professional

The length of the off-season in North American professional soccer, namely Major League Soccer and National Women's Soccer League, ranges from 12 to 16 weeks. The time spent during each phase will depend not only on athlete training age but also the needs of the individual athlete based on strength and power assessments done during the in-season or postseason. It is important to note that being a professional athlete is not equivalent to proficiency in the weight room and exceptional movement quality. Young athletes who are just beginning their professional careers still need a significant amount of education and support from strength and conditioning professionals in the weight room, in addition to closely monitored and individualized programs.

It is not uncommon for athletes coming from high school, collegiate, or semiprofessional programs in which movement competency, resistance training, and recovery were not prioritized to lack general strength and body awareness. These athletes might spend more time in GPP cycles with movement and activation in their warm-ups and to perform more unilateral training to gain proprioception and lay a more complete foundation of strength. More experienced athletes with higher training ages might require less time in the GPP phase, usually a few weeks, before advancing to the strength and power phases. However, these athletes can still demonstrate a variety of movement compensations throughout their careers, especially following periods of high fatigue or injury, which can create movement dysfunctions in the long term. A program that prioritizes improvement of movement and strength qualities on the field might be prioritized compared to focusing excessively on strength and power; this requires a focus on improving specific joint mobility, a cadence geared toward improving motor control, and the modification of certain exercises through progression and regression when individually appropriate. Again, postseason assessments and data-driven programming are needed to make sure productive, healthy goals are prioritized and achieved in the off-season protocol.

A 12-week professional off-season program might feature a two-week GPP phase, a six-week hypertrophy/strength endurance phase, a two-week basic strength and max strength phase, and a two-week strength and power phase. These cycles should vary according to individual needs, distributing time from hypertrophy/strength endurance to other microcycles as most beneficial.

Most professional European leagues feature a six- to eight-week combined postseason and off-season, creating the need for a hybrid program in which athletes spend less time in the GPP and hypertrophy/strength endurance microcycles and maximize time in the strength to power transition. Athletes on international duty often fall into this category, so programs have to be flexible around training camps and tournaments while also managing loads from club matches. A potential program for an accelerated off-season might require two weeks of hypertrophy, four weeks of strength, and two weeks of power. It should be noted that depending on club rules and international tournament schedules, it is sometimes possible to achieve many off-season training goals by expanding the strength and power phases into the preseason.

RECOMMENDED EXERCISES

When creating programs in the off-season, it is important that strength and conditioning professionals build their exercise selection based on what the team or individual athletes need based on position, instead of simple biased menu items, always going back to the KPIs of the sport and the results of postseason assessments. Athletes with less training experience might need movement regressions or other modifications to achieve the objectives of each session, while athletes with a higher training age likely will progress through exercises more quickly and be able to execute more challenging or technical movements.

Before the start of the program, athletes can be given individualized activation exercises so they can microdose specific work that will benefit them in the long-term. Those activation exercises can include work on the main priority areas of continuous improvement for soccer athletes such as the lower leg complex (foot and ankle), breathing and pelvic position awareness, hip intrinsic and deep core activation, lumbar pelvic control, and coordination and control of complex movement patterns.

While a balanced and structured program should emphasize all movement patterns of the entire body, some patterns are essential to a soccer off-season protocol to develop often-neglected areas while providing measurable benefits to athlete strength, speed, and resilience. These categories include hip extension (e.g., deadlift and hip thrust), unilateral strength (e.g., single-leg deadlift and split squat), and rotational power (e.g., chop and medicine ball throw).

INTENSITY

Equally important to the overall program structure and specific exercise selection is the intensity, also termed *load*, at which movements are prescribed and performed. This is especially relevant in the **basic strength phase**, when the objective is to increase athletes' maximal strength and a lack of intensity in the long term will not maximize strength gains. Intensity is most commonly prescribed in workouts as a percentage of the athlete's 1RM, the maximum load an individual can lift for one repetition, in the primary core and power exercises, namely the squat, deadlift, bench press, shoulder press, and clean (3). Assigning load based on percentage is beneficial when working with less experienced athletes, because it is individualized and ensures that the intensity goal will be achieved in each set and workout, and with groups or teams, because each athlete can calculate the prescribed intensity based on his or her 1RM. If a 1RM or maximal strength assessment is not performed before the start of the off-season or between the hypertrophy/strength endurance phase and the basic strength phase, an athlete's 1RM in any exercise can be estimated based on multirepetition maximal exercises, such as a 3RM or 5RM, which equal approximately 93% and 85% of an individual's 1RM respectively (21). This is also appropriate for athletes with a lower training age, who are not yet experienced in lifting weights above 80% intensity and thus cannot reliably execute or assess a 1RM.

When designing training programs for more experienced athletes (who should be accustomed to a higher training intensity and possess greater body awareness) as well as when designing individual training programs instead of general team protocols, it might be appropriate to prescribe load based on the athletes' **rating of perceived exertion** (RPE); that is, athletes select their own weight for the assigned exercise according to their individual rating of the intensity of each set, exercise, and session (9). This allows athletes a level of autonomy in their training sessions regardless of periodization model, which might in itself create more intensity while also accounting for and adapting to individual differences and day-to-day physiological and psychological fluctuations (17). Usage of the RPE scale for set and session intensity might also avoid or give early notice of overreaching and overtraining syndrome. However, this method of assigning intensity should be used almost exclusively for athletes with adequate training experience, motivation, and proprioception.

VOLUME

Volume is the total amount of work performed during a set, session, week of training, or training cycle. Thus, in resistance training, volume is the product of the number of repetitions, sets, and load used. During the GPP phase, volume within training and frequency of sessions remains relatively high through the postseason and into the hypertrophy/strength endurance phase, dropping to moderate volume with the basic strength phase and decreasing even more with the power phase.

SAMPLE PROGRAMS

The following sample programs are divided into two categories and their microcycles. Goalkeepers have unique and specific positional demands that are not entirely met by field athlete protocols and are therefore programmed separately (tables 9.1, 9.2, 9.3, and 9.4). Field athletes (i.e., forwards, midfielders, and defenders) are grouped into a different protocol, because the demands of the game on their strength and power qualities are very similar and athletes often move between positions (tables 9.5, 9.6, 9.7, and 9.8). Three workouts per week are proposed for each microcycle. The first two programs are divided into complementary focuses: lower body push and upper body pull followed by lower body pull and upper body push. The third session of the week is a velocity-power-based workout.

Perform all sets assigned for the first group of exercises (1a, 1b, 1c) before moving on to the second group of exercises (2a, 2b, 2c). To ensure optimal muscle recovery between sets, exercises alternate between upper and lower body or between antagonist muscle groups (3).

Interpreting the Sample Program Tables

BB = Barbell

BW = Body weight

DB = Dumbbell

MB = Medicine ball

KB = Kettlebell

RDL = Romanian deadlift

Side hang = Holding BB, DB, or KB with the arms hanging down, palms facing legs, and elbows extended

Rack position = Holding BB, DB, or KB in the catch or rack position on the anterior shoulder

Goblet = Holding DB or KB with both hands below the chin and elbows pointed out to the side in the midline of the body

Order = Performing one set of each exercise (1a, 1b, 1c) in the group one after the other. After the first set is completed, go back to the first exercise in the group and do the second set of each exercise. If certain exercises call for fewer sets than others in the group, perform those sets on the back end of the grouping. For example, if exercise 1a calls for 4 sets and exercise 1b calls for 3 sets, perform exercise 1b during sets 2 through 4 of exercises 1a.

Tempo (E:I:C) = Timing or duration (in seconds) of the eccentric phase (E), the isometric hold or pause between the eccentric and concentric phases (I), and the concentric phase (C); an "x" means explosive (12b).

Table 9.1   Goalkeepers: Off-Season Microcycle, Weeks 1-2

Day 1: Lower Body Push and Upper Body Pull

Order	Exercise	Tempo (E:I:C)	Intensity	Sets	Reps or distance	Rest
1a	Goblet squat	3:1:1	70%-75% 1RM	3	8-10	3 min
1b	Lat pulldown (neutral grip)	1:2:1	—	3	8-10	3 min
1c	Two-arm DB row (head supported)	1:2:1	—	3	8-10	3 min
2a	Lateral lunge	3:1:1	—	3	8-10 each	2 min
2b	Farmer's walk	—	—	3	20 yd (18 m)	1 min
2c	Suspension Y's, T's, W's	1:2:1	—	3	8-10	1 min

Day 2: Lower Body Pull and Upper Body Push

Order	Exercise	Tempo (E:I:C)	Intensity	Sets	Reps or time	Rest
1a	KB deadlift	3:1:1	70%-75% 1RM	3	8-10	3 min
1b	Lateral plank	—	—	3	30 sec each	3 min
1c	DB bench press	1:2:1	70%-75% 1RM	3	8-10	3 min
2a	Two-arm single-leg RDL	1:2:1	—	3	8-10	2 min
2b	Tall kneeling chop	1:2:1	—	3	8-10	1 min
2c	Dead bug (legs only)	1:2:1	—	3	8-10	1 min

Day 3: Velocity-Power

Order	Exercise	Tempo (E:I:C)	Intensity	Sets	Reps or time	Rest
1a	Rear foot–elevated split squat	1:3:1	70%-75% 1RM	3	8 each	1 min
1b	KB swing	—	—	3	8	2 min
1c	Band GHR prone iso hold	—	—	3	30 sec	1 min
2a	Push-up	1:2:1	—	3	8	1 min
2b	MB rotational throw	—	8-10 lb (3.6-4.5 kg)	3	6 each	2 min
2c	Turkish get-up	1:2:1	—	3	4 each	1 min

Table 9.2   Goalkeepers: Off-Season Microcycle, Weeks 3-6

Day 1: Lower Body Push and Upper Body Pull

Order	Exercise	Tempo (E:I:C)	Intensity	Sets	Reps	Rest
1a	Back squat	3:1:1	60%-80% 1RM	2-3	8-10	2-3 min
1b	MB rotational throw	—	8-10 lb (3.6-4.5 kg)	2-3	8-10 each	1-2 min
1c	Inverted row	3:2:x	—	2-3	8-10	1-2 min
2a	Front foot–elevated split squat	3:1:1	—	2-3	8-10 each	2-3 min
2b	Lat pulldown (neutral grip)	3:2:1	—	2-3	8-10	1-2 min
2c	Suspension Y's, T's, W's	1:2:1	—	2-3	8-10	1-2 min

Day 2: Lower Body Pull and Upper Body Push

Order	Exercise	Tempo (E:I:C)	Intensity	Sets	Reps	Rest
1a	Trap bar deadlift	3:1:1	60%-80% 1RM	2-3	8-10	2-3 min
1b	Half-kneeling chop	—	—	2-3	8-10	1-2 min
1c	One-arm DB bench press	3:1:1	70%-75% 1RM	2-3	8-10 each	1-2 min
2a	One-arm single-leg RDL	3:1:1	—	2-3	8-10 each	1-2 min
2b	One-arm landmine overhead press	1:1:1	—	2-3	8-10 each	1-2 min
2c	Anti-rotation lift (low split stance)	1:5:1	—	2-3	8-10	1-2 min

Day 3: Velocity-Power

Order	Exercise	Tempo (E:I:C)	Intensity	Sets	Reps or distance	Rest
1a	One-arm DB snatch	x:x:x	70%-75% 1RM	3	4-6 each	2-3 min
1b	Lift from low split stance	1:3:1	—	2-3	6-10	1-2 min
1c	Hip thrust	1:1:3	Heavy	2-3	6-10	1-2 min
2a	Crossover (lateral) sled push	1:1:1	Moderate	2-3	10-20 yd (9-18 m)	1-2 min
2b	Sliding leg curl	1:3:2	—	2-3	6-10	1-2 min
2c	Reverse crunch (on floor)	1:1:1	—	3	10-12	1-2 min

Table 9.3 Goalkeepers: Off-Season Microcycle, Weeks 7-10

Day 1: Lower Body Push and Upper Body Pull

Order	Exercise	Tempo (E:I:C)	Intensity	Sets	Reps	Rest
1a	Front squat	1:2:1	80%-95% 1RM	3-4	2-5	2-3 min
1b	One-arm DB row	1:2:1	—	3-4	3-5 each	1-2 min
1c	Tall kneeling chop	1:2:1	—	3	6-8	1-2 min
2a	Reverse lunge	2:2:1	—	2-4	3-5	2-3 min
2b	Lat pulldown (neutral grip)	1:2:1	—	3-4	3-5	1-2 min
2c	Dead bug (ipsilateral)	1:1:1	—	3	6-10	1-2 min

Day 2: Lower Body Pull and Upper Body Push

Order	Exercise	Tempo (E:I:C)	Intensity	Sets	Reps or time	Rest
1a	Trap bar deadlift	1:2:1	80%-95% 1RM	3-4	2-5	2-3 min
1b	DB incline bench press	1:1:1	—	3-4	3-5	1-2 min
1c	Stability ball leg curl	1:1:2	—	3	6-8	1-2 min
2a	One-arm single-leg RDL	1:1:1	—	3-4	3-5 each	2-3 min
2b	One-arm landmine overhead press	1:1:1	—	3-4	3-5 each	1-2 min
2c	Prone plank (on slideboard)	—	—	3	30 sec	1-2 min

Day 3: Velocity-Power

Order	Exercise	Tempo (E:I:C)	Intensity	Sets	Reps or distance	Rest
1a	Sled push	1:3:1	—	3-4	20 yd (18 m)	2-3 min
1b	KB swing	—	—	3	4-6	2-3 min
1c	Prone plank with one-arm row	—	—	3	8-10 each	1-2 min
2a	Rack pull	x:1:1	80%-95% 1RM	3-4	3-5	2-3 min
2b	Single-leg hip thrust	x:1:2	80%-95% 1RM	3-4	3-5 each	1-2 min
2c	Reverse crunch (hanging)	1:1:1	—	3-4	10-15	1-2 min

Table 9.4   Goalkeepers: Off-Season Microcycle, Weeks 11-12

Day 1: Lower Body Push and Upper Body Pull

Order	Exercise	Tempo (E:I:C)	Intensity	Sets	Reps or time	Rest
1a	Back squat	1:2:x	80%-85% 1RM	3	6	3 min
1b	DB hang snatch	—	—	3	4	2 min
1c	Half-kneeling chop	—	—	3	6	2 min
2a	Lateral lunge	1:2:x	—	3	6 each	2 min
2b	MB rotational throw	—	8-10 lb (3.6-4.5 kg)	3	5 each	1 min
2c	Single-leg GHR prone iso hold	—	—	2-3	10 sec	1 min

Day 2: Lower Body Pull and Upper Body Push

Order	Exercise	Tempo (E:I:C)	Intensity	Sets	Reps	Rest
1a	Trap bar deadlift	C only	80%-95% 1RM	4	3-5	3 min
1b	MB granny toss	—	8-10 lb (3.6-4.5 kg)	3	4	2 min
1c	Pull-up (neutral grip)	1:1:1	—	3	6	2 min
2a	One-arm DB bench press	1:1:1	—	3	8 each	2 min
2b	Nordic leg curl	3:x:x	—	3	4	2 min
2c	Dead bug (contralateral)	2:1:1	—	3	8-10	1 min

Day 3: Velocity-Power

Order	Exercise	Tempo (E:I:C)	Intensity	Sets	Reps or time	Rest
1a	Rear foot–elevated split squat	2:1:x	70%-75% 1RM	3	5 each	2 min
1b	KB swing	—	—	3	5	2 min
1c	GHR prone iso hold	—	—	3	30 sec	2 min
2a	One-arm DB row	1:2:2	—	3	6 each	1 min
2b	MB rotational throw	—	8-10 lb (3.6-4.5 kg)	3	6 each	2 min
2c	Prone plank (on slideboard)	—	—	3	8	1 min

Table 9.5 Field Players: Off-Season Microcycle, Weeks 1-2

Day 1: Lower Body Push and Upper Body Pull

Order	Exercise	Tempo (E:I:C)	Intensity	Sets	Reps or distance	Rest
1a	Goblet squat	3:1:1	—	3	8-10	1 min
1b	Quadruped birddog	1:2:1	—	3	8-10	1 min
1c	Two-arm DB row (head supported)	1:2:1	—	3	8-10	1 min
2a	Lateral lunge	3:1:1	—	3	8-10 each	1 min
2b	Farmer's walk	—	—	3	20 yd (18 m)	1 min
2c	Suspension Y's, T's, W's	1:2:1	—	3	9-10	1 min

Day 2: Lower Body Pull and Upper Body Push

Order	Exercise	Tempo (E:I:C)	Intensity	Sets	Reps or time	Rest
1a	KB deadlift	3:1:1	70%-75% 1RM	3	8-10	1 min
1b	Lateral plank	—	—	3	30 sec each	1 min
1c	DB bench press	1:2:1	—	3	8-10	1 min
2a	Two-arm single-leg RDL	1:2:1	—	3	8-10 each	1 min
2b	Tall kneeling chop	1:2:1	—	3	8-10	1 min
2c	Dead bug (legs only)	1:2:1	—	3	8-10	1 min

Day 3: Velocity-Power

Order	Exercise	Tempo (E:I:C)	Intensity	Sets	Reps or time	Rest
1a	Rear foot–elevated split squat	1:3:1	70%-75% 1RM	3	8	1 min
1b	KB swing	—	—	3	6	1 min
1c	Band GHR prone iso hold	—	—	2-3	30 sec	1 min
2a	MB rotational throw	—	8-10 lb (3.6-4.5 kg)	3	6 each	1 min
2b	Push-up	1:2:1	—	3	8	1 min
2c	Turkish get-up	1:2:1	—	3	4	1 min

Table 9.6   Field Players: Off-Season Microcycle, Weeks 3-6

Day 1: Lower Body Push and Upper Body Pull

Order	Exercise	Tempo (E:I:C)	Intensity	Sets	Reps	Rest
1a	Back squat	3:1:1	60%-80% 1RM	2-3	8-10	2-3 min
1b	MB rotational throw	—	8-10 lb (3.6-4.5 kg)	2-3	6-10 each	1-2 min
1c	Inverted row	3:2:x	—	2-3	6-10	1-2 min
2a	Front foot–elevated split squat	3:1:1	—	2-3	6-10 each	2-3 min
2b	Half-kneeling lift	1:2:1	—	2-3	6-10	1-2 min
2c	Lat pulldown (neutral grip)	3:2:1	—	2-3	6-10	1-2 min

Day 2: Lower Body Pull and Upper Body Push

Order	Exercise	Tempo (E:I:C)	Intensity	Sets	Reps	Rest
1a	Landmine deadlift	3:1:1	60%-75% 1RM	2-3	6-10	2-3 min
1b	Tall kneeling chop	—	—	2-3	6-10	1-2 min
1c	One-arm DB bench press	3:1:1	—	2-3	6-10 each	1-2 min
2a	One-arm single-leg RDL	3:1:1	—	2-3	6-10 each	1-2 min
2b	One-arm landmine overhead press	1:1:1	—	2-3	6-10 each	1-2 min
2c	Anti-rotation press (low split stance)	1:5:1	—	2-3	6-10	1-2 min

Day 3: Velocity-Power

Order	Exercise	Tempo (E:I:C)	Intensity	Sets	Reps or distance	Rest
1a	One-arm snatch	—	—	3	4-6 each	2-3 min
1b	Half-kneeling lift	1:3:1	—	2-3	6-10	1-2 min
1c	Leg curl (on slideboard)	3-5:1:1	—	2-3	6-10	1-2 min
2a	Crossover (lateral) sled push	1:1:1	—	2-3	20 yd (18 m)	2-3 min
2b	Hip thrust	1:3:2	—	2-3	6-10	2-3 min
2c	Reverse crunch	1:1:1	—	3	10-12	1-2 min

Table 9.7   Field Players: Off-Season Microcycle, Weeks 7-10

Day 1: Lower Body Push and Upper Body Pull

Order	Exercise	Tempo (E:I:C)	Intensity	Sets	Reps	Rest
1a	Front squat	1:2:1	80%-95% 1RM	3-4	2-5	3-4 min
1b	One-arm DB row	1:2:1	—	3-4	3-5 each	2-3 min
1c	Tall kneeling chop	1:2:1	—	3	6-8	1-2 min
2a	Reverse lunge	2:2:1	—	3-4	2-5 each	2-3 min
2b	Dead bug (ipsilateral)	1:2:1	—	3	6-8	2 min
2c	Lat pulldown (supinated grip)	1:2:1	—	3-4	2-5	2 min

Day 2: Lower Body Pull and Upper Body Push

Order	Exercise	Tempo (E:I:C)	Intensity	Sets	Reps or time	Rest
1a	Trap bar deadlift	1:2:1	80%-95% 1RM	3-4	2-5	3 min
1b	DB bench press	1:1:1	—	3-4	3-5	2-3 min
1c	Stability ball leg curl	1:1:2	—	3	6-8	2-3 min
2a	One-arm landmine overhead press	1:1:1	—	3-4	3-5 each	1-2 min
2b	One-arm single-leg RDL	1:1:1	—	3-4	3-5 each	1-2 min
2c	Prone plank (on slideboard)	—	—	—	30 sec	1-2 min

Day 3: Velocity-Power

Order	Exercise	Tempo (E:I:C)	Intensity	Sets	Reps	Rest
1a	Lateral lunge	1:2:1	—	3-4	3-5 each	2-3 min
1b	KB swing	—	—	3	4-6	2-3 min
1c	Prone plank with one-arm row	—	—	3	8-10 each	1-2 min
2a	Rack pull	x:1:1	—	3-4	2-5	2-3 min
2b	Single-leg hip thrust (elevated foot)	x:1:2	—	3-4	3-5 each	1-2 min
2c	Reverse crunch (hanging)	1:1:1	—	3	10-15	1-2 min

Table 9.8   Field Players: Off-Season Microcycle, Weeks 11-12

Day 1: Lower Body Push and Upper Body Pull

Order	Exercise	Tempo (E:I:C)	Intensity	Sets	Reps or time	Rest
1a	Reverse lunge	1:2:x	—	3	6	3-4 min
1b	MB rotational throw	—	8-10 lb (3.6-4.5 kg)	3	4 each	2-3 min
1c	Pull-up (neutral grip)	1:1:1	—	3	6	2-3 min
2a	Lateral lunge	1:2:x	—	3	6 each	2-3 min
2b	Half-kneeling chop	—	—	3	5	2 min
2c	Single-leg GHR prone iso hold	—	—	2-3	10 sec each	2 min

Day 2: Lower Body Pull and Upper Body Push

Order	Exercise	Tempo (E:I:C)	Intensity	Sets	Reps	Rest
1a	Trap bar deadlift	3-5:x:x	80%-95% 1RM	4	3-5	3-4 min
1b	MB granny toss	—	8-10 lb (3.6-4.5 kg)	3-4	4	2-3 min
1c	Lateral plank with one-arm row	1:3:1	—	3	8 each	2-3 min
2a	One-arm landmine overhead press	1:1:1	—	3	8 each	2-3 min
2b	Band-assisted Nordic leg curl	3-5:x:x	—	2-3	4-6	2-3 min
2c	Dead bug (contralateral)	1:2:1	—	3	6-8	1 min

Day 3: Velocity-Power

Order	Exercise	Tempo (E:I:C)	Intensity	Sets	Reps or time	Rest
1a	Back squat	x:1:1	—	4	2-4	1 min
1b	KB swing	—	—	3	4	1 min
1c	MB granny toss	—	8-10 lb (3.6-4.5 kg)	3	4	1-2 min
2a	Alternating DB bench press	x:1:1	—	3	6	2-3 min
2b	MB rotational throw	—	8-10 lb (3.6-4.5 kg)	3	6-8 each	1-2 min
2c	GHR prone iso hold	—	—	2	30 sec	1-2 min

CONCLUSION

During the off-season, it is critical to program as specifically, productively, and individually as possible in order to raise athletes' baseline of strength, movement competency, and overall athleticism. Programs should reflect individual needs, including weaknesses, injury history, biological and training age, and postseason assessment data, as well as time constraints and preseason schedules. Athletes with less training experience should spend more time on improving foundational movement and strength in the GPP and hypertrophy/strength endurance phases, while more trained athletes will move into the basic strength and power phases more quickly and with more progressed exercises. However, it is important to keep in mind that not all experienced athletes move perfectly, and they should be challenged constantly. The primary objective of the off-season program is to allow athletes to recover from the season and then prepare them for their upcoming competitive phase.

PRESEASON PROGRAMMING

DANIEL GUZMAN AND JOEY HARTY

Soccer is a dynamic sport that requires an athlete to use various aspects of strength, power, agility, speed, and aerobic endurance in situational moments. The athlete needs to be able to shift between and execute these skills and tasks during 90-plus minutes of competition while covering great distances. For example, professional male athletes travel an average total distance of 5.0 to 7.5 miles (8.0-12.1 km) per game. Games include many high-force and high-velocity movements: sprinting, accelerating, jumping, decelerating, and changing direction at multiple angles with the possibility of contact at any time. This chapter will not go in depth about an athlete's soccer intelligence or field vision, but it does recognize that the ability to process and anticipate a movement outcome is highly important when expressing the physical qualities of strength, power, and speed.

Resistance training is an important piece in a soccer athlete's holistic program. The systemic implementation of a training process to unveil an athlete's physical strength characteristics and areas to improve are key in the developmental outcomes of the resistance training program and transferability into match play. Possessing strength in multiple planes of movement and robust joint and tissue tolerance in force absorption and production potentially decrease injury incidence. It must be noted that the physical adaptations that occur from preseason resistance training exposure are especially beneficial to an athlete. The movement phases of sprinting, jumping, decelerating, and changing direction can be broken down to focus on the individual phases of force absorption and rate of force development to design the most holistic performance program for each athlete. These movements also must be taken into account during the periodization of the resistance training prescription.

GOALS AND OBJECTIVES

When beginning to periodize the preseason phase it is best to reverse engineer the process with the end goal in mind. Understanding the limitations of scheduling is one aspect, but an entire other challenge exists regarding the comfortability of the athlete and coach in this process. Each level of the game presents different scenarios in which the coach needs to be mindful of the transition period that occurs for the athlete to adapt to a new system. At the collegiate level, a coach might need to manage a first-year athlete or new transfer differently than one who has been in the system for an extended period of time. Similarly, at the professional level coaches might deal with a new athlete to the team who was acquired through a trade or transfer or with a rookie athlete. Lastly, the demands of the sport at various levels help frame the entire preseason conversation. These different levels of competition and league rules are important when programming a preseason. Length of the match, number of substitutions, number of days between matches, and different environmental exposures are all limitations that need to be defined clearly because each situation will differ.

LENGTH, STRUCTURE, AND ORGANIZATION

The goal of the chapter is not to dissect the sport's demands but to determine optimal resistance training organization and structure for the preparatory period including frequency, intensity, duration, and volume.

When structuring a preseason resistance training program, the biggest constraint is managing the shift from biasing weight room dominance during the off-season period to the increased demands of sport practice. Other considerations of periodization involve the quantity of training days, preseason match schedule, travel plans, equipment availability, off-season health status, and resistance training time constraints. As time spent on the soccer field increases, resistance training must complement and enhance the training environment while helping maintain or improve tissue and joint tolerance.

Needs Analysis

Determining optimal length and organization depends on the evaluation of the game itself and how it pertains to the individual athlete. Preseason provides the ideal timing for testing and evaluating in relation to the soccer training plan. A needs analysis of the individual and team as a whole allows for more precise periodization. It is the role of the strength and conditioning professional to choose evaluations that will aid prescription (see chapter 3). The result of all this data can lead to conversations with athletes, medical staff, and coaching staff to build a line of communication about goals and timelines. Additionally, understanding injury history is a vital piece of an athlete's initial intake, which helps to improve program design and establish communication with the sports medicine staff. Discussing *where the athlete is now* and *where the athlete wants to be* improves the strength and conditioning professional's ability to implement specific plans on the team and individual level. Above all, the most important thing to do during the planning and preparation period is to measure the components of the sport that have an intentional effect on decision-making. Collection of data without a system of design outputs and then follow-up based on results is not a complete system. Data inputs that lead to better conversations, designs, education, and group morale and competition ultimately will be able to provide a better framework to achieve the desired outcome.

When beginning to assess proper resistance training intensity prescriptions for athletes of any level during this phase, the discussion surrounds how to evaluate large groups of athletes safely and effectively. For evaluating muscular strength for a variety of reasons, the traditional 1RM resistance training assessment might not be the optimal method for a variety of reasons including athletes' various training backgrounds and a higher risk of injury than other assessment options. Using training as a means to testing might be a more practical method to the strength and conditioning professional at any level. **Autoregulated progressive resistance exercise** (APRE) periodization can provide a more practical solution by allowing the athlete to determine progression through repetitions completed, rather than forcing a percentage of 1RM on them (6). This method can benefit athletes in preseason by allowing them to dictate total volume load achieved during the session based on how they feel. For example, if the strength and conditioning professional wanted to assess the athlete's 3RM, he or she might do so by prescribing four sets. After performing the first two sets, with the first set being six repetitions at 50% of the 1RM and the second being three repetitions at 75% of the 1RM, the athlete would then choose a weight that could be lifted three to five times (80%-90% of the 1RM). On the third set the athlete would attempt as many repetitions as possible at the chosen weight, then add 5 to 10 pounds (2.3-4.5 kg) and perform a fourth set in a similar fashion. The weight used during the fourth set becomes the new 3RM and is used for the third set the following week. When using APRE, strength and conditioning professionals must understand that this system can be implement in many ways and that they must use discretion when determining optimal 1RM estimation ranges based on the needs of the athlete. Another option is to use different velocity-based training devices for assessing optimal load ranges targeting specific strength adaptations. Though this option can be a safer alternative to traditional 1RM testing, the associated financial constraints with many of these devices might not be realistic for the masses. Ultimately, resistance training opportunities during preseason are limited and must be prioritized accordingly. As with any preseason assessment, the strength and conditioning professional needs to use his or her best judgment in weighing the risk versus reward and determining what is most important to guide the training process.

Methods and Timing

When considering key movements for the sport of soccer, a holistic program should include multi-joint and involve multi-planar attributes. Muscular strength improvements have been linked to two primary adaptations: muscle (myofibrillar) hypertrophy and neural adaptations (9). Muscle hypertrophy is reflected by an increase in a muscle's cross-sectional area, which can result in an increase in body mass that might not be desirable during this period (13). Neural adaptations include increased recruitment of motor units and increased discharge rates (**rate coding**). Emphasizing neural drive via the use of high intensities, explosive movements, or complex movement patterns might also improve athlete explosiveness, coordination, and proprioception throughout the kinetic chain. This proves extremely valuable during this period because specificity is key, and the sport relies on the ability to produce force in the shortest amount of time possible.

Understanding the force–velocity curve and the methods that affect this can be beneficial in prescribing training methods that increase potential power output of the soccer athlete. Methods targeting maximum strength, strength speed, speed strength, and speed all involve neural factors of intramuscular coordination, intermuscular coordination, and the various components of the stretch-shortening cycle (SSC) (4a). Assessing the athlete's needs to understand if the focus needs to be on increasing force output or the rate at which force is produced allows for optimal improvements in the force–velocity profile of each athlete. Resistance training for strength (≥85% 1RM) relies on high force output to improve motor unit recruitment and rate coding (9). Training emphasizing the external intensity improves the ability to produce and absorb force, but contractile velocity likely is not improved. The opposite is true by only emphasizing attaining high movement velocities in the weight room. The formula for power (force × velocity) enforces the need to focus on the adaptations that can be obtained by training focused on high forces and high velocities. For general training, surfing the curve through each session during the preparatory period provides the best-case scenario for complementing field training. However, with better assessments come smarter and more efficient training prescriptions.

In general, resistance training in preseason should aim for two training opportunities per seven-day cycle, though depending on the age and level of the group of athletes, this might vary.

Managing the timing for organizing resistance training relative to field training is a worthwhile consideration depending on the resources available. Sometimes the resistance training session can be placed immediately after the field training session based on time constraints as well as access to a weight room at the training location. Other times, the resistance training session might be held in the afternoon after a morning field session. Due to the intense nature of soccer field training, separating resistance training sessions from the on-field work, if possible, allows for proper recovery in between, maximizing the potential for strength adaptation to occur.

Aiming for one power (technique) exercise, two multi-joint core exercises, and three or four assistance exercises provides a well-rounded program. One way to improve resistance training exposures during the preseason period is to add mobility and activation drills as substitutes to core or assistance exercises. This allows the coach to break up what might have been one longer resistance training session into two separate sessions, allowing for more training to occur over time while minimizing fatigue. In any case, movement skill and technique always should be the priority in any phase of training, but especially with athletes who have been away from the coach's eye or are new to the system. The preseason is a time to build a foundation of efficient movement technique (this varies per athlete) around core movements that will be important in their program. Movements such as bilateral and unilateral squatting and deadlifting are important staples that transfer for soccer athletes. Prioritizing these movements in a program will improve movement quality to the rest of the system as a whole.

Recent Training Exposure

It is important to understand the variety of different training phases or environments from which the athlete is coming into preseason. Professional team coaches and strength and conditioning professionals might have worked with athletes all off-season, but this is typically not the case for most. Many athletes leave to spend time at home and might have trained individually or with other individuals, while some might have recently finished international duty and not had a typical off-season. Similarly, most collegiate athletes leave to train in different environments during the off-season period or participate in other amateur soccer leagues. For either scenario, the strength and conditioning professional always needs to be aware of the athlete's status relative to the group, whether a rookie or first-year versus a veteran. When dealing with high school athletes, relying on the long-term athletic development model is imperative to ensuring these athletes are being trained relative to their training age rather than their chronological age. Being aware of the individual athlete's training age is critical not only to understanding their long-term training history but also to understand participation in relation to their most recent development period (7).

Even with an older athlete and a higher training age (>2-3 years), starting with foundational movements and periodization strategies can be effective during this period before progressing to more complex variations. Additionally, for an athlete with low weight room training experience or recent strength exposure, general physical preparedness volume and intensities for muscular strength are a recommended starting place. For example, at the high school level, the off-season might have been occupied by another sport (e.g., seasonal sports such as American football and swimming). In other high school and collegiate settings, weight room opportunities might be limited due to family travel priorities or intentional non-training prescription by a coach or strength and conditioning professional. In the men's and women's professional leagues, off-season training often can be a very short period of time, which can be limited to less than six weeks in some instances. Depending on the athlete, this could be cut even shorter with international responsibilities or playing in multiple leagues with overlapping competition.

All these factors contribute to the available exposures a strength and conditioning professional feels is correct to dose the athlete within preseason.

Understanding that an athlete can be trained in many ways to render a desired outcome is important. Strength and conditioning professionals need to be aware of their personal preferences and sideline them so that athletes receive the best training prescription possible. Keeping an athlete-centered focus allows the strength and conditioning professional to choose the right method or training tool for that individual.

VOLUME, INTENSITY, FREQUENCY, AND REST PERIODS

As stated previously, when understanding the appropriate prescription for resistance training volume and intensity during preseason, the strength and conditioning professional must begin to account for the increased demands of soccer team training, organization travel requirements, and the introduction of preseason matches. Strength and conditioning professionals must work alongside sport coaches in ensuring all training stimuli work in congruence to increase adaptation. Reiterating the goal of this period, resistance training should act as a supplemental complement to soccer training itself. The volume of resistance training during the off-season program should be much higher than that of the preseason period. Off-season goals are to address work capacity, hypertrophy, and muscular endurance, which all aid in resisting fatigue. As a result, the resistance training volume during this phase must be lower and progressed incrementally to avoid causing excess fatigue. Here, the primary focus is to provide the minimal effective dose for increasing both strength and power.

Resistance training variables of frequency, intensity, duration, and exercise selection are all important to consider when overloading athletes during preseason. Frequency of two resistance training sessions per weekly cycle is sufficient to increase strength and power during the preparatory phase (4a, 8). Intensity presented as a percent of 1RM is usually the primary mode for progression during the preseason phase. However, duration and exercise selection are two often-overlooked factors in progressing resistance training demands for the soccer athlete. Duration, as time under tension, can be manipulated through the introduction of isometric pauses or the use of eccentric tempos while always focusing on maximal intent of concentric phase velocity. Additionally, eccentric and isometric muscle contractions can enhance tendon stiffness through an increase in cross-sectional area, which aids in tolerance to ballistic activities involving the SSC on the field (3, 5). Exercise selection, perhaps the most underrated variable, increases demand through exercise progressions during this phase. For example, athletes might begin by performing a kettlebell deadlift before progressing to a trap bar deadlift. Simple progressions of this nature allow adaptation to occur organically for the less experienced or undertrained athlete.

The training age and needs analysis of the athlete should dictate the appropriate intensity prescription during any resistance training phase. Strong correlation has been observed between maximum strength and peak power in soccer athletes (11). Maximum strength development has also been linked to improvements in jump height, acceleration performance (33 ft [10 m]), and improvements in maximum velocity (98 ft [30 m]) (10, 11). Ideally, during the preparatory phase, a higher percentage of a 1RM with a lower number of sets and fewer repetitions should be used to increase strength and power while minimizing residual fatigue. More specifically, these suggested three to five sets with high load (>80%-85% 1RM) and fewer repetitions (4-6) also will not cause unnecessary increases in body mass while developing strength (1). Additionally, these prescriptions should be reserved only for core exercises (multi-joint movements) at the beginning of the resistance training session. Keep in mind that the prescription for the higher intensities should be for trained athletes with the requisite training history.

When using methods in the aforementioned intensity ranges it is important to provide adequate rest periods of two to five minutes between sets. Many strength and conditioning professionals are forced to work with large groups of athletes at a time, not making it feasible to manage these rest periods. To combat this constraint, one option is to superset a multi-joint lower body core exercise with a multi-joint upper body core exercise. This provides additional rest for the working muscle groups. Another option that can increase intra-set rest intervals, as well as increase the ability of achieving effective range of motion for the prescribed movement, is the addition of complementary stability or mobility exercises as active recovery. By combining these options, the strength and conditioning professional will be able to have larger groups of athletes (4-6) in one station at a time. If the situation allows, teams could be split up into separate groups of smaller numbers during the preseason period, allowing for more supervision per athlete.

It is important to note that any exercise prescription adds stress to the individual athlete. While preseason is about adapting to stressors in a progressive manner, stress also needs to be viewed from a holistic perspective. As matches are introduced during the preseason period, minute progressions usually apply. Each coaching staff has their expert opinion on the addition of match play. Depending on the opinion of staff, athletes might start at 30 to 45 minutes for a preseason match in either the first or second week. However, every athlete responds to the same training stress exposure individually. The strength and conditioning professional will have to navigate this gray area when determining the appropriate days to introduce resistance training sessions.

Being mindful of variation between high and low loads remains invaluable during this period in order to avoid causing excess fatigue for the athlete. It is important to understand the soccer microcycle and the different physical, mental, and emotional demands as it pertains to each day of the week. High load days on the field might be paired with similar demands in the weight room; the same goes for low load days. For example, a day involving a large number of small-sided games likely exposes the athletes to high amounts of change-of-direction tasks, involving high-intensity accelerations and decelerations. The mechanical demands associated with these actions can elicit higher amounts of delayed onset muscle soreness. This type of session, which typically occurs at least 72 hours away from preseason match play, pairs well with lower body, higher-intensity loading in the weight room. However, a day closer to a match it might be better to focus on upper body core exercises or lower body assistance exercises in the weight room. This allows match day to be a high-stress day in and of itself. Though the prior scenario provides one option, it might not always be feasible to match high days on the field with high days in the weight room. The coach and the strength and conditioning professional must continually evaluate the athlete's response to the session. If the on-field work excessively taxed the athlete, changing the resistance training session to upper body emphasis might allow for improved adaptation. Another option is to implement a high-intensity resistance training session after a preseason match with minute restrictions in place. Each strength and conditioning professional has his or her own methodology in terms of training periodization. The goal here is to shape a framework to adapt to the setting. By understanding the coordinative nature of stress in the weight room as it pertains to stress on the field, the options are endless for optimal volume, intensity, frequency, and duration during this phase. Ultimately, this all serves the purpose of viewing preseason load (stress) in a holistic manner.

As strength and conditioning professionals at any level, it is important to be stress managers by knowing when and where to implement specific exercises at different intensities. Factoring in the response of the individual to soccer training or match play might present the need for a wellness questionnaire to understand the resultant effect of the training stimulus on the athlete. Another tool to improve the coach and the strength and conditioning professional's understanding of each athlete's internal response to the session itself is a **session rating of perceived exertion** (sRPE). Using the wellness questionnaire alongside sRPE provides holistic insight of the demands placed on the individual. Due to the delicate nature of this phase and programming team resistance training around the introduction of new demands, adjustments at an individual level likely will be needed. Adjusting does not always mean removing the stimulus, but potentially altering the intensity and volume or regressing exercise selection itself. In keeping the athlete's health in mind, enhancing movement quality remains the number one priority.

Note that the development of a preseason resistance program begins with a needs analysis of the athlete and sport coach. This is consistent across levels of play (i.e., high school, collegiate, and professional).

High School

Youth soccer around the world has varying levels of structure within a governing body. Opportunities exist to play in an academy or club setting that might have an affiliation with a professional club. Also, a small season (e.g.., winter or spring) during the academic year offers athletes the chance to play for their high school–level team. (Of course, some athletes at this age group have opportunities to play on a higher-level professional team; however, this section focuses on the high school–level opportunities.) The professional academy and club teams can have two seasons (e.g., fall and spring) that compete in a large volume of matches. High school teams have a condensed schedule, depending on the location in the United States. Resistance training is an essential piece of a soccer athlete's holistic program and one that can directly increase performance attributes. This age group of soccer athletes likely has a low training age and would benefit from a starting foundation. In the long-term development of high school soccer athletes, it is important to expose them to a multitude of movement skills that provide a multi-planar approach in which a foundation can be developed to improve core exercises. This lays a foundation of movement skills that can be applied to the variety of match decisions that take place. The idea is to build a foundation that is an inch wide and a mile deep, as opposed to a mile wide and an inch deep. Simply put, athletes must become proficient in foundational movements before expanding to a trained library.

During a high sport training volume period (i.e., preseason), it is necessary to find the maximum effect with the minimum dose. During preseason coaches and strength and conditioning professionals must be wise when to push and when to pull. It is important to recognize the outside stressors that high school soccer athletes face: full academic schedules, limited training sessions, and the many other challenges that come with being a teenager. Preseason phases are designed to prepare athletes for the seasonal workload to come and not to develop toughness by means of strength tests and fitness evaluations. Grit is developed through consistency of character and hard work, not exercising to physiological failure.

Consider organizing resistance training around sport training time when possible. Aiming for 30 to 45 minutes of resistance training allows adequate time to teach, educate, and answer questions. Allow athletes to explore a movement pattern at low intensities and gain confidence through repetition and time under tension.

Preseason periods can be as short as three to four weeks in some youth academy settings. In that period of time, a good goal is to aim for six to nine resistance training exposures. As a starting point, try prioritizing a few core exercises that could be programmed several times over nine exposures. Understand that multi-joint lower body exercises provide the greatest benefit to an athlete. Try providing a simple program, and choose two core exercises and four assistance exercises, spreading them out over two days. The high school soccer athlete would get four or five resistance training sessions to groove those patterns and potentially be able to progressively load depending on their movement quality. Remember, time is a precious commodity for the high school athlete who is juggling academics, sports, family, and important developmental life stages. The same mindset must align in the weight room when calculating the total resistance training time. This includes working sets, rest periods, transitions, and other distractions that might occur.

College

The collegiate soccer athlete might have more resistance training experience than the high school athlete, but a needs analysis helps the strength and conditioning professional understand the level of that experience. At this level, collegiate soccer athletes typically have a two- to four-week preseason period to prepare for the regular season. It is important to understand the varying levels of preparation for each athlete to best program their preseason resistance training phase. A freshman or transfer athlete needs time to adjust to the coach's style of play and strength and conditioning staff philosophy. A veteran collegiate soccer athlete has an understanding of the environment and might be further ahead depending on his or her compliance with the off-season program prescription. Division I athletes might return for a second summer session as a lead-in to the preseason, which could be very beneficial for athletes who are new to the program. In any event, it seems the most plausible route to improve performance, while respecting preseason sport volume, is to start everyone with a foundational program. The academic workload should be very low at this point, and the "controllables" of a preseason can be managed with little external interruptions.

A major controllable for the strength and conditioning professional is to understand the governing laws of their league and how that influences training time. In some academic settings, there might be an hourly amount that is allocated to sport training each week. Be prepared to adjust programming as needed when resistance training time is constrained. A strength and conditioning professional should view these moments as opportunities rather than threats to develop trust with the coaching staff and academic advisors allowing flexibility in the program management. Find moments to have follow-up discussions with these groups of people to reflect on the aspects of the strength and conditioning program that were achieved or surrendered due to the time constraints. Abiding by these collegiate rules will provide wisdom and understanding in achieving an appropriate holistic program.

Once an athlete's training background as it relates to his or her previous injury history and training experience has been evaluated, a progressive program can begin to take shape. Aim for two or three sessions each seven-day cycle focusing on movement quality to build a foundation from which the athlete can grow. These sessions can range anywhere from 45 to 60 minutes to allow adequate coaching time. Additionally, the strength and conditioning professional must keep in mind the aspects of volume, intensity, and duration when programming preseason sessions. If coaching staff is limited, consider a segmented start by organizing the athletes into three groups to maintain a smaller strength and conditioning professional–to–athlete ratio. This will allow more opportunities to coach athletes in and out of positions through visual and verbal cues. Again, as the group size varies, structure the blocks of exercises to efficiently manage intensity, by means of work and rest periods, to give the athlete the highest performance benefit.

Professional

Professional leagues around the world hold various lengths of time for preseason training. In most leagues, five to nine weeks is common to prepare for the first league or tournament match. Of course, an athlete could have a shorter preseason period due to international duty. Understanding the head sport coach's goals of the preseason, along with the demands of the sport and position, helps guide program structure. At this point, the minimal effective dose plays a huge role in programming by foreshadowing where training stress comes from. For example, an athlete who is new to the club takes on much more stress to adapt to the head coach's style, along with the strength and conditioning program. These athletes might benefit from a simplified approach that focuses on one or two main movements in the foundation of the program. The timeline for an athlete's adaptation to a new environment operates in the gray area of coaching and demands wisdom in the prescription of volume and intensity. Do not feel the need to force volume on an athlete because of the program; rather, an athlete-centric view aids decision-making surrounding questions of pushing or pulling intensity.

Structuring a preseason resistance training session around the sport training session helps the strength and conditioning professional reach the outcomes toward which he or she is working. Although strength and power sessions have the best outcomes as a separate event from training, it is possible to hold resistance training sessions immediately after the sport session. In this instance, it is helpful to have conversations with the technical coaches to best understand the demands of sport training for that day.

Toward the end of a preseason, a group of 11 to 14 athletes might start to see the majority of match minutes as the first league or tournament match approaches. This affects the organization of resistance training because some athletes might be able to be trained on match day. If they start to fall outside of the starting group or reserve group of athletes, they might begin to use the match day as a third resistance training session in a seven-day cycle. In this instance, volume and intensity can rise with the lack of high match minutes. At any point, athletes will move around the depth chart due to congested match fixtures or injury incidence and always will need to be prepared to step into match minutes.

RECOMMENDED EXERCISES

The preseason is a great time to focus on specific movements that can cause injury if not managed well. According to the UEFA injury study, the highest incidence of noncontact injury occurs in the posterior thigh, hip and groin, anterior thigh, and lower leg (2). Hamstring muscle groups and adductor muscle groups strains are perhaps the most widely discussed area of focus for injury risk mitigation in the sport of soccer. As a result, both muscle groups need to be an important marker on all strength and conditioning professionals' 10,000-foot view. Focusing on a few resistance exercises can improve performance greatly and contribute to a holistic preseason strength and conditioning program. In order to recommend appropriate exercises as solutions it is important to consider factors that would increase injury risk.

While the pathologies associated with the hip joint in many soccer athletes is beyond the scope of this chapter, it is worthwhile in helping understand adductor strains and groin pain in soccer. Adductor involvement during soccer actions such as ball striking and change-of-direction tasks have proven to be high. Specifically, for ball-striking moments, electromyography (EMG) analysis has shown high activity in the adductor muscle group for both the kicking leg as well as the support leg (12). The preseason is the first time many soccer athletes will be reintroduced to high-intensity ball striking in weeks or perhaps months in some cases, which can cause potential spikes in injury incidence. Providing a program to improve strength alongside increasing mobility through the hips proves most effective to mitigate adductor injury risk. Prescribing frontal plane–biased movements and addressing stability in the torso through exercises involving cocontraction of the adductor muscle groups and abdominal musculature can help strengthen these areas effectively. Three categories of exercises that train the adductor muscle groups in this manner are anti-flexion, anti-extension, and anti-lateral flexion exercises.

When implementing any frontal plane–associated pattern, it is important to address the athlete's ability to control a single-leg stance and the stability demands of the movement before progressing to more dynamic progressions. The strength and conditioning professional might first begin with a single-leg squat to bench, emphasizing posture and stability. Progression from there might begin to include a reverse lunge with ipsilateral loading and then a slideboard lateral lunge, keeping the stance leg kinematics similar to that in the single-leg squat. A final step is to add a bit more of a dynamic pattern such as a free-moving lateral lunge. As with any exercise, based on the level of the athlete, the strength and conditioning professional can manipulate the load through many implements such as bungee resistance, landmine attachments, dumbbells, or weight vests.

The Copenhagen adduction bridge (CAB) is widely touted as a great way to mitigate groin pain and adductor injury incidence for soccer athletes. While the transferability of this exercise is arguable, it is popularly believed that the ability to avoid energy leaks in ballistic actions enables the transfer of force to be safer and more effective. Understanding the research done on the efficacy for including this exercise in a soccer athlete's program certainly presents the case for inclusion. While the demand on the adductor muscle groups is high when executing the CAB, following proper progressions avoids excessive soreness for the athlete. One example for progression is to begin with a side-lying adductor raise or supine hook-lying position adduction squeeze using a Pilates ring or other implements such as a foam roller. Both exercises introduce time under tension in a supportive manner for further progressions. From there the CAB might be introduced in a short lever position with support at the knee or with light to moderate assistance from the bottom leg. A final progression is to increase the lever length with position of support at the ankle in addition to removing support from the bottom leg. Dosage needs to be progressed in an intelligent manner, with an optional starting point at two sets of 10 to 15 seconds.

Hamstring involvement plays an important role during maximum velocity and sprinting movements in soccer. In the preseason, an increase in intensity and volume of high-speed running can contribute to hamstring injury incidence. In addition to high-speed running exposure, the athlete's mechanics contribute to injury risk factors as well. It is important to provide a balanced approach to hamstring training. Including exercises that focus on movements at both the hip and knee provides the best-case scenario for hamstring resilience alongside addressing absolute speed sprinting mechanics. Two exercises that train hamstrings at the hip and knee are RDL (Romanian deadlift) variations and the NHE (Nordic hamstring exercise) or NHC (Nordic hamstring curl).

The RDL can be coached from a bilateral or unilateral stance depending on the goal and training age of the athlete. In the early stages of coaching the hinge movement, a more stable base is found in a bilateral position. This exercise can start from a body-weight hinge to wall or regressed to a tall kneeling position. It is up to the strength and conditioning professional to decide which progression is most appropriate for his or her athletes. Later progressions might use a medicine ball, kettlebell, dumbbell, barbell or other equipment. As in any other exercise, progressively overloading those muscle groups combined with proper mechanics increases strength in those areas.

The NHE is widely debated for its transfer to sport and functionality in a strength and conditioning program. Although this chapter does not get into that debate, acknowledging the research showing that athletes who have used this movement have a lower hamstring injury incidence remains important. This exercise will not be the sole reason hamstring injury incidence might decrease, because coaching and periodizing sprinting in soccer athletes have exponential benefits. The NHE, as other exercises, can play a supporting role in sprinting moments during sport training activities. Implementing this exercise must begin with caution because the eccentric demand imposed on the hamstring muscle groups is extremely high. Providing a proper progression to introduction, as with any exercise, enables the strength and conditioning professional to properly plan dosage. One example of a progression to an NHE is to start with the supine eccentric-only hamstring slide. This movement has been found to support the high-force eccentric demand of the NHE down the road. From there, a band-assisted NHC can be used with a volume prescription starting at two sets of three repetitions. (Note that this recommendation is for the eccentric-only version of the NHC and is not for the concentric movement in this discussion). This can be performed two to four days from a preseason match depending on the volume prescription and training experience of the athlete. As athletes progress, the prescription might transition to bodyweight NHC's and eventually plate-loaded NHC's, varying the lever length with overhead plate-hold progressions. Lastly, the NHE can be measured by different technologies to give a force or torque measurement that can also aid in progression and programming.

Again, using exercise progression and regression without manipulating sets and repetitions provides a safe and effective way to manage increased demands for the soccer athlete during the preseason phase. No exercise can be claimed to prevent injury, because competitive play has a variety of variables that contribute to the reactive demands of each individual situation on the field. These exercises are an addition to a holistic program addressing all movement patterns.

SAMPLE PROGRAMS

The following sample programs are split into two groups, goalkeepers (table 10.1) and field athletes (table 10.2). Goalkeepers present a unique situation in that their on-field training volume is different than that of field athletes, potentially allowing exposure to higher volumes and intensities of resistance training. Field athletes include forwards, midfielders, and defenders; the reason for grouping these athletes together is not that each position does not need different physical qualities. Rather, through the course of the preseason many factors affect how to train each position, the biggest of which is that the coach still might be figuring out where each athlete best fits into the system and might play the athlete in multiple positions during this time period.

Sample programs are split into two total body days, alternating between lower body and upper body push and pull emphasis. Each set of exercises should be performed in sequential order within their grouping before completing the next set within the grouping (e.g., 1a, then 1b, then 1c) before moving to the next group (e.g., 2a, then 2b, then 2c, and so on).

Interpreting the Sample Program Tables

BB = Barbell

BW = Body weight

DB = Dumbbell

MB = Medicine ball

KB = Kettlebell

RDL = Romanian deadlift

Side hang = Holding BB, DB, or KB with the arms hanging down, palms facing legs, and elbows extended

Rack position = Holding BB, DB, or KB in the catch or rack position on the anterior shoulder

Goblet = Holding DB or KB with both hands below the chin and elbows pointed out to the side in the midline of the body.

Order = Performing one set of each exercise (1a, 1b, 1c) in the group one after the other. After the first set is completed, go back to the first exercise in the group and do the second set of each exercise. If certain exercises call for fewer sets than others in the group, perform those sets on the back end of the grouping. For example, if exercise 1a calls for 4 sets and exercise 1b calls for 3 sets, perform exercise 1b during sets 2 through 4 of exercises 1a.

Tempo (E:I:C) = Timing or duration (in seconds) of the eccentric phase (E), the isometric hold or pause between the eccentric and concentric phases (I), and the concentric phase (C); an "x" means explosive (4b).

Table 10.1   Goalkeepers: Preseason Microcycle, Weeks 1-5

Day 1: Lower Body Push and Upper Body Pull

Order	Exercise	Tempo (E:I:C)	Intensity	Sets	Reps	Rest
1a	DB push press	x:x:x	—	2	5	4 min
1b	MB squat to vertical throw	x:x:x	8-10 lb (3.6-4.5 kg)	2	5	4 min
1c	Box jump	x:x:x	—	2	3	4 min
2a	Safety bar squat	x:1:1	80%-85% 1RM	4	4-6	2 min
Regression	*Goblet squat*	*3:1:1*	—	*3*	*8-10*	*1 min*
2b	Dead bug (legs only)	1:2:1	—	3	10-12 each	2 min
2c	One-arm DB row (3 points supported)	2:1:1	—	4	6-8 each	2 min
3a	Lateral lunge	1:1:1	Bungee	3	8-10 each	1 min
Regression	*Lateral split squat*	*3:1:1*	—	*3*	*8-10 each*	*1 min*
3b	Neutral grip pull-up (eccentric)	4:x:x	—	3	5-6	1 min
3c	Half-kneeling lift	1:1:1	—	3	10-12 each	1 min
3d	Prone Y's, T's, W's (chest supported on bench)	1:2:1	5 lb (3.6 kg)	3	5 each	1 min

Day 2: Lower Body Pull and Upper Body Push

Order	Exercise	Tempo (E:I:C)	Intensity	Sets	Reps	Rest
1a	One-arm DB snatch	x:x:x	—	2	5 each	4 min
1b	MB granny toss	x:x:x	8-10 lb (3.6-4.5 kg)	2	5	4 min
1c	Broad jump	x:x:x	x:x:x	2	3	4 min
2a	Trap bar deadlift	1:1:1	80%-85% 1RM	4	4-6	2 min
Regression	*DB or KB RDL*	*3:1:1*	—	*3*	*8-10*	*1 min*
2b	Reverse crunch (on floor)	1:1:1	—	3	10-12	2 min
2c	Barbell bench press	2:1:1	80%-85% 1RM	4	4-6	2 min
3a	Nordic leg curl	3:x:x	—	2	4	2 min
Regression	*Sliding leg curl (eccentric only)*	*4:2:x*	—	*3*	*4-6*	*1 min*
3b	One-arm DB shoulder press	3:1:1	—	3	8-10 each	1 min
3c	Half-kneeling chop	1:1:1	—	3	10-12 each	1 min
3d	Suspension I's, Y's, T's	2:2:1	—	3	3 each	1 min

Table 10.2   Field Players: Preseason Microcycle, Weeks 1-5

Day 1: Lower Body Push and Upper Body Pull

Order	Exercise	Tempo (E:I:C)	Intensity	Sets	Reps or time	Rest
1a	MB granny toss	x:x:x	8-10 lb (3.6-4.5 kg)	4	4	4 min
1b	Seated box jump	x:x:x	—	4	3	4 min
1c	Hip thrust	1:3:2	—	4	8	4 min
2a	DB rear foot–elevated split squat	2:1:1	—	3-4	6-8 each	2 min
Regression:	*DB split squat*	*2:1:1*	—	*3*	*8-10*	*2 min*
2b	Prone plank (on slideboard)	x:x:x	—	3	8	2 min
2c	One-arm DB row (3 points supported)	1:1:2	—	3	6-8 each	2 min
3a	BB hip thrust (shoulders elevated on box)	1:3:2	—	3	8	2 min
3b	Copenhagen adductor bridge	x:15:x	—	2	15 sec	2 min
3c	Suspension inverted row	1:1:2	—	3	10	2 min

Day 2: Lower Body Pull and Upper Body Push

Order	Exercise	Tempo (E:I:C)	Intensity	Sets	Reps or time	Rest
1a	Hang clean rack pull	x:x:x	—	3	4	4 min
1b	MB rotational throw	x:x:x	8-10 lb (3.6-4.5 kg)	3	6 each	4 min
1c	Dead bug (legs only)	1:2:1	—	3	10-12 each	
2a	Trap bar deadlift	1:1:1	—	4	5	2 min
Regression	*KB deadlift*	*1:1:1*	—	*3*	*8*	*2 min*
2b	Kneeling anti-rotation press	1:1:1	—	3	8	2 min
2c	DB bench press	2:1:1	—	3	6-8	2 min
3a	One-arm landmine overhead press	1:1:1	—	3	8 each	2 min
3b	Lateral plank with KB	x:20:x	—	3	20 sec each	2 min
4a	Nordic leg curl	3:x:x	—	2	4	3 min

CONCLUSION

Preseason plays the important transitional role from the general preparation period to the competitive season. As a result, in this period it is essential for the strength and conditioning professional to understand the physical level of each athlete as he or she rejoins the team. This can be accomplished through a needs analysis of each individual athlete to best inform the strength and conditioning staff. By considering factors of volume, intensity, duration, and exercise selection the strength and conditioning professional is able to better prescribe appropriate progressions for the individual athlete. Viewing stress holistically is essential to optimally planning and implementing resistance training during preseason.

11

IN-SEASON PROGRAMMING

MELISSA TERRY AND MATT HOWLEY

While the demands of a soccer season vary greatly from level to level, what remains consistent throughout is the importance of producing and following a resistance training program that attempts to carry over progress made from the previous programs (both off-season and preseason). Increases in strength, gains in aerobic and anaerobic fitness, and improvements in movement qualities made in the previous weeks or months are all important aspects to carry into an in-season program in order to increase durability and resiliency while minimizing the likelihood of injuries. Implementing a program that enhances the on-field performance provides the adequate balance between both recovery and stimulus exposure needed for both the team (or squad) as well as each individual, and doing so efficiently to a timeline of achieving positive outcomes requires a balance of art and science.

GOALS AND OBJECTIVES

Several factors go into the development of an in-season program for a soccer athlete, including training age, injury history, level of competition, travel schedule, length of season, and planned breaks, to name a few. Regardless of these factors, however, the aim of an in-season program is to build on progress made in preceding programs as well as enhance overall durability of the athlete so that they are able to adapt more efficiently to the overload of stress that compounds throughout the season.

The five components that encompass physical fitness can be broadly categorized as cardiovascular endurance, muscular strength, muscular endurance, flexibility and mobility, and body composition. If athletes are to improve their performance within a given sport across the span of their career, it stands to reason that improvements made in their physical fitness throughout the year will complement and enhance their abilities within their sport. It is then important to recognize which categories are prudent to improve during an in-season period. Significant gains in muscular strength or body composition are unlikely to occur during the rigors of a competitive season for a soccer athlete; however, positive changes in cardiovascular endurance, muscular endurance, and flexibility, with proper progression and load management, can be realized.

Further, it must be noted that teams will have different groups of athletes that will need various training foci based on their playing time, training level, and intensity. For example, each week, those athletes who played at least 60 minutes of the competition had a higher demand placed on them within the week and therefore require different physiological needs for recovery.

These groups typically can be organized into four main groups: the starting group (i.e., those who played at least 60 minutes), the substitute group that played some but not all minutes, the group that dressed for competition but did not see any game time, and the group that was not selected for the match-day squad. The latter two groups often complete technical, conditioning, and resistance training physical development–based work. In high school and even college, these groups might be more difficult to delineate due to more freedom with the substitution rule; however, in the professional game, these groups are quite distinct. Collegiate and high school athletes who play partial minutes often reincorporated into game simulation sessions the day following a game, should the schedule permit, along with those who were not selected for the match-day squad with the aim of keeping these athletes as best prepared for full-scale match play. For the purposes of this chapter and to make reference for their need for separation below, group 1 consists of the major-minute athletes, group 2 is the lesser-minute athletes, group 3 is the zero-minute athletes, and group 4 is athletes who did not make the match-day squad.

Lastly, because the movement qualities and physical demands for goalkeepers compared to outfield athletes are so vastly different, it is important to create a separate in-season plan for goalkeepers that meets the demand of their sporting tasks. These athletes require greater anaerobic power and total body strength and less cardiovascular endurance. Goalkeepers' plans also focus more on acceleration, deceleration, and change of direction rather than on maximum-velocity exposure because their injury risk related to this quality is much less.

LENGTH, STRUCTURE, AND ORGANIZATION

Depending on the level, the length of a soccer season varies greatly from high school to college to professional. Lower levels of competition might last three to four months, while professional athletes might have seasons lasting eight to ten months (including postseason competition). Because this is a substantial period of time for the athlete at any level, it is important to capitalize on the time in order to minimize deterioration of improvements made from the off-season program. For college and professional athletes, the in-season mesocycle is the greatest proportion of programming for the year; therefore, it is important to organize a resistance training program in such a way that decline is not seen. Across all ages and groups, a typical session can last 30 to 45 minutes including proper warm-up and activation as well as suitable cooldown movements that can be incorporated into recovery efforts.

High School

The highest-level high school soccer athletes' schedules in the United States are governed by U.S. Soccer or an elite competitive league that is outside of the individual's academic institution. For the purposes of this chapter, only the schedule and time demand created by high school athletic associations are discussed.

Depending on the region, not all high school soccer competes at the same time of year; however, they all typically last around 10 to 14 weeks, consisting of one to two games per week before the playoffs. This should allow for two total body sessions per week with a focus on movement qualities, with strength maintenance earlier in the week and whole-body movement patterns and mobility later in the week. Like all levels, it is important to break the team into groups 1, 2, and 3 in order to ensure group 1 gets the necessary amount of recovery and group 3 does not fall behind the physical requirements. With youth athletes it is important to consider their long-term development. Therefore, their actual age or school year might not be the only factor that affects programming. Biological age, peak height velocity, physical maturation, and where they lie within the movement and performance protocol also should drive programming for such athletes. Because of participation and substitution rules in high school soccer, it might be the case that only two groups are needed (i.e., if all team members participate in the games, both varsity and junior varsity, throughout the week). During a single-game week, goalkeepers might be able to get an additional session in to improve total body strength and reactive ability.

College

Programming for collegiate soccer athletes at the NCAA Division I (DI) level might consist of two separate in-season periods. The fall competitive season, when teams are ranked and compete for a spot in the national tournament, is the main competitive season, lasting 14 to 18 weeks (mid-August to beginning of December). The second period of in-season programming is the spring competitive season. This season is a non-competitive season of six to eight weeks in which five friendly matches are scheduled. These matches are designed for the development of the athlete and do not count toward NCAA rankings, nor are any results documented. However, even though no awards or achievements are gained during this period, many collegiate programs train and play at similar intensities because the hours allotted at the NCAA DI level are the same during the fall competitive season. During these periods it is recommended that athletes complete one or two total body sessions per week consisting of exercises that enhance total body power, improve or maintain movement qualities, and enhance recovery.

Because of demands placed on differing groups, it is important that groups 2 and 3 do not fall behind the top group in their fitness and power outputs, and that group 1 gets extra consideration for recovery.

Further, the programming for goalkeepers, as mentioned previously, must cater to their positional needs and might include more upper body work and a stronger emphasis on total body strength and power. This can include Olympic lifting variations (depending on the athlete's skill acquisition at said movements). Implementing such variations means more time can be dedicated to the development of muscular power through these movements and their variations while using higher intensities throughout the season through total body movements.

Lastly, one must take into consideration the schedule and time demands placed on a collegiate athlete. The NCAA stipulates that collegiate athletes not exceed 20 hours per week in required sporting activities. Their coursework, travel, game, and training schedules must all be balanced so as to create the requisite time and physical ability for the athletes to complete their twice-weekly resistance training sessions. This could mean that a maximum of 60 to 90 minutes per week is all that their schedules allow. Such sessions might need to be performed early in the morning or after training in the evening; therefore, exercise selection and efficiency is of utmost importance.

Professional

In-season programming for the professional soccer athlete depends on a number of factors, including but not limited to training age (previous resistance training experience), injury history, and group delineation (as mentioned earlier). In the professional game, a teenager might come from a youth development program in which resistance training was not a part of the regimen. Some athletes come from a collegiate program in which resistance training was a very important part of the development, and they might be both willing and capable of executing any and all exercises thrown their way. Some team members might be decades-long veterans of the game, have a wide array of injury histories, and have completed training programs and exercises that have helped make them successful across their career. Lastly, other athletes will have had experience but are not married to a specific methodology of training, so designing a program specific to such athletes is also important. Strength and conditioning professionals must recognize who fits in which groups and must determine progressions and regressions for all major movement exercises so that they are capable of delivering a program that can be customized to the differing needs of athletes, positions, and groups.

The season for Major League Soccer (MLS), the men's professional league in the United States, consists of a 34-game slate occurring over approximately 32 weeks, plus another four weeks for those who make the playoffs. The season for the National Women's Soccer League (NWSL), the women's professional league, consists of a 24-game slate occurring over approximately 28 weeks, plus a maximum of two more weeks for those who make the playoffs. Both leagues are affected by multiple international breaks, which is a part of the greater global game and set by the governing body of world soccer, FIFA. During these breaks athletes often depart for international duty for between 7 to 14 days, and on occasion athletes will miss club games. During FIFA World Cup years, both MLS and NWSL athletes might be away from their club teams for up to eight weeks. Management of athletes around these periods is paramount. Training weeks can be broken up into the following categories: off-weeks (in which no match takes place), one-game weeks (this makes up the majority of playing seasons), and two-game weeks. Rarely does a team have three games within a seven-day period. Contending with the travel and game schedule, roster availability, training versus gym locations, and training intensities are the major barriers to the delivery of a well-planned in-season program. While professional athletes have neither hours restrictions predetermined by the NCAA nor academic requirements, they do have other scheduling commitments outside of training and games that must be considered. Harmonizing the athlete's time demands by applying a program that enhances their physical qualities while promoting the necessary recovery is the ultimate balancing act for the strength and conditioning professional.

RECOMMENDED EXERCISES

When determining which exercises should be prescribed to the athlete, it is important to refer to the needs analysis for the sport as well as assessing the individual needs and training goals of the athlete (3a). The approach to programming for high school, college, and professional athletes follows the same framework while progressing in difficulty and specificity as the athlete develops, becomes stronger, and cultivates better movement competencies. Globally focusing on the fundamental movement patters of squatting, hinging, pulling, pushing, jumping, and landing is vital in all phases of training, especially during the in-season. Specifically, the program should focus on ground-based movements followed by incorporating single-leg, posterior chain, power, upper body, and core-strengthening exercises (3a). The exercises selected within a given workout should be aimed at maintaining or improving athlete development while limiting the orthopedic stress placed on the athlete. Throughout the in-season block of training, the strength and conditioning professional has the ability to manipulate volume and intensity of the exercises across each microcycle. When assessing exercises during the exercise selection process, identifying exercises that provide the greatest level of physical development or transferability in-season is vital. When programming for power development and maximal strength, the implementation of ground-based movements is usually advised. Such movements require the use of larger musculature, driving greater levels of physiological and muscular adaptations (4). These movements target the total body muscular recruitment, and for soccer athletes, the development of strength from the midsection down through the hips and legs is vital for improved technical and physical abilities. Exercises such as loaded jumping movements, Olympic lifts, and bilateral squatting and deadlift movements are often used (4).

Due to the movement capacities of the sport, completing technical demands at a high level, and the running-based nature of the sport, the implementation of single-leg movements is crucial for athletes of all levels and attributes. Single-leg movements can be performed in both the sagittal and frontal planes. Because of the 360-degree nature in which soccer is played, performing exercises in multiple planes is important for athletic development and mitigating injury risk. Single-leg movements and variations of the split squat, single-leg squat, step-up, and lunge in multiple planes are movements that can be implemented as assistance exercises within a resistance training program for a soccer athlete.

Due to the running and sprinting demands of the sport, having a well-developed posterior chain is crucial, and it helps mitigate injury risk in the hamstrings while contributing to speed development. Many approaches can be taken to selecting appropriate posterior chain exercises for an athlete's resistance training program. Implementing posterior chain exercises that are hip and knee dominant and that involve isotonic, isometric, or eccentric muscular actions are all factors that need to be considered. However, to have a component of eccentric strengthening is important for the hamstring muscles. It is known such training can decrease injury risk by assisting to increase muscle fascicle length and developing greater levels of strength (1). Exercises such as the Romanian deadlift and its many variations, hip/glute bridge, glute-ham raise, Nordic leg curl variations, and eccentric leg curl are all viable options for helping with posterior chain strength development. Such movements might also have variations that can assist with power and explosive training. Power and explosive exercises provide the strength and conditioning professional with the ability to more holistically train the athlete by training the entire force–velocity curve. By neglecting power exercises, even during the in-season period, athletes' ability to continually increase rate of force development can be limited. Jumping and landing variations are great options for developing power, explosiveness, and stiffness. Unloaded movements can be performed both on the field and in the resistance training program. Adding such exercises into the warm-up of a sport training session is advised when resistance training time is limited during the in-season period, especially if only one or two resistance training sessions will be performed each week. In conjunction, such movements along with loaded jumps, resisted jumps, and explosive hip hinge movements (e.g., kettlebell swing) can assist in developing power within a resistance training program.

Finally, exercises focusing on the core musculature and balance also should be considered when developing an in-season resistance training program. Such exercises, which are based on the premise of stabilization, anti-rotation, anti-flexion, and anti-extension, are strongly encouraged. These exercises can be performed by combining them with main movements within a resistance training session, or they can be performed in addition to any pretraining movements or completed after a resistance training session in a circuit.

INTENSITY

Many factors affect the intensity prescribed by the strength and conditioning professional throughout the in-season period. These factors include current on-field training volume, days between games, athlete training age, injury history, and the athlete's ability to handle training within the in-season period.

In the early stages of an in-season period, developmental programs for athletes should be the focus; intensities generally are higher as the strength and conditioning professional tries to drive adaptation. As the season progresses, though, it is important to provide athletes only with enough stimulus to maintain performance outcomes. Typically, lower volumes are prescribed while intensity is maintained. When teams are in periods of match congestion or are near postseason play, such that athletic development becomes increasingly a lower priority in comparison to sport performance, resistance training programs might focus on maintaining rather than developing.

That said, when considering the length of the in-season period of the professional athlete, although it is critical to apply the least amount of stress possible, maintenance is not an effective approach because the athlete's development would be limited over the course of many in-season periods throughout his or her career. The strength and conditioning professional should assist the athlete in continuing to develop and improve.

When developing an in-season program for a high school or collegiate athlete, the program generally should focus on maintaining physical development. Due to their seasons generally lasting between 12 and 16 weeks and the dense game and training schedule, development for these athletes generally occurs during the noncompetitive phases when the focus is on global development of all areas: physical, technical, and tactical.

Often, strength and conditioning professionals look to work within guidelines, which have been derived from research, to have athletes complete the least effective dose needed to maintain their physical abilities. Because power work might assist with neural priming, it is sometimes performed at a high intensity closer to the game, with the goal of driving sport performance through physical preparation.

Strength and conditioning professionals can use many options to moderate training within an in-season period. A more traditional measure includes Prilepin's chart (table 11.1), relative intensity scale, and the rating of perceived exertion scale.

Another approach strength and conditioning professionals have instituted is the use of velocity-based training. This enables the athlete to regulate the intensity of the work based on the speed at which he or she moves a given load within a given workout. This method uses objective data to provide feedback, reduces subjectivity, and provides research-validated loading schemes to prescribe loads based on what group an athlete is in. For example, different speed ranges might be issued for starters (group 1), reserves (group 2), and those who do not play (groups 3 and 4), therefore driving specific physiological adaptations.

Table 11.1   Prilepin's Chart

Percent (% 1RM)	Optimal number of reps per set per exercise	Optimal number of total reps* per exercise	Optimal range of total reps* per exercise
55-65	3-6	24**	18-30***
70-80	3-6	18	12-24
80-90	2-4	15	10-20
>90	1-2	4	4-10

*Total reps = sets × reps.

**For example, 8 × 3, 4 × 6, or 6 × 4.

***For example, 3 × 6, 4 × 5, 5 × 4, and so on as long as 3 to 6 reps per set are performed.

Based on Prilepin's Chart.

VOLUME

The factors that affect intensity throughout the in-season period also apply to volume. Higher training volumes increase the level of microtrauma and damage to the muscle and therefore the level of perceived fatigue, and they might decrease performance. Higher volumes can be used during other phases of training when the goal is to increase muscle mass or the cross-sectional area of a muscle, which can help with force and power production capabilities. In-season, especially for group 1 athletes, building muscle mass is not a priority, however. Soccer athletes are generally smaller in stature and carry less muscle mass than most other athletes. Therefore, in-season resistance training volumes for soccer athletes are near the lowest effective dose that enables athletes to maintain muscle mass and, ultimately, performance.

Strength and conditioning professionals can adhere to many methods and periodization strategies when developing the total volume within a resistance training program. As mentioned with intensity, Prilepin's chart is one method that can be used when planning and developing resistance training programs. Not only is this method based on intensity ranges, but it provides recommended volumes that the strength and conditioning professional should use in accordance with said intensity ranges. Tables 11.2 and 11.3 show the intensity ranges as well as the optimal volume and volume ranges for both sets and repetitions, and provides a guide to the strength and conditioning professional on what is considered high and low volume at a particular intensity. This enables the strength and conditioning professional to assess the phase of the season as it pertains to on-field training and game density, as well as the athlete's current readiness to train at the optimal volume to achieve the desired outcomes.

Another method to determine volume is microdosing, which involves the prescription of one or two exercises performed across three to four days of the week that coincide with the on-field training plan. This enables the strength and conditioning professional to specifically manage and moderate the volume within each exercise an athlete performs based on his or her training outputs during the on-field session and his or her current status as it pertains to previous playing time and upcoming matches. For example, one day an athlete might have a higher on-field output and be in a higher state of fatigue, so training volume is decreased. However, after an off day and a lighter on-field session, the athlete might be able to withstand a higher volume within the resistance training exercises. Therefore, volume can be adjusted on a day-to-day basis, and instead of the volume being dictated in one session, it can be specifically allocated across the training period by assessing the athlete's readiness to train. This philosophical approach is more commonly suited to the professional environment, where time with athletes is greater than with collegiate and high school athletes.

SAMPLE PROGRAMS

Tables 11.2 through 11.13 provide separate sample programs for high school, college, and professional goalkeepers and field athletes. Within those programs are two distinct phases of in-season resistance training: total body–focused sessions for high school and college athletes and a lower body–focused session and a lower body power and upper body strength–focused session for professional athletes.

Perform the sets assigned for the first group of exercises (1a, 1b, 1c) before moving to the next group of exercises (2a, 2b, 2c).

Interpreting the Sample Program Tables

BB = Barbell

BW = Body weight

DB = Dumbbell

MB = Medicine ball

KB = Kettlebell

RDL = Romanian deadlift

Side hang = Holding BB, DB, or KB with the arms hanging down, palms facing legs, and elbows extended

Rack position = Holding BB, DB, or KB in the catch or rack position on the anterior shoulder

Goblet = Holding DB or KB with both hands below the chin and elbows pointed out to the side in the midline of the body.

Order = Performing one set of each exercise (1a, 1b, 1c) in the group one after the other. After the first set is completed, go back to the first exercise in the group and do the second set of each exercise. If certain exercises call for fewer sets than others in the group, perform those sets on the back end of the grouping. For example, if exercise 1a calls for 4 sets and exercise 1b calls for 3 sets, perform exercise 1b during sets 2 through 4 of exercises 1a.

Tempo (E:I:C) = Timing or duration (in seconds) of the eccentric phase (E), the isometric hold or pause between the eccentric and concentric phases (I), and the concentric phase (C); an "x" means explosive (3b).

Table 11.2 Goalkeepers: In-Season, High School, Phase 1

Total Body Focus

Order	Exercise	Tempo (E:I:C)	Intensity	Sets	Reps	Rest
1a	KB sumo deadlift	2:0:1	—	4	8	2 min
1b	Hip thrust	2:1:1	BW	4	4	<40 sec
2a	Two-DB single-leg RDL	2:0:1	—	3	8	2 min
2b	Back extension	3:1:1	—	3	10	1 min
3a	DB bench press (neutral grip)	2:0:1	—	4	5	3 min
3b	One-arm DB row (hand and knee supported)	2:1:1	—	4	6 each	1 min

Table 11.3 Goalkeepers: In-Season, High School, Phase 2

Total Body Focus

Order	Exercise	Tempo (E:I:C)	Intensity	Sets	Reps	Rest
1a	Trap bar deadlift (concentric only)	0:0:1	—	4	6	2 min
1b	Single-leg hip thrust	2:1:1	BW	4	4	<40 sec
2a	One-arm single-leg DB RDL	2:0:1	—	3	8 each	2 min
2b	Split squat	3:1:1	—	3	6	1 min
3a	DB bench press (neutral grip)	2:0:1	—	3	5	3 min
3b	One-arm DB row (hand and knee supported)	2:1:1	—	3	6 each	1 min

Table 11.4 Goalkeepers: In-Season, College, Phase 1

Total Body Focus

Order	Exercise	Tempo (E:I:C)	Intensity	Sets	Reps	Rest
1a	Trap bar deadlift (concentric only)	0:0:1	—	4	4	3 min
1b	Lateral mini-band walk	—	—	3	10 each	<40 sec
2a	Hip thrust	2:1:1	—	3	8	3 min
2b	Deadlift	3:0:1	—	3	6	3 min
3a	DB bench press (neutral grip)	2:0:1	—	4	5	3 min
3b	One-arm DB row (hand and knee supported)	2:1:1	—	4	6 each	1 min
4a	Shoulder press	2:0:1	—	3	8	3 min
4b	Band pull-apart	2:1:1	—	3	10	1 min

Table 11.5 Goalkeepers: In-Season, College, Phase 2

Total Body Focus

Order	Exercise	Tempo (E:I:C)	Intensity	Sets	Reps or time	Rest
1a	Trap bar deadlift (concentric only)	0:0:1	—	4	4	3 min
1b	Lateral mini-band walk	—	—	3	10 each	<40 sec
2a	Hip thrust	2:1:1	—	3	6	3 min
2b	One-arm single-leg BB RDL	3:0:1	—	3	5 each	3 min
3a	DB bench press (neutral grip)	2:0:1	—	3	4	3 min
3b	Standing one-arm cable row	2:1:1	—	3	8 each	1 min
4a	Prone Y's, T's, W's	1:8:1	—	3	8 sec each	3 min
4b	Face pull (band)	2:1:1	—	3	10	1 min

Table 11.6 Goalkeepers: In-Season, Professional, Phase 1

Day 1: Lower Body Focus

Order	Exercise	Tempo (E:I:C)	Intensity	Sets	Reps or distance	Rest
1a	Trap bar deadlift (concentric only) (VBT >0.5 m/s [>1.6 ft/s])	0:1:1	75%-80% 1RM	5	5	3 min
1b	Lateral mini-band walk	—	—	3	10 each	<40 sec
2a	RDL	3:0:1	—	3	6	3 min
2b	Step-up	2:0:1	—	3	5	1 min
3a	Hip thrust	2:1:1	—	3	8	3 min
3b	Farmer's walk (with contralateral rack hold)	—	—	3	15 steps	1 min

Day 2: Lower Body Power and Upper Body Strength

Order	Exercise	Tempo (E:I:C)	Intensity	Sets	Reps	Rest
1a	KB swing	1:0:x	—	4	10	2 min
1b	Jump squat (bungee resisted)	1:0:x	—	4	4	<40 sec
2a	Safety bar speed box squat (VBT >0.8 m/s [>2.6 ft/s])	1:1:x	—	4	4	3 min
2b	Single-leg hip thrust	2:1:1	—	2	8 each	1 min
3a	DB bench press (neutral grip)	2:0:1	—	4	5	3 min
3b	Bench row (neutral grip)	2:1:1	—	4	5	1 min
4a	Cuban shoulder press	2:0:1	—	3	8	3 min
4b	Band pull-apart	2:1:1	—	3	10	1 min

Table 11.7   Goalkeepers: In-Season, Professional, Phase 2

Day 1: Lower Body Focus

Order	Exercise	Tempo (E:I:C)	Intensity	Sets	Reps or distance	Rest
1a	Trap bar deadlift (concentric only) (VBT >0.35 m/s [1.1 ft/s])	0:0:1	80%-90% 1RM	5	5|5|3|3|3	3 min
1b	Lateral mini-band walk	—	—	3	10 each	<40 sec
2a	One-arm single-leg BB RDL	3:0:1	—	3	4 each	3 min
2b	Single-leg hip thrust	2:1:1	—	3	6 each	3 min
3a	Reverse sled drag	—	—	3	20 steps	2 min
3b	Single-arm farmer's walk	—	—	3	15 steps each	1 min

Day 2: Lower Body Power and Upper Body Strength

Order	Exercise	Tempo (E:I:C)	Intensity	Sets	Reps	Rest
1a	KB swing (banded)	1:0:x	—	4	8	2 min
1b	Hip thrust (banded)	1:0:x	—	4	5	<40 sec
2a	Safety bar banded speed box squat (VBT >1.0 m/s [3.3 ft\s])	1:1:x	—	4	4	3 min
3a	DB bench press (neutral grip)	2:0:1	—	4	4	3 min
3b	Bench row (neutral grip)	2:1:1	—	4	4	1 min
4a	Suspension Y's, T's, W's	2:0:1	—	3	8 each	3 min
4b	Face pull (band)	2:1:1	—	3	10	1 min

Table 11.8   Field Players: In-Season, High School, Phase 1

Total Body Focus

Order	Exercise	Tempo (E:I:C)	Intensity	Sets	Reps	Rest
1a	Goblet squat	2:0:1	—	4	8	2 min
1b	Seated concentric jump	0:1:x	—	4	4	<40 sec
2a	DB split squat	2:0:1	—	3	8	2 min
2b	Back extension	3:1:1	—	3	10	1 min
3a	DB bench press	2:0:1	—	3	8	2 min
3b	One-arm DB row (hand and knee supported)	3:1:1	—	3	10 each	1 min
3c	Nordic leg curl	4:0:0	—	2	3	2 min

Table 11.9   Field Players: In-Season, High School, Phase 2

Total Body Focus

Order	Exercise	Tempo (E:I:C)	Intensity	Sets	Reps	Rest
1a	Goblet squat	2:0:1	—	4	8	2 min
1b	Box jump	1:0:x	—	4	4	<40 sec
2a	Pistol squat	2:0:1	—	3	5 each	2 min
2b	Glute-ham raise	3:1:1	—	3	6	1 min
3a	DB incline bench press	2:0:1	—	3	6	2 min
3b	Pull-up (supinated grip)	3:1:1	—	3	8	1 min
3c	Nordic leg curl	4:0:0	—	2	3	2 min

Table 11.10   Field Players: In-Season, College, Phase 1

Total Body Focus

Order	Exercise	Tempo (E:I:C)	Intensity	Sets	Reps	Rest
1a	DB jump squat	1:0:x	20%-30% 1RM	3	4	3 min
1b	Box jump	1:0:x	—	3	3	<40 sec
2a	Trap bar deadlift (concentric only)	0:0:1	—	4	4	3 min
3a	Pistol squat	2:0:1	—	3	4 each	3 min
3b	Glute-ham raise	3:0:1	—	3	6	1 min
4a	Bench press	2:0:1	70%-80% 1RM	3	5	3 min
4b	Pull-up (supinated grip)	3:1:1	—	3	6	1 min
4c	Nordic leg curl	4:0:0	—	1	3	NA

Table 11.11   Field Players: In-Season, College, Phase 2

Total Body Focus

Order	Exercise	Tempo (E:I:C)	Intensity	Sets	Reps	Rest
1a	Trap bar jump	1:0:x	20%-30% 1RM	3	4	3 min
1b	Broad jump	1:0:x	—	3	3	<40 sec
2a	Trap bar deadlift (concentric only)	0:0:1	—	4	3|3|2|2	3 min
3a	DB walking lunge	2:0:1	—	3	6	3 min
3b	One-arm single-leg DB RDL	3:0:1	—	3	6 each	1 min
4a	Bench press	2:0:1	80%-90% 1RM	3	4|3|2	3 min
4b	Weighted pull-up (supinated grip)	3:1:1	—	3	5	1 min
4c	Nordic leg curl	4:0:0	—	2	2	NA

Table 11.12   Field Players: In-Season, Professional, Phase 1

Day 1: Lower Body Focus

Order	Exercise	Tempo (E:I:C)	Intensity	Sets	Reps	Rest
1a	DB jump squat	1:0:x	20%-30% 1RM	3	3	2 min
1b	Box jump	1:0:x	BW	3	3	<40 sec
2a	Trap bar deadlift (concentric only) (VBT >0.45 m/s [1.5 ft/s])	0:0:1	75%-80% 1RM	5	5	3 min
2b	Lateral mini-band walk	—	—	3	10 each	<40 sec
3a	Reverse lunge	1:0:1	—	3	6	3 min
3b	One-arm single-leg DB RDL	3:0:1	—	3	8 each	1 min
4a	Nordic leg curl	4:0:0	—	2	3	3 min

Day 2: Lower Body Power and Upper Body Strength

Order	Exercise	Tempo (E:I:C)	Intensity	Sets	Reps	Rest
1a	KB swing	1:0:x	—	4	8	2 min
1b	Broad jump (bungee resisted)	1:0:x	—	4	4	<40 sec
2a	Speed box back squat (VBT >0.8 m/s [2.6 ft/s])	1:1:x	—	4	5	3 min
3a	Bench press	2:0:1	—	4	6	3 min
3b	Bench row	2:1:1	—	4	8	1 min
4a	DB shoulder press (seated)	2:0:1	—	3	6	3 min
4b	Pull-up (supinated grip)	2:1:1	—	3	8	1 min

Table 11.13 Field Players: In-Season, Professional, Phase 2

Day 1: Lower Body Focus

Order	Exercise	Tempo (E:I:C)	Intensity	Sets	Reps	Rest
1a	Trap bar jump (VBT >1.4 m/s [4.6 ft/s])	1:0:x	20%-30% 1RM	3	4	2 min
1b	Single-leg box jump	1:0:x	BW	3	3 each	<40 sec
2a	Trap bar deadlift (concentric only) (VBT >0.35 m/s [1.1 ft/s])	0:0:1	80%-90% 1RM	5	5|5|3|3|3	3 min
2b	Lateral shuffle (band resisted)	—	—	3	10 each	<40 sec
3a	Rear foot–elevated split squat	2:0:1	—	3	4 each	3 min
3b	One-arm single-leg BB RDL	3:0:1	—	3	5 each	1 min
4a	Nordic leg curl	4:0:0	—	1	3	3 min

Day 2: Lower Body Power and Upper Body Strength

Order	Exercise	Tempo (E:I:C)	Intensity	Sets	Reps	Rest
1a	KB swing	1:0:x	—	4	8	2 min
1b	Lateral bound (bungee resisted)	1:0:x	—	4	4 each	<40 sec
2a	Banded speed trap bar deadlift (VBT >1.0 m/s [3.3 ft/s])	1:1:x	—	4	5	3 min
3a	One-arm DB bench press	2:0:1	—	4	4 each	3 min
3b	One-arm DB row (hand and knee supported)	2:1:1	—	4	5 each	1 min
4a	Split stance one-arm shoulder press	2:0:1	—	3	5 each	3 min
4b	Weighted pull-up (supinated grip)	2:1:1	—	3	5	1 min

CONCLUSION

Due to a variety of factors, generalizing a productive, relevant in-season program for soccer athletes of all levels is an impossible task. It is possible, however, to design a program based on foundational principles and adapt that to each team's or group's individual needs, time demands, and overarching goals. It is the role of the strength and conditioning professional to create a standard program, based in sound scientific rationale, that allows for fluidity based on ever-changing scenarios brought on by the rigors of a competitive season. The principles and methodologies outlined in this chapter, if implemented tactically and with reasonable understanding as to how and when adjustments ought to be made, can aid in producing an effective in-season resistance training program that mitigates risk of injury and enhances the strength and durability of the athlete.

While an athlete's sport-specific focus and physical demands vary greatly from off-season to in-season, the exercise selection and movement qualities trained are surprisingly similar. Throughout the year, the same exercises remain, by and large, the most important exercises because of benefits they provide to overall athleticism, movement patterns, and strength maintenance. Understanding variations on the core movement selections and providing progressions, regressions, or unilateral adaptations to them is key in curating an in-season program that is highly transferable to sporting demands.

POSTSEASON PROGRAMMING

RYAN ALEXANDER

The postseason is the peak of the season and represents the cumulative work of staff and athletes across an annual program. Although around the world different formats of postseason play are instituted (e.g., home and away leg aggregates, group stage to knockouts, single-match knockout rounds), the concepts instituted for resistance training should remain relatively consistent. To this point in the competitive season athletes have performed a mixture of progressive loading, maintenance, and tapering in a multitude of combinations with the goal of progressing the team to this culminating stage in relatively good health, prepared to perform the potential multiple matches at or near top physical form.

FACTORS INFLUENCING POSTSEASON PROGRAMMING

Before addressing the postseason resistance training program for a soccer team, it is important to have a foundation of knowledge of the stimuli that has be expressed during the preceding phases of the season. The following variables should be considered prior to prescribing resistance training for postseason play:

- Time from last competition
- Length of the competitive season
- Individual athlete roles on the team
- Injury history of each athlete
- Longest continuous training period for each athlete
- Postseason format

It is crucial to understand how each of these variables affects the volume load scheme and exercise selection prescribed in an effort to achieve optimal physical preparation for competition.

Time From Last Competition

The immediate build-up that occurs just prior to the onset of the postseason is the last window of potential fatigue-accumulating activities that athletes experience. Consider the following scenarios.

Collegiate and high school campaigns might finish on a Saturday or Sunday night, and athletes typically have five days prior to the start of postseason play. In an ideal scenario, that timeline is extended to 12 or 13 days. To balance out the time prior to the beginning of the postseason, it is important to consider the format of the season. Often in collegiate campaigns the conference tournament is preceded by conference season play, which traditionally consists of two matches per week over a span of six to eight weeks. That is a significant amount of fatigue accumulated in an acute window to manage in a quick turnaround for postseason competition. High school soccer teams, although a little less consistent in schedule formats, typically play a match every three to four days, and during this time fatigue is accumulated. Prioritizing fatigue management and trying to use the modalities in the weight room to reverse the catabolic processes of a season-long overload likely result in conservative approaches that help reduce the risk of injury. However, these approaches might not reach the minimum threshold necessary for positive adaptations associated with traditional resistance training models.

In the amateur club setting, the competition format has evolved to a more professional format of season-long group or league play, culminating with a showcase or multimatch event that leads into a knockout (i.e., single-elimination) format. The amount of time leading up to these events varies based on level, but the typical time is one to two weeks. In general, success in these events can result in five to seven matches played across one to two weeks depending on the league affiliation. Given these competitions' unique formatting for both convenience of travel and budget, it is prudent to prescribe build-up resistance training prior to the event.

At the professional level, a few countries take on the traditional postseason play format, which can last three to four weeks in total. In 2019 in the United States the top division of men's soccer transitioned to a single-elimination knockout format that resulted in 14 teams playing through four rounds over the course of 23 days, with postseason play beginning 13 days after the final day of the regular season. The top division on the women's side in the United States separates their 24-match competitive season from the playoffs by one week, straight into semifinal matches between the top four teams of the league table. The semifinal and championship match are also separated by one week, mitigating the risk of fatigue at the end of their six-month campaign. Match density leading up to the final day of the regular season varies by club and is difficult to standardize, as are the dense periods of competition throughout the season for each team.

Length of the Competitive Season

Competitive seasons follow various formats. The density and volume of fixtures immediately ahead of the postseason are vital to the approach to training in the weight room leading up to the first meaningful competition. However, when prescribing postseason resistance training it is also crucial to measure athletes' acute versus chronic loading specific to the time frame of the regular season and to consider the preseason.

At the collegiate and high school level the seasons are compact, spanning two to three months with 15 to 22 competitions dispersed throughout. Based on governing bodies supervising the two levels, the time allotted for preseason is also limited. NCAA rules state that each institution is allotted 21 practice opportunities or units, which averages out to about 14 days, prior to the first official competition. For example, in 2019 the NCAA Division I women's and men's soccer seasons started on August 22 and August 30, respectively. The women's campaign came to a close with the national championship match on December 8, 2019. The majority of teams at the collegiate level end their season in the conference tournaments, which are typically the first week of November. The men's national championship match was played on December 15, 2019, and the conference tournaments started slightly after the women on November 4 or 5. Table 12.1 shows the typical campaign length and density of competition from the start of preseason to the beginning of the conference tournaments and to the national championship match date.

Table 12.1   Overview From Start of Preseason to Phases of Collegiate Competitive Season

	Preseason to first official match	Preseason to end of competition schedule	Preseason to start of conference tournament	Preseason to start of NCAA tournament	Preseason to NCAA championship match
Women	14 days	87 days	90 days	102 days	125 days
Men	14 days	81 days	85 days	101 days	125 days

Note: All dates presented are approximated based on general schedule interpretations from 2019.

Although similar, the men's and women's schedules are not uniform across all conferences. In 2019 the Stanford University women's soccer team won the national championship and posted a record of 24-1-0. From the start of the campaign to the completion they played 25 meaningful competitions, or a match every five days. On the men's side, the Virginia Cavaliers men's soccer team posted a record of 21-2-1 and won the national championship. From the start of the campaign to the completion they played 24 meaningful competitions across 125 days, averaging slightly more than five days between competitions. For both the men and women this is not an unreasonable match-to-day ratio. However, further inspection shows that from the start of the competitive season to its completion the ratio is altered.

The Stanford women's program played their first official competition on August 23, 2019, and finished their competitive season on November 8, 2019. That equates to 19 matches in 77 days for a match-to-day ratio of 4.05. The Virginia Cavaliers men's program began official competition on August 30, 2019, and completed the competitive season schedule on November 1, 2019, with 16 organized matches in 63 days, for a ratio of 3.9. The entire build-up to the postseason is two months of dense fixtures with a high potential of fatigue accumulation in the collegiate environment.

The high school time frame is similar to the collegiate time frames. The time of the season is not uniform across the country, but the general trend is for 15 to 18 competitions over a span of approximately 70 to 80 days prior to postseason competition. The time between matches is highly variable, with some clustering of matches at various times during the two-month season. It is also important to note that not all high school athletes are committed to a single sport. Based on the region of the country, soccer can be an attractive sport for multi-sport athletes, so such athletes have a separate set of considerations when programming the postseason resistance training program.

The amateur club and professional calendars have similar campaign lengths. The match-to-day ratios vary more than in the collegiate and high school environment. At these levels the main considerations when determining the aggressive nature of the resistance training program for the postseason are the longevity of the season and overall competition volume of each athlete. These long campaigns have an inevitable feeling of monotony and grind. This should heavily influence the exercise selection recommendations, as discussed later in the chapter.

Individual Athlete Roles on the Team

Independent of level, athletes are stratified based on minutes they accumulate during a competitive season. First, bench and role athletes do not accumulate the same volume of minutes during the year as starting athletes and therefore should be programmed differently during the postseason time because of the need to promote different adaptations (i.e., recovery versus strength endurance) for each group. Second, athletes in starting roles who have played the majority of matches during the season should have a separate and specific resistance training program during the postseason. The stimuli accumulated over the course of the competitive season result in a different presentation of fitness and fatigue. Therefore, the complexity (i.e., multi-joint versus isolated, unilateral versus bilateral) of the exercises prescribed in the postseason must be considered for this group. Although sometimes latent in a number of activities because of the natural decrease in the intensity of training during the postseason, fatigue in starting athletes can demand lower volumes and simpler or previously mastered movements during the postseason. A third categorization is the goalkeeping position, which is unlike any other position with respect to physical demands of competition. Goalkeeping is a less fatiguing position, but it is much more dependent on strength and power training to be an effective athlete.

Injury History of Each Athlete

At any level the injury history of the athlete, both acute and chronic, should be taken into consideration when designing their postseason resistance training programming. The stimulus during this phase is already so sensitive to fatigue because of the in-season volume of work. For example, an athlete who has been out for four to six weeks with a soft tissue injury has a less developed base fitness. Therefore, decreases in volume or intensity of the program might be appropriate to not overload the fatiguing aspects of the workout. Ultimately, for this phase of the season, independent of the categorization of athlete availability, injury history, level, and so on, nothing should diminish or sacrifice on-field performance. The reality is that the addition of positive adaptations in the areas of strength, power, or speed at this time of the season are minimal, especially considering the percentage of overall stimulus dedicated to soccer-specific training. The general recommendation considering injury history is to trend on the cautious side to decrease the risk of injury and increase the overall preparedness of the athlete for soccer-specific training and competition by keeping volumes low and exercise selection similar to the in-season programming.

Longest Continuous Training Period for Each Athlete

Because of a variety of factors, athletes likely enter the postseason with varying lengths of continuous training periods. For example, an athlete might have returned to full team training and competition two weeks prior to the postseason. With one or two full matches under the athlete's belt, a likely plan of action is to group him or her back into the full team activities and have the volume-load in the weight room be proportional to all non-limited athletes in the same category of participation. It might be tempting to put this athlete back into full team activities along with other non-limited athletes with no changes to their program. Doing so would not be recommended, though, because the returning athlete has not sustained a consistent loading pattern that is proportional to that of their teammates. It is important to consider the details of this athlete's activity. For example, the strength and conditioning professional knows that those two weeks of activity were highly productive, with no reported complaints or setbacks from the athlete. However, the injury was a soft tissue, non-contact injury to the hamstring, and the athlete's position is fullback. With the physical demands in the match, he or she likely is getting an increased stimulus from competition, and from working with the athlete through rehab the strength and conditioning professional knows an aggressive return-to-play process prepared the athlete for the postseason. However, the athlete's overall ability to recover might be suboptimal relative to the abilities of an athlete who has been training consistently for more than 10 weeks. Increased specific fatigue or soreness responses to stimuli that the athlete has not been accustomed to acutely can cause a significant spike in fatigue that might have deleterious impacts on his or her body. Therefore, the strength and conditioning professional must approach this time with caution and organize all programming accordingly.

Postseason Format

The least surprising variable of a resistance training program is the postseason format. Consider a single knockout format that spans three weeks versus a group stage progressing to knockout that spans two weeks. Density and volume of matches and total duration of the postseason are critically important when designing the program. Progressions to volume load should be dosed and always individualized for any athletes lacking resiliency, as well as being complementary to the physical demands of the team's style of play.

POSTSEASON PROGRAMMING FOR HIGH SCHOOL AND COLLEGE SOCCER

Specific examples of programming are provided here for each of the environments described, with high school and college soccer grouped together because of their similar natures. Postseason formats for the two typically are single-elimination, knockout rounds that continue for a certain number of rounds based on the size of the district, conference, region, division, and so on. The initial phase of postseason matches traditionally begins within six days of the last meaningful competition of the season. Therefore, athletes rarely have an opportunity to recover optimally and build up after having competed in 16 to 18 competitions in the last two to two and a half months, with match-to-day ratios between 3 and 4. Both the collegiate- and high school–level periods of competition are dense, and athletes have the potential to accumulate fatigue at increasing rates as the competitive season progresses.

High School

With multiple progressive rounds—traditionally broken up into districts, regions, and statewide brackets with two or three rounds per section—resistance training can be used as a recovery modality following matches at the high school level. Unfortunately, a reality of this level is that a weight room is not always readily available to the soccer programs based on the size of the school and the time of year in which soccer competes. For the programs that are fortunate to have the resource of a traditional weight room, it is ideal to plan a resistance training session in combination with the team recovery session.

Table 12.2 on page 237 is an example of a workout for the starting athletes to complete following a match. The idea of resistance training the day following a match, and also one or two days ahead of the next match, might be novel. This is not a resistance training session with the objective of inducing hypertrophic adaptations to the working muscle. Instead, this session offers a reversal of the accumulative catabolic breakdown of the body over the course of continuous training and competition. This is achieved by prescribing only exercises with which the group is familiar and has shown mastery over during previous phases of the program. All lower body exercises have a low load assignment, so barely enough weight is used to produce tension in the muscle. Upper body exercises have more freedom in the loading in an attempt to achieve a response in the body that can promote repair and growth.

Similar to the field-based session, the non-starters can perform a gym-based session with minor modifications to increase overall volume load and achieve a slightly higher stimulus (see table 12.3 on page 238). Small changes to the exercise selection also benefit athletes who are looking to maintain strength and power.

With each week that the team advances, the set and repetition scheme changes minimally. The program already documents a repetition range, which allows athletes the freedom to perform the exercise within a range that will not force or motivate them to push outside of their comfort. Remember, resistance training should not affect on-field performance. Everything prescribed in the weight room needs to promote positive on-field performance (see the footnote for table 12.3 on page 238). During the postseason phase that means approaching with caution and taking very measured progressions.

Table 12.4 on page 238 shows how sets, repetitions, and loads can be progressed within a four-week program for a high school postseason.

College

The college-level format can be advantageous, with just a single match per six to seven days. The college postseason has two distinct phases. First, the conference tournament is a time when the mid-majors fight for their automatic qualifying spot. These tournaments can be three or four rounds, with matches played every other day throughout a week. Second, the NCAA tournament traditionally begins the week after the conference tournaments have finished and the field of teams has been selected. The women's programs play one round the first week then two matches over three days for the second and third rounds. The quarterfinal round is a single match in a week, then the Final Four event is two matches in three days for the advancing teams. The men's programs play one match per week until the Final Four event, which, like the women's programs, is two matches in three days.

Following the same progression from week to week that is presented in table 12.4, the only modification recommended when transitioning to a postseason with a one-match-per-week format is to include a second resistance training session in the week. Ideally, the team does resistance training on their first day back to training to promote recovery. A second session, ideally three days prior to the next competition, adds some strength and power derivatives to prime the body for the next competition. Table 12.5 on page 238 is an example of a program for the second session of the week in a postseason format of one match per week. The exercises in table 12.5 are designed to be completed in pairs, or miniature complexes, by doing a resistance training exercise focused on technique and a concentrated load, followed by an explosive exercise that uses similar movements as the exercise with which it is paired.

Inherent in the in-season schedule of roughly two matches per week is the potential for injuries, inconsistent training periods, and only a minimal sport-specific training stimuli. It is important to be mindful of these realities and to learn to adapt the programming. In these instances when athletes have a weak strength foundation due to injury or inconsistent training, a prioritization of the training prescription is needed. Based on the level of confidence in the return-to-play process, these athletes should start at low volumes and intensities. Once the athlete has shown an ability to manage volume and load, first increase volume. As the weeks progress through the postseason, the final variable to increase to match the rest of the team is the intensity. All exercise selection should be prescribed in collaboration with the sports medicine professionals supervising the rehabilitation process to be certain the program has no contraindications.

POSTSEASON PROGRAMMING FOR CLUB-LEVEL ATHLETES

As mentioned previously, club-level athletes experience the biggest variety of postseason competition format. Some levels of club soccer hold a large, formatted tournament at a single site with single-elimination knockout rounds lasting between three and seven days. Others adopt the tournament or showcase format that follows an extremely dense period of matches progressing from group play to knockout rounds. During this time, because of the lack of significant time between matches, it is not realistic to accomplish anything more than a movement-focused session on the field. A program that focuses on movement and joint mobility more than loading is the most practical approach for a number of clubs. It is important to promote full range-of-motion movements that work through the fatigue that muscle groups accumulate from the competitions.

Balance the bilateral and unilateral exercises for the lower body with many of the exercises that have been introduced in this book. The objective is to only prescribe exercises with which the athletes are familiar. This is not the time to introduce a new stress to the system because that increases the likelihood of soreness or maladaptation to a movement. Set and repetition schemes should be low; the aim is not to induce fatigue, but instead to promote neuromuscular drive. The upper body exercise selection is limited due to being at a field with no traditional resistance training equipment. The strength and conditioning professional should be smart with variations and creativity without increasing the difficulty of the overall workout through exercise selection. Each exercise should be simple to promote recovery, success, and confidence.

Modifications for inconsistent training, long-term rehabilitations, or other injuries are the same at this level as for the collegiate and high school environments. First, such athletes should have modified workout volumes and loads. Once a baseline for total volume load has been established, volume can increase, then load can increase. Especially if such an athlete is accumulating minutes in matches during this dense time period, it is best to minimize as much as possible all other stimuli through resistance training sessions that potentially could fatigue the athlete.

POSTSEASON PROGRAMMING FOR PROFESSIONAL-LEVEL ATHLETES

In the United States, the men's professional-level postseason is a mix of the one-match-per-week format and some dense periods with a match every three days. The balance of resistance training sessions should be determined by using resistance training as recovery as opposed to preparation. Using resistance training as a means of recovery is accomplished by using low volume set and repetition schemes and low to moderate percentages for load assignments on the first or second day following a competition. With a one-match-per-week format, the second session, similar to the collegiate level, is recommended to fall two or three days ahead of the next competition. Similar to the programming for college athletes, table 12.6 on page 239 is made up of two-exercise complexes of complementary movements that follow a progressive loading scheme from week to week and have a balance of upper body (push and pull) and lower body exercises. At this level, strength and conditioning professionals should be mindful of the on-field stimulus because specific tactics might have a greater fatiguing effect on some positions than on others. It is critical during the postseason phase that all athletes' stimuli are taken into consideration to avoid unnecessary overloads of any muscle group unless they are intentionally prescribed.

When the match schedule permits it, two resistance training workouts can be done weekly, with one session planned for early in the week focusing on total body, bilateral and unilateral work with full range of motion and a higher-intensity loading on the upper body, and a second session planned for later in the week, two or three days ahead of the next competition, to keep athletes balanced between recovery and preparation without increasing risk of fatigue or injury. The same concepts of familiarity with exercise selection and very conservative progression in volume load apply. The level of specificity is the main difference of the programming demands at the professional level versus those at the collegiate, high school, or club level.

Lastly, athletes have preferences for exercises that they are good at. As mentioned in previous sections, it is good to prescribe exercises that promote success and confidence. This is not an excuse to vary from the key concepts in this book, but if an athlete enjoys a certain exercise, it is permissible to alter his or her individual program. For example, if an athlete enjoys a medicine ball overhead toss versus a medicine ball slam, that is an easy substitution. Overall, strength and conditioning professionals should not stray from the basic concepts presented here, but where necessary, modify for the purpose of reaping increased psychological benefits.

SPECIFIC POSTSEASON RECOMMENDATIONS FOR GOAL-KEEPERS

The final topic to discuss for postseason programming is uniqueness of the goalkeeping position. This specifically pertains to the top club, collegiate, and professional levels, where position specialization is evident. The postseason is a prime time to use resistance training for recovery and preparation to keep athletes performing their best on field. For the goalkeeping position that looks slightly different for one main reason: goalkeepers rely primarily on those high-end motor units to perform in competition, whereas field athletes use low-, mid, and high-end motor units to complete activities ranging from walking and jogging to sprinting, jumping, and striking the ball. Goalkeepers consistently are called on to complete maximal efforts as in diving to make a save, jumping to claim a cross, or accelerating off the line to close off an opponent's angle for shot. Therefore, goalkeepers' programming must be adjusted to focus on these higher-end motor units in a standardized and controlled manner.

In the instance of the goalkeeper, the exercise selection is modified to include focused lateral movements because of the prevalence of those movements in the success of the position. Additionally, the objective loading ranges are increased to recruit a higher portion of the top-end motor units. However, it is important to note that this is not a departure from the overall concepts of postseason resistance training. Using small modifications in exercise selection, volume load, or set and repetition schemes addresses all the variables introduced in this chapter while maintaining a safe and efficient program to promote positive adaptations.

SAMPLE PROGRAMS

Tables 12.2 through 12.6 provide examples of postseason workouts and programming guidelines for high school, college, and professional athletes. Readers should take note of the additional detail provided for tables 12.2 and 12.3 and the directions for pairing exercises in tables 12.5 and 12.6.

Interpreting the Sample Program Tables

BB = Barbell

BW = Body weight

DB = Dumbbell

MB = Medicine ball

KB = Kettlebell

RDL = Romanian deadlift

Side hang = Holding BB, DB, or KB with the arms hanging down, palms facing legs, and elbows extended

Rack position = Holding BB, DB, or KB in the catch or rack position on the anterior shoulder

Goblet = Holding DB or KB with both hands below the chin and elbows pointed out to the side in the midline of the body.

Order = Performing one set of each exercise (1a, 1b, 1c) in the group one after the other. After the first set is completed, go back to the first exercise in the group and do the second set of each exercise. If certain exercises call for fewer sets than others in the group, perform those sets on the back end of the grouping. For example, if exercise 1a calls for 4 sets and exercise 1b calls for 3 sets, perform exercise 1b during sets 2 through 4 of exercises 1a.

Tempo (E:I:C) = Timing or duration (in seconds) of the eccentric phase (E), the isometric hold or pause between the eccentric and concentric phases (I), and the concentric phase (C); an "x" means explosive (King, 1998).

Table 12.2 High School: Post-Match Recovery Programming for Starters

Exercise	Tempo (E:I:C)	Intensity	Sets	Reps or time	Rest
Trap bar deadlift	1:1:1	40%-60% 1RM	3	5-12*	3 min
One-arm single-leg RDL	2:1:1	PVC	3	4-6 each	3 min
One-arm DB bench press	1:1:1	60%-70% 1RM	3	4-8	2 min
KB lateral lunge	3:1:1	30%-40% 1RM	3	3-5 each	3 min
One-arm DB row	1:1:1	60%-70% 1RM	3	4-8	2 min
Explosive floor press	2:0:1	Soccer ball	3	4-6	2 min
MB sit-up	1:0:2	10-25 lb (5-11 kg)	3	6-15	2 min
Prone plank	—	BW	2	30-60 sec	2 min

*The large gap for repetitions is to account for the various physical demands at each position. For example, an external player such as a wide midfielder, winger, or external defender with a high muscle load would be prescribed a higher volume (e.g., 10-12 reps) at 40% to 50% of the 1RM to work the lower-end motor units to serve as a flush instead of having them perform a 20-to-30-minute jog, run, or cycle. A central defender or striker with significantly less muscle load, with a higher dependence on acceleration and deceleration resulting in joint load, and who has just come off a match would be prescribed a lower volume (e.g., 5-6 reps) at closer to 60% of the 1RM. Central midfielders that with a balance of muscle and joint load, depending on the tactical role within the team, would be in the intermediate repetition range (e.g., 6-9 reps) at 50% to 60% of the 1RM.

Table 12.3 High School: Postseason Programming for Non-Starters

Exercise	Tempo (E:I:C)	Intensity	Sets	Reps or time	Rest
Trap bar deadlift	1:1:1	60%-75% 1RM	3*	8-12*	3 min
One-arm single-leg RDL	2:1:1	30%-50% 1RM	3	4-6 each	3 min
One-arm DB bench press	1:1:1	70%-80% 1RM	3	8-12*	2 min
Drop jump to box jump	1:0:x	BW	3*	2-4 each	2 min
One-arm DB row	1:1:1	70%-80% 1RM	3*	8-12*	2 min
Explosive floor press	2:0:1	5-10 lb (2.3-4.5 kg)**	3	4-6	3 min
MB sit-up	1:0:2	10-25 lb (5-11 kg)	3	12-20	2 min
Prone plank	—	BW	2	30-60 sec	2 min

* Traditionally, resistance training volume is reduced during the postseason. However, non-starters, for whom the overall stimulus of the season has been lower, have a greater need for an elevated stimulus to account for their individualized needs to stay physically prepared. Reducing their volume proportionally, or in line with, the starters has the potential to serve as a detraining mechanism because they are completely void of the overload that traditionally comes on match day. Specifically for this session, the goal is to achieve a higher stimulus than what might be perceived as traditional for the non-starters because the previous day or two days was in the range of 10% to 40% of the 1RM of the stimulus the starters achieved. However, if a non-starter might be called into play at the next match, the repetitions and loading could be reduced (e.g., 2 or 3 sets of 5 to 8 reps at 60% to 75% of the 1RM), especially in the lower body core exercises to reduce residual fatigue while still providing a stimulus.

** To promote rate of force development.

Table 12.4 High School: Progressions for Postseason Programming for Non-Starters

Week	Sets	Reps	Loading (lower)	Loading (upper)
1	3	6-12	40%-60% 1RM	60%-75% 1RM
2	3-4	6-12	45%-65% 1RM	62.5%-77.5% 1RM
3	3-4	6-12	47.5%-67.5% 1RM	65%-80% 1RM
4	3	6-12	40%-60% 1RM	60%-75% 1RM

Table 12.5 College: Postseason Programming: Second Weekly Session*

Order**	Exercise	Tempo (E:I:C)	Intensity	Sets	Reps or time	Rest
1a	Back squat	1:1:1	60%-75% 1RM	3	3-5	0 min
1b	Box jump	1:0:x	BW	3	2-4	3 min
2a	DB shoulder press	1:1:1	50%-60% 1RM	3	8-12	0 min
2b	MB chest press	2:0:1	10-20 lb (5-9 kg)	3	2-4	3 min
3a	BB upright row	1:1:1	70%-80% 1RM	3	8-12	0 min
3b	MB slam	x:x:x	10-25 lb (5-11 kg)	3	2-4	3 min
4a	MB sit-up to throw	x:x:x	10-25 lb (5-11 kg)	3	8-12	0 min
4b	Prone plank	—	BW	2	30-60 sec	2 min

* Within a one-match-per-week format.

** Complete the exercises in pairs, with the second exercise performed immediately after the first exercise before resting.

Table 12.6   Professional: Postseason Programming: Second Weekly Session*

Order**	Exercise	Tempo (E:I:C)	Intensity	Sets	Reps or time	Rest
1a	Back squat	1:1:1	70%-80% 1RM	3	3-5	0 min
1b	Box jump	2:x:x	BW	3	2-4	3 min
2a	KB lateral lunge	3:1:1	15%-30% 1RM	3	2-4 each	0 min
2b	Lateral shuffle to box jump	—	BW	3	2-4 each	3 min
3a	BB upright row	1:1:1	75%-85% 1RM	3	6-8	0 min
3b	MB slam	x:x:x	20-35 lb (9-16 kg)	3	2-4	2 min
4a	MB sit up to throw	x:x:x	10-25 lb (5-11 kg)	3	8-12	0 min
4b	Prone plank	—	BW	2	30-60 sec	2 min

*Within a one-match-per-week format; two or three days ahead of the next competition.

** Complete the exercises in pairs, with the second exercise performed immediately after the first exercise before resting.

CONCLUSION

In general, the theme in postseason programming is to be conservative. It is always easier to increase volume or intensity in small increments from week to week than it is to take away once an athlete has experienced an adverse physiological response of soreness or worse. Any progressions in the overall program should be completed in small doses; 2.5% to 5% increases by week are more than enough to stave off monotonous stimulus.

REFERENCES

Chapter 1

1. Alvehus, M, Boman, N, Söderlund, K, Svensson, MB, and Burén, J. Metabolic adaptations in skeletal muscle, adipose tissue, and whole-body oxidative capacity in response to resistance training. *Eur J Appl Physiol* 114(7):1463-1471, 2014.

2. Amonette, WE, Brown, D, Dupler, TL, Xu, J, Tufano, JJ, and De Witt, JK. Physical determinants of interval sprint times in youth soccer players. *J Hum Kinetics* 40(1):113-120, 2014.

3. Angeli, A, Minetto, M, Dovio, A, and Paccotti, P. The overtraining syndrome in athletes: A stress-related disorder. *J Endocrinol Invest* 27(6):603-612, 2004.

4. Asadi, A. Effects of six weeks depth jump and countermovement jump training on agility performance. *Sport Sci J* 5(1):67-70, 2012.

5. Burgomaster, KA, Heigenhauser, GJ, and Gibala, MJ. Effect of short-term sprint interval training on human skeletal muscle carbohydrate metabolism during exercise and time-trial performance. *J Appl Physiol* 100(6):2041-2047, 2006.

6. Carroll, TJ, Riek, S, and Carson, RG. Neural adaptations to resistance training. *Sport Med* 31(12):829-840, 2001.

7. Chesley, A, MacDougall, JD, Tarnopolsky, MA, Atkinson, SA, and Smith, K. Changes in human muscle protein synthesis after resistance exercise. *J Appl Physiol* 73(4):1383-1388, 1992.

8. Cormie, P, McCaulley, GO, Triplett, NT, and McBride, JM. Optimal loading for maximal power output during lower-body resistance exercises. *Med Sci Sport Exerc* 39(2):340-349, 2007.

9. Church, DD, Hoffman, JR, Mangine, GT, Jajtner, AR, Townsend, JR, Beyer, KS, Wang, R, La Monica, MB, Fukuda, DH, and Stout, JR. Comparison of high-intensity vs. high-volume resistance training on the BDNF response to exercise. *J Appl Physiol* 121(1):123-128, 2016.

10. Cook, G. *Movement: Functional Movement Systems: Screening, Assessment, Corrective Strategies.* Santa Cruz, CA: On Target Publications, 2010.

11. DeLorme TL. Heavy resistance exercises. *Arch Phys Med Rehabil* 27:607-630, 1946.

12. DeWitt, JK, Gonzales, M, Laughlin, MS, and Amonette, WE. External loading is dependent upon game state and varies by position in professional women's soccer. *Sci Med Football* 2(3):225-230, 2018.

13. Gibala, MJ, Little, JP, Van Essen, M, Wilkin, GP, Burgomaster, KA, Safdar, A, Raha, S, and Tarnopolsky, MA. Short-term sprint interval versus traditional endurance training: Similar initial adaptations in human skeletal muscle and exercise performance. *J Physiol* 575(3):901-911, 2006.

14. Gilchrist, J, Mandelbaum, BR, Melancon, H, Ryan, GW, Silvers, HJ, Griffin, LY, Watanabe, DS, Dick, RW, and Dvorak, J. A randomized controlled trial to prevent noncontact anterior cruciate ligament injury in female collegiate soccer players. *Am J Sport Med* 36(8):1476-1483, 2008.

15. Gómez-Pinilla, F, Ying, Z, Roy, RR, Molteni, R, and Edgerton, VR. Voluntary exercise induces a BDNF-mediated mechanism that promotes neuroplasticity. *J Neurophysiol* 88(5):2187-2195, 2002.

16. Hewett, TE. Neuromuscular and hormonal factors associated with knee injuries in female athletes. *Sport Med* 29(5):313-327, 2000.

17. Hewett, TE, Lindenfeld, TN, Riccobene, JV, and Noyes, FR. The effect of neuromuscular training on the incidence of knee injury in female athletes. *Am J Sport Med* 27(6):699-706, 1999.

18. Hill, AV. (The heat of shortening and the dynamic constants of muscle. *Proceed Roy Soc London. Series Biol Sci* 126(843):136-195, 1938.

19. Jones, K, Bishop, P, Hunter, G, and Fleisig, G. The effects of varying resistance-training loads on intermediate- and high-velocity-specific adaptations. *J Strength Cond Res* 15(3):349-356, 2001.

20. Koopman, R, Manders, RJ, Zorenc, AH, Hul, GB, Kuipers, H, Keizer, HA, and van Loon, LJ. A single session of resistance exercise enhances insulin sensitivity for at least 24 h in healthy men. *Eur J Appl Physiol* 94(1-2):180-187, 2005.

21. Kraemer, WJ, and Ratamess, NA. Hormonal responses and adaptations to resistance exercise and training. *Sport Med* 35(4):339-361, 2005.

22. Kraemer, WJ, Ratamess, NA, and Komi, P. Endocrine responses and adaptations to strength and power training. In *Strength and Power in Sport.* 2nd ed. Komi, P, ed. Hoboken, NJ: Wiley, 361-386, 2003.

23. Krzysztof, M, and Mero, A. A kinematics analysis of three best 100 m performances ever. *J Hum Kin* 36(1):149-160, 2013.

24. Kuipers, H, and Keizer, HA. Overtraining in elite athletes. *Sport Med* 6(2):79-92, 1988.

25. Keiner, M, Sander, A, Wirth, K, and Schmidtbleicher, D. Long-term strength training effects on change-of-direction sprint performance. *J Strength Cond Res* 28(1):223-231, 2014.

26. McGuigan, MR, Egan, AD, and Foster, C. Salivary cortisol responses and perceived exertion during high intensity and low intensity bouts of resistance exercise. *J Sport Sci Med* 3(1):8, 2004.

27. Morin, JB, Gimenez, P, Edouard, P, Arnal, P, Jiménez-Reyes, P, Samozino, P, Brughelli, M, and Mendiguchia, J. Sprint acceleration mechanics: The major role of hamstrings in horizontal force production. *Front Physiol* 6:404, 2015.

28. Panagoulis, C, Chatzinikolaou, A, Avloniti, A, Leontsini, D, Deli, CK, Draganidis, D, Stampoulis, T, Oikonomou, T, Papanikolaou, K, Rafailakis, L, and Kambas, A. In-season integrative neuromuscular strength training improves performance of early-adolescent soccer athletes. *J Strength Cond Res* 34(2):516-526, 2020.

29. Pullinen, T, Mero, A, MacDonald, E, Pakarinen, A, and Komi, PV. Plasma catecholamine and serum testosterone responses to four units of resistance exercise in young and adult male athletes. *Eur J Appl Occup Physiol* 77(5):413-420, 1998.

30. Ratamess, NA, Alvar, BA, Evetoch, TE, Housh, TJ, Ben Kibler, W, Kraemer, WJ, and Triplett, NT. Progression models in resistance training for healthy adults. *Med Sci Sport Exerc* 41(3):687-708, 2009.

31. Reilly, T, Bangsbo, J, and Franks, A. Anthropometric and physiological predispositions for elite soccer. *J Sport Sci* 18(9):669-683, 2000.

32. Risso, FG, Jalilvand, F, Orjalo, AJ, Moreno, MR, Davis, DL, Birmingham-Babauta, SA, Stokes, JJ, Stage, AA, Liu, TM, Giuliano, DV, and Lazar, A. Physiological characteristics of projected starters and non-starters in the field positions from a Division I women's soccer team. *Int J Exerc Sci* 10(4):568, 2017.

33. Selye, H. *The Stress of Life*. New York: McGraw Hill, 1956.

34. Selye, H. Stress without distress. In *Psychopathology of Human Adaptation*. Serban, G, ed. Boston: Springer, 137-146, 1976.

35. Sonchan, W, Moungmee, P, and Sootmongkol, A. The effects of a circuit training program on muscle strength, agility, anaerobic performance and cardiovascular endurance. *Int J Med, Health, Biomed, Bioengineer Pharmaceut Engineer* 11(4):170-173, 2017.

36. Spiering, BA, Kraemer, WJ, Anderson, JM, Armstrong, LE, Nindl, BC, Volek, JS, and Maresh, CM. Resistance exercise biology. *Sport Med* 38(7):527-540, 2008.

37. Stone, MH, O'Bryant, H, Garhammer, J, McMillan, J, and Rozenek, R. A theoretical model of strength training. *NSCA J* 4(4):36-39, 1982.

38. Sutton, L, Scott, M, Wallace, J, and Reilly, T. Body composition of English Premier League soccer players: Influence of playing position, international status, and ethnicity. *J Sport Sci* 27(10):1019-1026, 2009.

39. Todd, JS, Shurley, JP, and Todd, T.C. Thomas L. DeLorme and the science of progressive resistance exercise. *J Strength Cond Res* 26(11):2913-2923, 2012.

40. Tesch, P. Skeletal muscle adaptations consequent to long-term heavy resistance exercise. *Med Sci Sport Exerc* 20(5 Suppl):S132-134, 1988.

41. Thiel, TV, Shepherd, J, Espinosa HG, Kenny, M, Fischer K, Worsey, M, Matsuo, A, Wada, T. Predicting ground reaction forces in sprint running using a shank mounted inertial measurement unit. *Proceedings* 2:199, 2018.

42. Varlet, M, and Richardson, MJ. What would be Usain Bolt's 100-meter sprint world record without Tyson Gay? Unintentional interpersonal synchronization between the two sprinters. *J Experiment Psych: Hum Perc Perf* 41(1):36, 2015.

43. Waldén, M, Hägglund, M, Werner, J, and Ekstrand, J. The epidemiology of anterior cruciate ligament injury in football (soccer): A review of the literature from a gender-related perspective. *Knee Surg Sport Traum Arthroscop* 19(1):3-10, 2011.

44. Weyand, PG, Sternlight, DB, Bellizzi, MJ, and Wright, S. Faster top running speeds are achieved with greater ground forces not more rapid leg movements. *J Appl Physiol* 89(5):1991-1999, 2000.

45. Weyand, PG, Sandell, RF, Prime, DN, and Bundle, MW. The biological limits to running speed are imposed from the ground up. *J Appl Physiol* 108(4):950-961, 2010.

46. Wilson, GJ, Murphy, AJ, and Giorgi, A. Weight and plyometric training: Effects on eccentric and concentric force production. *Can J Appl Physiol* 21(4):301-315, 1996.

Chapter 2

1. Bangsbo, J, and Mohr, M. *Individual Training in Football*. Copenhagen: Bangsbosport, 19, 2014.

2. Bangsbo, J, and Mohr, M. *Fitness Testing in Football: Fitness Training in Soccer II*. Copenhagen: Bangsbosport, 36, 2012.

3. Bangsbo, J, and Mohr, M. *Fitness Testing in Football: Fitness Training in Soccer II*. Copenhagen: Bangsbosport, 74, 2012.

4. Bangsbo, J, and Mohr, M. *Fitness Testing in Football: Fitness Training in Soccer II*. Copenhagen: Bangsbosport, 78, 2012.

5. Bradley, P. The physical demands of elite soccer match play. In *Fitness in Soccer: The Science and Practical Application in Soccer*. Van Winckel, J, Helsen, W, McMillian, K, Tenney, D, Meert, JP, Bradley, P, eds. Brooklyn, NY: Moveo Ergo Sum/Klein-Gelman, 33, 2014.

6. Carling, C, Le Gall, F, and Dupont, G. Analysis of repeated high-intensity running in professional soccer. *J. Sport Sci* 30(4):325-336, 2012.

7. Dupont, G, and McCall, A. Targeted systems of the body for training. In *Soccer Science: Using Science to Develop Players and Teams*. Strudwick, A, ed. Champaign, IL: Human Kinetics, 221, 2016.

8. Dupont, G, and McCall, A., Targeted systems of the body for training. In *Soccer Science: Using Science to Develop Players and Teams*. Strudwick, A, ed. Champaign, IL: Human Kinetics, 228, 2016.

9. Mascio, M, and Bradley, PS. Evaluation of the most intense high-intensity running period in English FA Premier League soccer matches. *J. Strength Cond Res* 27(4):909-915, 2013.

10. Mohr, M, Krustrup P, and Bangsbo, J. Match performance of high-standard soccer players with special reference to development of fatigue. *J Sport Sci* 21:439-449, 2003.

11. Rampinini, E, Sassi, A, Morelli, A, Mazzoni, S, Fanchini, M, and Coutts, A. Repeated-sprint ability in professional and amateur soccer players. *Appl Physiol Nutr Metab* 34(6):1048-1054, 2009.

12. Sheppard, JM, and Young, WB. Agility literature review: Classifications, training and testing. *J Sports Sci* 24(9):919-932, 2006.

13. Verstegen, M, Marcello, B. Agility and coordination. In *High-Performance Sports Conditioning: Modern Training for Ultimate Athletic Development*. Foran, B, ed. Champaign, IL: Human Kinetics, 141, 2001.

Chapter 3

1. Altmann, S, Ringhof, S, Neumann, R, Woll, A, and Rumpf, MC. Validity and reliability of speed tests used in soccer: A systematic review. *PLOS One* 14, 2019.

2. Arnason, A, Sigurdsson, SB, Gudmundsson, A, Holme, I, Engebretsen, L, and Bahr, R. Physical fitness, injuries, and team performance in soccer. *Med Sci Sports Exerc* 36:278-285, 2004.

3. Askling, C, Karlsson, J, and Thorstensson, A. Hamstring injury occurrence in elite soccer players after preseason strength training with eccentric overload. *Scand J Med Sci Sports* 13:244-250, 2003.

4. Bangsbo, J, Iaia, FM, and Krustrup, P. The yo-yo intermittent recovery test. *Sports Med* 38:37-51, 2008.

5. Berthoin, S, Gerbeaux, M, Turpin, E, Guerrin, F, Lensel-Corbeil, G, and Vandendorpe, F. Comparison of two field tests to estimate maximum aerobic speed. *J Sports Sci* 12:355-362, 1994.

6. Billat, LV. Interval training for performance: A scientific and empirical practice. *Sports Med* 31:13-31, 2001.

7. Bishop, C, Read, P, Chavda, S, and Turner, A. Asymmetries of the lower limb: The calculation conundrum in strength training and conditioning. *Strength Cond J* 38:27-32, 2016.

8. Bloomfield, J, Polman, R, and O'Donoghue, P. Physical demands of different positions in FA Premier League soccer. *J Sports Sci Med* 6:63, 2007.

9. Bourne, MN, Opar, DA, Williams, MD, and Shield, AJ. Eccentric knee flexor strength and risk of hamstring injuries in rugby union: A prospective study. *Am J Sports Med* 43:2663-2670, 2015.

10. Brady, CJ, Harrison, AJ, and Comyns, TM. A review of the reliability of biomechanical variables produced during the isometric mid-thigh pull and isometric squat and the reporting of normative data. *Sports Biomech* 19:1-25, 2020.

11. Brady, CJ, Harrison, AJ, Flanagan, EP, Haff, GG, and Comyns, TM. A comparison of the isometric midthigh pull and isometric squat: Intraday reliability, usefulness, and the magnitude of difference between tests. *Int J sports Physiol Perform* 13:844-852, 2018.

12. Buchheit, M. The 30-15 intermittent fitness test: Accuracy for individualizing interval training of young intermittent sport players. *J Strength Cond Res* 22:365-374, 2008.

13. Buchheit, M. The 30-15 intermittent fitness test: 10-year review. *Myorobie J* 1:278, 2010.

14. Buchheit, M, Cholley, Y, Nagel, M, and Poulos, N. The effect of body mass on eccentric knee-flexor strength assessed with an instrumented Nordic hamstring device (Nordbord) in football players. *Int J Sports Physiol Perform* 11:721-726, 2016.

15. Buchheit, M, Simpson, BM, Hader, K, and Lacome, M. Practical solutions to submaximal Nordics: Insights for exercise familiarization and return to train following knee flexors injury. *Sport Perf Sci Reports* 1, 2019.

16. Castagna, C, Impellizzeri, FM, Chamari, K, Carlomagno, D, and Rampinini, E. Aerobic fitness and yo-yo continuous and intermittent tests performances in soccer players: A correlation study. *J Strength Cond Res* 20:320-325, 2006.

17. Cometti, G, Maffiuletti, N, Pousson, M, Chatard, J-C, and Maffulli, N. Isokinetic strength and anaerobic power of elite, subelite and amateur French soccer players. *Int J Sports Med* 22:45-51, 2001.

18. Comfort, P, Dos'Santos, T, Beckham, GK, Stone, MH, Guppy, SN, and Haff, GG. Standardization and methodological considerations for the isometric midthigh pull. *Strength Cond J* 41:57-79, 2019.

19. Currell, K, and Jeukendrup, AE. Validity, reliability and sensitivity of measures of sporting performance. *Sports Med* 38:297-316, 2008.

20. Datson, N, Hulton, A, Andersson, H, Lewis, T, Weston, M, Drust, B, and Gregson, W. Applied physiology of female soccer: An update. *Sports Med* 44:1225-1240, 2014.

21. Deprez, D, Fransen, J, Boone, J, Lenoir, M, Philippaerts, R, and Vaeyens, R. Characteristics of high-level youth soccer players: Variation by playing position. *J Sports Sci* 33:243-254, 2015.

22. Dos'Santos, T, Thomas, C, Comfort, P, McMahon, JJ, Jones, PA, Oakley, NP, and Young, AL. Between-session reliability of isometric midthigh pull kinetics and maximal power clean performance in male youth soccer players. *J Strength Cond Res* 32:3364-3372, 2018.

23. Dos'Santos, T, Thomas, C, Comfort, P, McMahon, JJ, and Jones, PA. Relationships between isometric force-time characteristics and dynamic performance. *Sports* 5:68, 2017.

24. Dupont, G, Defontaine, M, Bosquet, L, Blondel, N, Moalla, W, and Berthoin, S. Yo-yo intermittent recovery test versus the Université de Montreal Track Test: Relation with a high-intensity intermittent exercise. *J Sci Med Sport* 13:146-150, 2010.

25. Ekstrand, J, Hägglund, M, and Waldén, M. Injury incidence and injury patterns in professional football: The UEFA injury study. *Br J Sports Med* 45:553-558, 2011.

26. Emmonds, S, Sawczuk, T, Scantlebury, S, Till, K, and Jones, B. Seasonal changes in the physical performance of elite youth female soccer players. *J Strength Cond Res* 34(9):2636-2643, 2018.

27. Faude, O, Koch, T, and Meyer, T. Straight sprinting is the most frequent action in goal situations in professional football. *J Sports Sci* 30:625-631, 2012.

28. Gabbett, TJ. The development of a test of repeated-sprint ability for elite women's soccer players. *J Strength Cond Res* 24:1191-1194, 2010.

29. Gabbett, TJ, Kelly, JN, and Sheppard, JM. Speed, change of direction speed, and reactive agility of rugby league players. *J Strength Cond Res* 22:174-181, 2008.

30. Gerodimos, V, Karatrantou, K, Paschalis, V, Zafeiridis, A, Katsareli, E, Bilios, P, and Kellis, S. Reliability of concentric and eccentric strength of hip abductor and adductor muscles in young soccer players. *Biol* 32:351, 2015.

31. Girard, O, Mendez-Villanueva, A, and Bishop, D. Repeated-sprint ability—Part I. *Sports Med* 41:673-694, 2011.

32. Halperin, I, Williams, KJ, Martin, DT, and Chapman, DW. The effects of attentional focusing instructions on force production during the isometric midthigh pull. *J Strength Cond Res* 30:919-923, 2016.

33. Haugen, T, and Buchheit, M. Sprint running performance monitoring: Methodological and practical considerations. *Sports Med* 46:641-656, 2016.

34. Haugen, TA, Breitschädel, F, and Seiler, S. Sprint mechanical properties in soccer players according to playing standard, position, age and sex. *J Sports Sci* 17:1-7, 2020.

35. Helgerud, J, Engen, LC, Wisløff, U, and Hoff, J. Aerobic endurance training improves soccer performance. *Med Sci Sports Exerc* 33:1925-1931, 2001.

36. Hetzler, RK, Stickley, CD, Lundquist, KM, and Kimura, IF. Reliability and accuracy of handheld stopwatches compared with electronic timing in measuring sprint performance. *J Strength Cond Res* 22:1969-1976, 2008.

37. Hori, N, Newton, RU, Andrews, WA, Kawamori, N, McGuigan, MR, and Nosaka, K. Does performance of hang power clean differentiate performance of jumping, sprinting, and changing of direction? *J Strength Cond Res* 22:412-418, 2008.

38. Jordan, MJ, Aagaard, P, and Herzog, W. Anterior cruciate ligament injury/reinjury in alpine ski racing: A narrative review. *Open Access J Sports Med* 8:71, 2017.

39. Krustrup, P, Zebis, M, Jensen, JM, and Mohr, M. Game-induced fatigue patterns in elite female soccer. *J Strength Cond Res* 24:437-441, 2010.

40. Kuki, S, Sato, K, Stone, MH, Okano, K, Yoshida, T, and Tanigawa, S. The relationship between isometric mid-thigh pull variables, jump variables and sprint performance in collegiate soccer players. *J Trainol* 6:42-46, 2017.

41. Langhout, R, Weir, A, Litjes, W, Gozeling, M, Stubbe, JH, Kerkhoffs, G, and Tak, I. Hip and groin injury is the most common non-time-loss injury in female amateur football. *Knee Surg Sports Traumatol Arthrosc* 27:3133-3141, 2019.

42. Laursen, P, and Buchheit, M. *Science and Application of High-Intensity Interval Training.* Champaign, IL: Human Kinetics, 2019.

43. Layer, JS, Grenz, C, Hinshaw, TJ, Smith, DT, Barrett, SF, and Dai, B. Kinetic analysis of isometric back squats and isometric belt squats. *J Strength Cond Res* 32:3301-3309, 2018.

44. Lockie, RG, Liu, TM, Stage, AA, Lazar, A, Giuliano, DV, Hurley, JM, Torne, IA, Beiley, MD, Birmingham-Babauta, SA, and Stokes, JJ. Assessing repeated-sprint ability in Division I collegiate women soccer players. *J Strength Cond Res* 26, 2018.

45. Lodge, C, Tobin, D, O'Rourke, B, and Thorborg, K. Reliability and validity of a new eccentric hamstring strength measurement device. *Arch Rehabil Res Clin Transl* 2:100034, 2020.

46. Malone, S, Hughes, B, Doran, DA, Collins, K, and Gabbett, TJ. Can the workload–injury relationship be moderated by improved strength, speed and repeated-sprint qualities? *Journal Sci Medicine Sport* 22:29-34, 2019.

47. Markovic, G, Sarabon, N, Boban, F, Zoric, I, Jelcic, M, Sos, K, and Scappaticci, M. Nordic hamstring strength of highly trained youth football players and its relation to sprint performance. *J Strength Cond Res* 34:800-807, 2020.

48. McGawley, K, and Andersson, P-I. The order of concurrent training does not affect soccer-related performance adaptations. *Int J Sports Med* 34:983-990, 2013.

49. McMahon, JJ, Stapley, JT, Suchomel, TJ, and Comfort, P. Relationships between lower body muscle structure and isometric mid-thigh pull peak force. *J Trainol* 4:43-48, 2015.

50. Moeskops, S, Oliver, JL, Read, PJ, Cronin, JB, Myer, GD, Haff, GG, and Lloyd, RS. Within- and between-session reliability of the isometric mid-thigh pull in young female athletes. *J Strength Cond Res* 32:1892, 2018.

51. Morin, J-B, Jiménez-Reyes, P, Brughelli, M, and Samozino, P. When jump height is not a good indicator of lower limb maximal power output: Theoretical demonstration, experimental evidence and practical solutions. *Sports Med* 49:999-1006, 2019.

52. Morin, J-B, and Samozino, P. Interpreting power-force-velocity profiles for individualized and specific training. *Int J Sports Physiol Perform* 11:267-272, 2016.

53. Morin, J-B, Samozino, P, Murata, M, Cross, MR, and Nagahara, R. A simple method for computing sprint acceleration kinetics from running velocity data: Replication study with improved design. *J Biomech* 94:82-87, 2019.

54. Morris, RO, Jones, B, Myers, T, Lake, J, Emmonds, S, Clarke, ND, Singleton, D, Ellis, M, and Till, K. Isometric midthigh pull characteristics in elite youth male soccer players: Comparisons by age and maturity offset. *J Strength Cond Res* 34(10):2947-2955, 2018.

55. Nimphius, S, Callaghan, SJ, Spiteri, T, and Lockie, RG. Change of direction deficit: A more isolated measure of change of direction performance than total 505 time. *J Strength Cond Res* 30:3024-3032, 2016.

56. O'Brien, M, Bourne, MN, Heerey, J, Timmins, RG, and Pizzari, T. A novel device to assess hip strength: Concurrent validity and normative values in male athletes. *Phys Ther Sport* 35:63-68, 2019.

57. Pardos-Mainer, E, Casajús, JA, and Gonzalo-Skok, O. Reliability and sensitivity of jumping, linear sprinting and change of direction ability tests in adolescent female football players. *Sci Med Footb* 3:183-190, 2019.

58. Ramos-Campo, DJ, Rubio-Arias, J, Carrasco-Poyatos, M, and Alcaraz, P. Physical performance of elite and subelite Spanish female futsal players. *Biol Sport* 33:297, 2016.

59. Romero-Franco, N, Jiménez-Reyes, P, Castaño-Zambudio, A, Capelo-Ramírez, F, Rodríguez-Juan, JJ, González-Hernández, J, Toscano-Bendala, FJ, Cuadrado-Peñafiel, V, and Balsalobre-Fernández, C. Sprint performance and mechanical outputs computed with an iPhone app: Comparison with existing reference methods. *Eur J Sport Sci* 17:386-392, 2017.

60. Ryan, S, Kempton, T, Pacecca, E, and Coutts, AJ. Measurement properties of an adductor strength-assessment system in professional Australian footballers. *Int J Sports Physiol Perform* 14:256-259, 2019.

61. Sayers, SP, Harackiewicz, DV, Harman, EA, Frykman, PN, and Rosenstein, MT. Cross-validation of three jump power equations. *Med Sci Sports Exerc* 31:572-577, 1999.

62. Schmitz, B, Pfeifer, C, Kreitz, K, Borowski, M, Faldum, A, and Brand, S-M. The yo-yo intermittent tests: A systematic review and structured compendium of test results. *Front Physiol* 9:870, 2018.

63. Sheppard, JM, and Young, WB. Agility literature review: Classifications, training and testing. *J Sports Sci* 24:919-932, 2006.

64. Slimani, M, and Nikolaidis, PT. Anthropometric and physiological characteristics of male soccer players according to their competitive level, playing position and age group: A systematic review. *J Sports Med Phys Fitness* 59:141-163, 2019.

65. Spencer, M, Pyne, D, Santisteban, J, and Mujika, I. Fitness determinants of repeated-sprint ability in highly trained youth football players. *Int J Sports Physiol Perform* 6:497-508, 2011.

66. Stølen, T, Chamari, K, Castagna, C, and Wisløff, U. Physiology of soccer. *Sports Med* 35:501-536, 2005.

67. Thomas, C, Comfort, P, Chiang, C-Y, and Jones, PA. Relationship between isometric mid-thigh pull variables and sprint and change of direction performance in collegiate athletes. *J Trainol* 4:6-10, 2015.

68. Thomas, C, Dos'Santos, T, Cuthbert, M, Fields, C, and Jones, PA. The effect of limb preference on braking strategy and knee joint mechanics during pivoting in female soccer players. *Sci Med Footb* 4:30-36, 2020.

69. Thomas, C, Dos'Santos, T, Comfort, P, and Jones, PA. Relationships between unilateral muscle strength qualities and change of direction in adolescent team-sport athletes. *Sports* 6:83, 2018.

70. Thomas, C, Dos'Santos, T, and Jones, PA. A comparison of dynamic strength index between team-sport athletes. *Sports* 5:71, 2017.

71. Thorborg, K, Bandholm, T, and Hölmich, P. Hip- and knee-strength assessments using a hand-held dynamometer with external belt-fixation are inter-tester reliable. *Knee Surg Sports Traumatol Arthrosc* 21:550-555, 2013.

72. Thorborg, K, Couppé, C, Petersen, J, Magnusson, S, and Hölmich, P. Eccentric hip adduction and abduction strength in elite soccer players and matched controls: A cross-sectional study. *Br J Sports Med* 45:10-13, 2011.

73. Thorborg, K, Serner, A, Petersen, J, Madsen, TM, Magnusson, P, and Hölmich, P. Hip adduction and abduction strength profiles in elite soccer players: Implications for clinical evaluation of hip adductor muscle recovery after injury. *Am J Sports Med* 39:121-126, 2011.

74. Toohey, LA, De Noronha, M, Taylor, C, and Thomas, J. Is a sphygmomanometer a valid and reliable tool to measure the isometric strength of hip muscles? A systematic review. *Physiother Theory Pract* 31:114-119, 2015.

75. Tummala, SV, Chhabra, A, Makovicka, JL, Patel, KA, and Hartigan, DE. Hip and groin injuries among collegiate male soccer players: The 10-year epidemiology, incidence, and prevention. *Orthopedics* 41:e831-e836, 2018.

76. Turner, A, Brazier, J, Bishop, C, Chavda, S, Cree, J, and Read, P. Data analysis for strength and conditioning coaches: Using Excel to analyze reliability, differences, and relationships. *Strength Cond J* 37:76-83, 2015.

77. Turner, A, Walker, S, Stembridge, M, Coneyworth, P, Reed, G, Birdsey, L, Barter, P, and Moody, J. A testing battery for the assessment of fitness in soccer players. *Strength Cond J* 33:29-39, 2011.

78. Vescovi, JD, Rupf, R, Brown, T, and Marques, M. Physical performance characteristics of high-level female soccer players 12–21 years of age. *Scand J Med Science Sports* 21:670-678, 2011.

79. Walker, S, and Turner, A. A one-day field test battery for the assessment of aerobic capacity, anaerobic capacity, speed, and agility of soccer players. *Strength Cond J* 31:52-60, 2009.

80. Wik, EH, Auliffe, SM, and Read, PJ. Examination of physical characteristics and positional differences in professional soccer players in Qatar. *Sports* 7:9, 2019.

81. Williams, DA, Hall, CD, Cantor, P, Williams, J, Brown, N, Dulling, R, and Egbujor, O. Reliability of two alternative methods for the standard mid-thigh isometric pull. *International Conference of Biomechanics in Sports.* Johnson City, TN, 2014.

82. Young, WB, and Rath, DA. Enhancing foot velocity in football kicking: The role of strength training. *J Strength Cond Res* 25:561-566, 2011.

Chapter 4

1. French, DN. Advanced power techniques. In *Developing Power.* McGuigan, M, ed. Champaign, IL: Human Kinetics, 191, 2017.

2. Gentil, P, Bottaro, M, Oliveira, E, Veloso, J, Amorim, N, Saiuri, A, and Wagner, DR. Chronic effects of different between-set rest durations on muscle strength in nonresistance trained young men. *J Strength Cond Res* 24(1):37-42, 2010.

3. Haff, GG, and Haff, EE. Resistance training program design. In *NSCA's Essentials of Personal Training.* 2nd ed. Coburn, JW, and Malek, MH, eds. Champaign, IL: Human Kinetics, 345-388, 2012.

4. Harries, SK, Lubans, DR, and Callister, R. Systematic review and meta-analysis of linear and undulating periodized resistance training programs on muscular strength. *J Strength Cond Res* 29(4):1113-1125, 2015.

5. Issurin, V. Block periodization versus traditional training theory: A review. *J Sports Med Phys Fitness* 48(1):65, 2008.

6. Mann, B. *The APRE: The Scientifically Proven Fastest Way to Get Strong.* London, OH: EliteFTS, 2011.

7. Mann, JB, Ivey, PA, and Sayers, SP. Velocity-based training in football. *Strength Cond J* 37(6):52-57, 2015.

8. Mann, JB, Thyfault, JP, Ivey, PA, and Sayers, SP. The effect of autoregulatory progressive resistance exercise vs. linear periodization on strength improvement in college athletes. *J Strength Cond Res* 24(7):1718-1723, 2010.

9. Otero-Esquina, C, de Hoyo Lora, M, Gonzalo-Skok, Ó, Domínguez-Cobo, S, and Sánchez, H. Is strength-training frequency a key factor to develop performance adaptations in young elite soccer players? *Eur J Sport Sci* 17(10):1241-1251, 2017.

10. Ratamess, NA. Resistance training. In *NSCA's Guide to Program Design.* Hoffman, J, ed. Champaign, IL: Human Kinetics, 71-94, 2012.

11. Rhea, MR, Phillips, WT, Burkett, LN, Stone, WJ, Ball, SD, Alvar, BA, and Thomas, AB. A comparison of linear and daily undulating periodized programs with equated volume and intensity for local muscular endurance. *J Strength Cond Res* 17(1):82-87, 2003.

12. Ribeiro, J, Afonso, J, Camões, M, Sarmento, H, Sá, M, Lima, R, Oliveira, R, and Clemente, FM. Methodological characteristics, physiological and physical effects, and future directions for combined training in soccer: A systematic review. *Healthcare* 9(8):1075, 2021.

13. Rønnestad, BR, Nymark, BS, and Raastad, T. Effects of in-season strength maintenance training frequency in professional soccer players. *J Strength Cond Res* 25(10):2653-2660, 2011.

14. Schoenfeld, BJ, Pope, ZK, Benik, FM, Hester, GM, Sellers, J, Nooner, JL, Schnaiter, JA, Bond-Williams, KE, Carter, AS, Ross, CL, and Just, BL. Longer interset rest periods enhance muscle strength and hypertrophy in resistance-trained men. *J Strength Cond Res* 30(7):1805-1812, 2016.

15. Sheppard, JM, and Triplett, NT. Program design for resistance training. In *Essentials of Strength Training and Conditioning*. 4th ed. Haff, G, Triplett, NT, eds. Champaign, IL: Human Kinetics, 439-470, 2016.

16. Silva III, JM. An analysis of the training stress syndrome in competitive athletics. *J App Sport Psych* 2(1):5-20, 1990.

17. Zatsiorsky, VM, Kraemer, WJ, and Fry, AC. *Science and Practice of Strength Training*. 3rd ed. Champaign, IL: Human Kinetics, 2021.

Chapter 5

1. Caulfield, S, and Berninger, D. Exercise technique for free weight and machine training. In *Essentials of Strength Training and Conditioning*. 4th ed. Haff, GG, and Triplett, NT, eds. Champaign, IL: Human Kinetics, 351-408, 2016.

2. National Strength and Conditioning Association. *Exercise Technique Manual for Resistance Training*. 3rd ed. Champaign, IL: Human Kinetics, 2016.

Chapter 6

1. Caulfield, S, and Berninger, D. Exercise technique for free weight and machine training. In *Essentials of Strength Training and Conditioning*. 4th ed. Haff, GG, and Triplett, NT, eds. Champaign, IL: Human Kinetics, 351-408, 2016.

2. Mann, B. *The APRE: The Scientifically Proven Fastest Way to Get Strong*. London, OH: EliteFTS, 2011.

3. National Strength and Conditioning Association. *Exercise Technique Manual for Resistance Training*. 3rd ed. Champaign, IL: Human Kinetics, 2016.

4. Sheppard, JM, and Triplett, NT. Program design for resistance training. In *Essentials of Strength Training and Conditioning*. 4th ed. Haff, GG, and Triplett, NT, eds. Champaign, IL: Human Kinetics, 439-470, 2016.

Chapter 7

1. Caulfield, S, and Berninger, D. Exercise techniques for free weight and machine training. In *Essentials of Strength Training and Conditioning*. 4th ed. Haff, GG, and Triplett, NT, eds. Champaign, IL: Human Kinetics, 351-408, 2016.

2. Haff, GG, Caulfield, S, and Berninger, D. Exercise techniques for alternative modes and nontraditional implement training. In *Essentials of Strength Training and Conditioning*. 4th ed. Haff, GG, and Triplett, NT, eds. Champaign, IL: Human Kinetics, 409-438, 2016.

3. Jeffreys, I, and Goodwin, J. Developing speed and agility for sports performance. In *Strength and Conditioning for Sports Performance*. Jeffreys, I, and Moody J, eds. London: Routledge, 341-371, 2016.

Chapter 8

1. Biel, A. *Trail Guide to the Body: A Hands on Guide to Locating Muscles, Bones, and More*. 4th ed. Boulder, CO: Books of Discovery, 2010.

2. Bien, DP. Rationale and implementation of anterior cruciate ligament injury prevention warm-up programs in female athletes. *J Strength Cond Res* 25:271-285, 2011.

3. Boden, BP, Dean, GS, Feagin Jr., JA, and Garrett Jr, WE. Mechanisms of anterior cruciate ligament injury. *Orthopedics* 23:573-578, 2000.

4. Callaghan, JP, and McGill, SM. Intervertebral disc herniation: Studies on a porcine model exposed to highly repetitive flexion/extension motion with compressive force. *Clin Biomech* 16:28-37, 2001.

5. Gunning, JL, Callaghan, JP, and McGill, SM. Spinal posture and prior loading history modulate compressive strength and type of failure in the spine: A biomechanical study using a porcine cervical spine model. *Clin Biomech* 16:471-480, 2001.

6. Hewett, TE, Myer, GD, Ford, KR, Paterno, MW, and Quatman, CE. The 2012 ABJS Nicolas Andry Award: The sequence of prevention: A systematic approach to prevent anterior cruciate ligament injury. *Clin Orthop Relat Res* 470:2930-2940, 2012.

7. McGill, SM. Core training: Evidence translating to better performance and injury prevention. *Strength Cond J* 32:33-46, 2010.

8. McGill, SM. *Ultimate Back Fitness and Performance*. 4th ed. Waterloo, Canada: Backfitpro, 84-86, 2009.

9. Mendrin, N, Lynn, S, Griffith-Merritt, H, and Noffal, G. Progressions of isometric core training. *Strength Cond J* 38:50-65, 2010.

10. Meyers, T. *Anatomy Trains: Myofascial Meridians for Manual and Movement Therapists*. 1st ed. London: Churchill Livingstone, 2001.

11. Neumann, D. *Kinesiology of the Musculoskeletal System: Foundations for Physical Rehabilitation*. 3rd ed. St. Louis: Mosby, 2002.

12. Snell, P. *Case Study-Lateral Elbow Pain through a DNS/Functional Lens*. MyRehabExercise.com. https://myrehabexercise.com/blog/tag/phillip-snell/. Accessed November 29, 2021.

13. Zazulak, BT, Hewett, TE, Reeves, NP, Goldberg, B, and Cholewicki J. The effects of core proprioception on knee injury: A prospective biomechanical-epidemiologic study. *Am J Sports Med* 35:368-373, 2007.

14. Zazulak, BT, Ponce, PL, Straub, SJ, Medvecky, MJ, Avedisian, L, and Hewett, TE. Gender comparison of hip muscle activity during single-leg landing. *J Orthop Sports Phys Ther* 35:292-299, 2005.

15. Zebis, MK, Bencke, J, Anderson, LL, Dossing, S, Alkjaer, T, Magnusson, SP, Kjaer, M, and Aagaard, P. The effects of neuromuscular training on knee joint motor control during sidecutting in female elite soccer and handball players. *Clin J Sport Med* 18:329-337, 2008.

Chapter 9

1. Alexander, RM. Mechanics of the skeleton and tendons. In *Handbook of Physiology, Section I: The Nervous System.* Brookhardt, JM, Mountcastle, VB, Brooks, VB, and Greiger, SR, eds. Bethesda, MD: American Physiological Society, 17-142, 1981.

2. Behm, DG, and Sale DG. Intended rather than actual movement velocity determines velocity-specific training response. *J Appl Physiol* 74(1):359-68, 1993.

3. Bompa, T, and Buzzichelli, CA. *Periodization Training for Sports.* Champaign, IL: Human Kinetics, 108-296, 2015.

4. Brumitt, J, Engilis, A, Eubanks, A, Mattocks, A, Peet, J, and Bush, N. Risk factors associated with noncontact time-loss lower-quadrant injury in male collegiate soccer players. *Sci Med Footb* 1(2):96-101, 2017.

5. Brumitt, J, Mattocks, A, Engilis, A, Sikkema, J, and Loew, J. Off-season training habits and BMI, not preseason jump measures, are associated with time-loss injury in female collegiate soccer players. *Sports* 8(3):36, 2020.

6. Buchheit, M, Morgan, W, Wallace, J, Bode, M, and Poulos, N. Physiological, psychometric, and performance effects of the Christmas break in Australian football. *Int J Sports Physiol Perform* 10(1):120-123, 2015.

7. Chiu, LZF, Fry, AC, Weiss, LW, Schilling, BK, Brown, LE, Smith, SL. Postactivation potentiation response in athletic and recreationally trained individuals. *J Strength Cond Res* 17(4):671-677, 2003.

8. Favero, TG, and White, J. Periodization in college soccer. *Strength Cond J* 40(3):33-44, 2018.

9. Foster, C. Monitoring training in athletes with reference to overtraining syndrome. *Med Sci Sports Exerc* 30:1164-1168, 1998.

10. Haff, GG. The essentials of periodisation. In *Strength and Conditioning for Sports Performance.* Jeffreys, I, and Moody, J, eds. London: Routledge, Taylor & Francis, 409-435, 2016.

11a. Haff, GG, and Triplett, NT. *Essentials of Strength Training and Conditioning.* 4th ed. Champaign, IL: Human Kinetics, 107-595, 2016.

11b. Hewett, TE, Myer, GD, Ford, KR, Heidt, RS, Colosimo, AJ, McLean, SG, Van den Bogert, AJ, Paterno, MV, and Succop, P. Biomechanical measures of neuromuscular control and valgus loading of the knee predict anterior cruciate ligament injury risk in female athletes: A prospective study. *Amer J Sport Med* 33(4):492-501, 2005.

12a. Hopper, A, Haff, EE, Barley, OR, Joyce, C, Lloyd, RS, and Haff, GG. Neuromuscular training improves movement competency and physical performance measures in 11-13-year-old female netball athletes. *J Strength Cond Res* 31:1165-1176, 2017.

12b. King, I. *How to Write Strength Training Programs.* Toowong (AUS): Kings Sport Publishing, 123, 1998.

12. Ranson, C, and Joyce, D. Enhancing movement efficiency. In *High-Performance Training for Sports.* Joyce, D, ed. Champaign, IL: Human Kinetics, 33, 2013.

13. Lloyd, RS, and Oliver, JL. The youth physical development model: A new approach to long-term athletic development. *Strength Cond J* 34:61-72, 2012.

14. Loturco, I, Pereira, LA, Kobal, R, Maldonado, T, Piazzi, AF, Bottino, A, Kitamura, K, Cal Abad, CC, de Arruda, M, and Nakamura, FY. Improving sprint performance in soccer: Effectiveness of jump squat and Olympic push press exercises. *PLOS One* 11(4):e0153958, 2016.

15. Macdonald, B, O'Neill, J, Pollock, N, and Hooren, BV. Single-leg Roman chair hold is more effective than the Nordic hamstring curl in improving hamstring strength-endurance in Gaelic footballers with previous hamstring injury. *J Strength Cond Res* 33(12):3302-3308, 2019.

16. McNamara, JM, and Stearne, DJ. Flexible nonlinear periodization in a beginner college weight training class. *J Strength Cond Res* 24:17-22, 2010.

17. Pichardo, AW, Oliver, JL, Harrison, CB, Maulder, PS, Lloyd, RS, and Kandoi, R. The influence of maturity offset, strength, and movement competency on motor skill performance in adolescent males. *Sports* 7(7):168, 2019.

18. Bogdanis, G, Papaspyrou, A, Souglis, A, Theos, A, Sotiropoulos, A, and Maridaki, M. Effects of hypertrophy and a maximal strength training programme on speed, force and power of soccer players. In *Science and Football VI, the Proceedings of the Sixth World Congress on Science and Football, Antalya, Turkey, January 2007.* Reilly, T, and Korkusuz, F, eds. New York: Routledge, 290-295, 2008.

19. Requena, B, González-Badillo, J, Villareal, E, Ereline, J, García, I, Gapeyeva, H, and Pääsuke, M. Functional performance, maximal strength, and power characteristics in isometric and dynamic actions of lower extremities in soccer players. *J Strength Cond Res* 23(5):1391-1401, 2009.

20. Reynolds, JM, Gordon, TJ, and Roberg, RA. Prediction of one repetition maximum strength from multiple repetition maximum testing and anthropometry. *J Strength Cond Res* 20(3):584-582, 2006.

21. Ryan D, McCall A, Fitzpatrick G, Hennessy L, Meyer T, and McCunn R. The influence of maturity status on movement quality among English Premier League academy soccer players. *Sport Perf Sci Rep* 32:1-3, 2018.

22. Ryan, D, Lewin, C, Forsythe, S, and McCall, A. Developing world-class soccer players: An example from the academy physical development program from an English Premier League team. *Strength Cond J* 40:2-11, 2017.

23. Stone, MH, Sanborn, K, O'Bryant, HS, Harman, M, Stone, ME, Proulx, C, Ward, B, and Hruby, J. Maximum strength-power-performance relationship in collegiate throwers. *J Strength Cond Res* 17:739-745, 2003.

24. Suchomel, TJ, Nimphius, S, Bellon, CR, and Stone, MH. The importance of muscular strength: Training considerations. *Sports Med* 48(4):765-785, 2018.

25. Støren, O, Helgerud, J, Støa, E, and Hoff, J. Maximal strength training improves running economy in distance runners. *Med Sci Sports Exerc* 40(6):1087-1092, 2008.

26. Tumilty, D. Physiological characteristics of elite soccer players. *Sports Med* 16(2):80-96, 1993.

27. Wing, CE, Turner, AN, and Bishop, CJ. The importance of strength and power on key performance indicators in elite youth soccer. *J Strength Cond Res* 34(7):2006-2014, 2020.

Chapter 10

1. Baechle, TR, Earle, RW, and Wathen, D. Resistance training. In *Essentials of Strength Training and Conditioning*. 2nd ed. Baechle, TR, and Earle, RW, eds. Champaign, IL: Human Kinetics, 395-426, 2000.

2. Ekstrand, J, Bengtsson, H, and Hallen, A. UEFA. UEFA Elite Club Injury Study—2018/19 Season Report. www.uefa.com/MultimediaFiles/Download/uefaorg/Medical/02/61/67/86/2616786_DOWNLOAD.pdf. Accessed September 27, 2020.

3. Franchi, MV, Atherton, PJ, Reeves, ND, Flück, M, Williams, J, Mitchell, WK, Selby, A, Beltran Valls, RM, and Narici, MV. Architectural, functional and molecular responses to concentric and eccentric loading in human skeletal muscle. *Acta Physiologica* 210(3):642-654, 2014.

4a. Gamble, P. *Training for Sports Speed and Agility: An Evidence-Based Approach*. Oxon, UK: Routledge, 7-19, 2012.

4b. King, I. *How to Write Strength Training Programs*. Toowong (AUS): Kings Sport Publishing, 123, 1998.

5. Magnusson, SP, and Kjaer, M. The impact of loading, unloading, ageing and injury on the human tendon. *J Physiol* 597:1283-1298, 2019.

6. Mann, B. *The APRE: The Scientifically Proven Fastest Way to Get Strong*. London, OH: EliteFTS, 2011.

7. Peterson, MD, Rhea, MR, and Alvar, BA. Applications of the dose-response for strength development: A review of meta-analytic efficacy and reliability for designing training prescription. *J Strength Cond Res* 19:950-958, 2005.

8. Rønnestad, BR, Nymark, BS, and Raastad, T. Effects of in-season strength maintenance training frequency in professional soccer players. *J Strength Cond Res* 25(10):2653-2660, 2011.

9. Sheppard, JM, and Triplett, TN. Program design for resistance training. In *Essentials of Strength Training and Conditioning*. 4th ed. Haff, GG, and Triplett, NT, eds. Champaign, IL: Human Kinetics, 440-470, 2016.

10. Silva, JR, Nassis, GP, and Rebelo, A. Strength training in soccer with a specific focus on highly trained players. *Sports Med Int Open* 1(1):1-17, 2015.

11. Turner, AN, and Stewart, PF. Strength and conditioning for soccer players. *Strength Cond J* 36(4):1-13, 2014.

12. Watanabe, K, Nunome, H, Inoue, K, Iga, T, and Akima, H. Electromyographic analysis of hip adductor muscles in soccer instep and side-foot kicking. *Sports Biomech* 19(3):295-306, 2020.

13. Wong, PL, Chaouachi, A, Chamari, K, Dellal, A, and Wisloff, U. Effect of preseason concurrent muscular strength and high-intensity interval training in professional soccer players. *J Strength Cond Res* 24(3):653-660, 2010.

Chapter 11

1. Bourne, MN, Timmins, RG, Opar, DA, Pizzari, T, Ruddy, JD, Sims, C, Williams, MD, and Shield, AJ. An evidence-based framework for strengthening exercises to prevent hamstring injuries. *Sports Med* 2:251-267, 2018.

2. Laputin, NP, and Oleshko, VG. *Managing the Training of Weightlifters*. Kiev, Ukraine: Zdorov'ya Publishers, 1982.

3a. Kraemer, WJ, and Ratamess, NA. Fundamental of resistance training: Progression and exercise prescription. *Med Sci Sports Exerc* 4:674-688, 2004.

3b. King, I. *How to Write Strength Training Programs*. Toowong (AUS): Kings Sport Publishing, 123, 1998.

4. Silva, JR, Nassis, GP, and Rebelo, A. Strength training in soccer with a specific focus on highly trained players. *Sports Med Int Open* 1(1):1-17, 2015.

Chapter 12 Recommended Reading

Alexander, R. *Complete Conditioning for Soccer*. Champaign, IL: Human Kinetics, 2021.

Haff, GG. Periodization. In *Essentials of Strength Training and Conditioning*. 4th ed. Haff, GG, and Triplett, NT, eds. Champaign, IL: Human Kinetics, 583-604, 2016.

King, I. *How to Write Strength Training Programs*. Toowong (AUS): Kings Sport Publishing, 123, 1998.

McGuigan, M. Team sport power training. In *Developing Power*. McGuigan, M, ed., Champaign, IL: Human Kinetics, 204-205, 2017.

Sheppard, JM, and Triplett, TN. Program design for resistance training. In *Essentials of Strength Training and Conditioning*. 4th ed. Haff, GG, and Triplett, NT, eds., Champaign, IL: Human Kinetics, 440-470, 2016.

Silva, JR, Nassis, GP, and Rebelo, A. Strength training in soccer with a specific focus on highly trained players. *Sports Med Int Open* 1(1):1-17, 2015.

Turner, AN, and Stewart, PF. Strength and conditioning for soccer players. *Strength Cond J* 36(4):1-13, 2014.

INDEX

A

abductor strength 46-48
absolute speed 32
acceleration 7, 11, 20-22, 31-32, 117
ACL (anterior cruciate ligament) 14, 15, 97
action, movement and 19-20
activation exercises 139-144
adaptation 4-7, 67-68
adductor strength 46-48
adenosine triphosphate (ATP) 4, 27, 185
adolescent awkwardness 187
advanced exercises 70-71
aerobic fitness testing 58-64
aerobic systems 5, 26-27
agility 12, 13, 24, 28, 29, 30
agility tests 51-54
amortization period 9
anaerobic capacity 28
anaerobic system 27-28
anatomical core. *See* core exercises
angle of attack 25
ankle mechanics 21, 22
anterior cruciate ligament (ACL) 14, 15, 97
APRE (autoregulatory progressive resistance exercise) protocol 73, 98, 202
arm swing 22, 24
assistance exercises 185
asymmetries 50
athlete assessment. *See also* testing protocols
    data range appropriateness in 40
    guidelines for 39-40
    reasons for 39
    systematic bias in 43
    test finder 41
athletes
    continuous training of 232-233
    genetics 20, 22, 23, 25, 28
    injury history 69, 232
    needs analysis 202-203
    role on team 231-232
    training age 68-69
ATP (adenosine triphosphate) 4, 27, 185
autoregulatory progressive resistance exercise (APRE) protocol 73, 98, 202

B

backpedaling 33
back squat 102-103
ballistic training 13, 70, 71, 187
band-assisted Nordic leg curl 112
band glute-ham raise (GHR) prone isometric hold 113
barbell glute-ham raise (GHR) prone isometric hold 113
barbell split squat 105-106
baselines 39
base phase, of deceleration 23
base stance 23
basic agility 29
basic strength phase 185-186, 190
BDNF (brain-derived neurotrophic factors) 7
bear crawl 165-166
belt squat 102
bench press 121-123
bent-over row 129-130
bias 43, 47
bilateral asymmetry 50
biomechanical analysis 17-25
block periodization 78
body composition 13
bounding 70
brain-derived neurotrophic factors (BDNF) 7

C

central nervous system (CNS) 70, 72, 185
cerebellum 6
change of direction 24-25, 29
change-of-direction deficit 54
chin-ups 136
chop and lift from low split stance 173-175
closed skills 30
club-level athletes 235
CMJ (countermovement jump) 43, 49-50
CNS (central nervous system) 70, 72, 185
college level
    in-season programming 217, 223-224, 226
    off-season programming 188
    postseason programming 230, 234, 238
    preseason programming 208
    seasonal overview 231

combination sets 76
competitive season. *See* in-season programming
compound movements 10
concentric contractions 8, 23
concurrent model of periodization 78
contact phase 21
Copenhagen adductor exercise 114-115, 210
core exercises 185
    description 145
    exercise finder 146
    exercises 146-178
cortisol 6
countermovement jump (CMJ) 43, 49-50
coupling time 9
creatine phosphate 4
crossover 34
curtsy lunge 110

D

daily undulating periodization 78
dead bug (contralateral and ipsilateral) 176-177
deceleration 12-13, 22-24, 33
decline push-ups 121
defenders 26, 36. *See also* field players
deloading 76
DeLorme, Thomas 3
direction changes 24-25, 29
drive phase 22
drop step 35
dumbbell bench press 123-124
duration 5, 205
dynamic strength index 43
dynamometers 45, 47

E

eccentric actions 8, 23, 186
eccentric-only Nordic leg curl 111-112
endurance 25, 26-27, 58
energy 4
energy leaks 145
energy pathways 4-5, 26-28
environmental factors 30-31
exercise
    frequency 71-72, 205-207
    order 72
    selection 68-71, 119
explosive actions 18, 19, 27, 70
explosive strength 186

F

face pull 139-140
farmer's walk 161
farmer's walk–double rack hold 163
farmer's walk–single-bell rack hold 164
farmer's walk with contralateral rack hold 162

fatigue 26, 28, 221, 230, 232
field players
    in-season 225-228
    off-season microcycle 196-199
    position requirements 26, 36, 81
    preseason microcycle 214
fitness assessment. *See* athlete assessment
505 test 52
foot location 24, 25
foot position 24, 25
force 6, 7, 11
force plates 42, 44, 49
force–velocity curve 7, 8, 9, 80, 81
forward lunge 109-110
forwards 36. *See also* field players
foundation building 14, 20
frequency 71-72, 205-207
front foot-elevated split squat 106
front squat 100-101

G

gender differences 14-15
general adaptation syndrome 4
general physical preparation 183-184
genetics 20, 22, 23, 25, 28
glute-ham raise (GHR) prone isometric hold 112-113
goalkeepers
    in-season 223-225
    off-season microcycle 192-195
    position requirements 37, 80-81
    postseason programming for 236
    preseason microcycle 213
goals 75, 78, 181, 201, 205, 215
goblet squat 101
Golgi tendon organs 6
goniometers 42
grip variations 136, 138
ground reaction force 11, 12
growth hormone 6

H

half-kneeling chop and lift 170-172
hamstring strength 45-46
hanging reverse crunch 149
hang power clean 86-87
hang power snatch 88-89
high-intensity actions 18, 19, 26
high school
    in-season programming 216-217, 223, 225-226
    off-season 187-188
    postseason programming 233-234, 237-238
    preseason programming 207-208
hip-dominant focus 69
hip thrust 104-105

hops 70
hormonal stress 5-6
hypertrophy/strength endurance phase 184-185

I

inertia 7, 8, 118
injuries 7, 12, 13-14, 15, 69, 119, 209-210, 232
in-season programming
    college level 217
    goals and objectives 215-216
    high school 216-217
    intensity 219-220
    length of 216, 230-231
    professional level 217-218
    recommended exercises 218-219
    sample programs 222-228
    structure and organization 216
    volume 221
intensity 5, 18, 25, 73-74
    in-season programming 219-220
    off-season programming 190
    preseason programming 205-207
30-15 intermittent fitness test 62-64
interval training programs 63
inverted row 138-139
isometric belt-squat 44-45
isometric contractions 8, 9
isometric mid-thigh pull 42-43
isometric training 185-186
isotonic movements 187

J

joint angle measurement 42
joint mobility 14
jumps 9, 70

K

kettlebell swing 92-93
kickstand RDL 107
knee-dominant focus 69
knee injuries 7, 14-15, 97, 145

L

lateral lunge 110
lateral plank 155
lateral plank (kettlebell loaded) 156-157
lateral plank (partner or bench supported) 160
lateral plank with arm extended 157-158
lateral plank with one-arm row 158-159
lat pulldown 137-138
linear periodization 78
load. *See* intensity
loaded Nordic leg curl 112
lower body exercise technique 71
    description 97-98

exercise finder 98
exercises 98-115
lowering phase, of deceleration 23
low-intensity actions 18, 26

M

match play analysis 18-19, 35
maximal aerobic speed 63
maximal strength 185
maximum velocity 11-12
medicine ball exercises 70
medicine ball granny toss 95
mesocycles 77, 216
metabolic stress 4-5
microcycles 71, 77
midfielders 26, 36
mobility 13-14
modified 505 52-53
motor cortex 6
motor pattern development 6
movement
    action and 19-20
    compensations 14
    foundation of 14
    fundamental 20
    patterns of 14
    quality of 20, 28
    skills 28-29, 36-37, 79-80
    term 19
multidirectional speed 30-31
muscle
    contractions 8-9, 23
    glycogen storage in 4, 5
    hypertrophy 13, 76, 203
    pH 5
muscular strength. *See* strength

N

needs analysis 202-203
neurological stress 6-7, 70, 203
neuromuscular recruitment 6
Newton's laws 7, 8, 10, 97, 117
NHE (Nordic hamstring exercise) 45, 112, 210, 211
non-contact injuries 12, 13-14, 232
nonlinear periodization 78
Nordic hamstring exercise (NHE) 45, 112, 210, 211

O

off-season programming 181
    basic strength phase 185-186
    college level 188
    general physical preparation 183-184
    goals and objectives of 181-182
    high school 187-188
    hypertrophy/strength endurance phase 184-185

off-season programming *(continued)*
   intensity 190
   length of 182
   power phase 186-187
   professional level 188-189
   recommended exercises 189-190
   sample programs 191-199
   structure and organization 182-183
   volume 190
Olympic weightlifting movements 71, 85
one-arm dumbbell bench press 125-126
one-arm dumbbell row (hand and knee supported) 131
one-arm dumbbell row (three points supported) 132
one-arm landmine overhead press 126-127
one-arm single-leg RDL 106-107
one repetition maximum (1RM) 8, 9, 10, 73, 202, 203
open skills 30
open step 34
overload 67-68
overtraining 4, 6
oxidative stress 5

P

Pallof press kneeling anti-rotation press 177-178
partner bear crawl 166-167
patterns 14
peak height velocity 188
peak power 9
performance data 18, 35
periodization 76, 77-78
pH 5
phase potentiation 68
phosphagen system 27
physiological analysis 25-28
planning 77
plyometric exercises 13, 70, 71, 187
positions (end-point range of motions) 14
position-specific analysis 25-26, 28-35
position-specific programming 80-81
possession games 28
postseason format 233
postseason programming
   club-level athletes 235
   college level 234, 238
   factors influencing 229-233
   for goalkeepers 236
   high school level 233-234, 237-238
   professional level 235-236, 239
   sample programs 236-239
power 9-10, 16, 79
power exercises 70, 71
power phase 186-187
power tests 49-50
preparatory period 181, 183

preseason programming 201
   college level 208
   goals and objectives of 201-202
   high school 207-208
   length of 202-205
   methods and timing factors 203-204
   needs analysis 202-203
   professional level 209
   recent training exposure and 204-205
   recommended exercises 209-211
   sample programs 211-214
   structure and organization 202-205
   training variables 205-207
Prilepin's chart 220
professional level
   in-season programming 217-218, 224-225, 227
   off-season 188-189
   postseason programming 235-236, 239
   preseason programming 209
program design 67, 81
program variables 3, 68-77
progressive overload 67-68
prone plank on hands 150
prone plank (on slideboard)–body saw 152-153
prone plank (partner or bench supported) 154
prone plank with one-arm row 151-152
prone T 142-143
prone W 143-144
prone Y 140-141
pulling exercises 69, 119, 129-139
pull-up 135-136
pushing exercises 69, 119, 120-129
push phase 21
push-up 120-121

Q

quadruped birddog 146-148

R

range of motion 14
rate coding 203
rate of force development 186
rating of perceived exertion (RPE) 207.190
RDL (Romanian deadlift) variations 210-211
reactive agility 29, 31
rear foot-elevated split squat 106
recovery 4, 76, 77, 182. *See also* rest periods
recovery phase of acceleration 22
regressions 121
rehabilitation 3, 39, 47, 50, 65, 69
repeated sprint ability test 55-58
repetition maximum 73
repetition-volume 74
resistance bands 141, 142, 143

resistance training
    benefits of 3, 7
    improvement in physical capabilities with 7-15
    principles of 67-68
    program variables 3, 5, 68-77, 205
    sport-specific goals of 78-81
rest periods 76-77, 205-207
return to sport 39, 50, 65, 69, 234
reverse crunch (floor) 148-149
reverse lunge 109-110
Romanian deadlift (RDL) variations 210-211
rotational lunge 110
rotational movement skills 33-35
RPE (rating of perceived exertion) 190
Russian lean 45

S

safety bar squat 102
SAID principle 14, 67
sample programs
    in-season 222-228
    off-season 191-199
    postseason 236-239
    preseason 211-214
Selye, Hans 4
session rating of perceived exertion (sRPE) 207
sex differences 14-15
shoulder press 128-129
should joint function 119
shuffle and cut 33
single-leg glute-ham raise (GHR) prone isometric hold 113
single-leg leg curl 108
single-leg stance 24
6 × 30-meter (33 yards) repeated sprint ability test 55-58
sled drag 94
sled push 94
sliding leg curl 108-109
soccer environment 30
specificity 67
speed 10-13
    absolute 32
    multidirectional 30-31
    testing 51-58, 63
sphygmomanometers 47
split squat 105-106
split stance 23
sport-specific goals 78-81
sprint mechanical properties 55
sprint tests 51, 54-58
sRPE (session rating of perceived exertion) 207
SSC (stretch-shortening cycle) 9, 10, 203
staggered stance 23
stance phase, of acceleration 21

stances 23-24
standing cable row 134-135
steroid hormones 5
sticking point 99
strength 7-9, 16, 79
strength exercises 69, 70-71
strength testing 41-48
stretch-shortening cycle (SSC) 9, 10, 203
stride frequency 22, 24
stride length 12, 22, 24
supersets 72
suspension leg curl 108
swing phase 22
systematic bias 43

T

tactical concepts 17, 30
tall kneeling chop and lift 168-170
testing protocols 40
    aerobic fitness testing 58-64
    power tests 49-50
    speed and agility 51-58
    strength tests 41-48
testosterone 5, 6
30-15 intermittent fitness test 62-64
30-meter (33 yards) sprint 54-55
time motion analysis 18
timers 53
torso lean 22, 24
total body exercise technique 71
    description 85-86
    exercise finder 86
    exercises 86-95
training age 67, 68-69
training phases 69-70, 77
transition phase. *See* off-season programming
transitions, movement 13
trap bar deadlift 98-99
Turkish get-up 90-91
two-arm dumbbell row 133
two-arm single-leg RDL 107

U

underloading 76
undulating periodization 78
unloading 76
upper body exercises 69, 71
    activation exercises 139-144
    cost-benefit analysis of 117-118
    exercise finder 120
    exercise selection 119
    focus on force and function 118-119
    pulling exercises 69, 129-139
    pushing exercises 69, 120-129
    supersets 72
upper crossed syndrome 130

V

velocity
    force and 7-8, 9
    maximum 11-12
    power and 9-10
    speed 10-12, 22, 24
velocity-based training 73-74, 203, 220
$\dot{V}O_2$ kinetics 26
volume 74-75, 76
    in-season programming 221
    off-season programming 190
    preseason programming 205-207
volume-load method 74-75

W

work 9, 26

Y

yo-yo test 58-61

ABOUT THE NSCA

The National Strength and Conditioning Association (NSCA) is the world's leading organization in the field of sport conditioning. Drawing on the resources and expertise of the most recognized professionals in strength training and conditioning, sport science, performance research, education, and sports medicine, the NSCA is the world's trusted source of knowledge and training guidelines for coaches and athletes. The NSCA provides the crucial link between the lab and the field.

Daniel Guzman, MS, CSCS, is one of the most respected strength and conditioning coaches in American soccer. He started as the youngest head strength and conditioning coach in Major League Soccer with the Los Angeles Galaxy in 2014; they went on to win the MLS Cup. In 2017 Daniel joined the United States men's national soccer team on the journey to the 2018 FIFA World Cup 2018 in Russia. He served that team as they won the Concacaf Gold Cup in the summer of 2017. Lastly, he served the Los Angeles Football Club (LAFC) from 2018 to 2021 as the head performance coach. LAFC won the Supporters' Shield trophy in 2019 and set a record for most points in a single season. In 2022, Daniel decided to leave the team side of professional sports and start his own business, Guzman Performance, which strives to train and educate soccer athletes and coaches using the top strength and conditioning strategies for the sport. Daniel wants to leave a legacy as a servant leader in the field of strength and conditioning who lived to lift others up. He lives in Orange County, California, with his wife and three kids. He enjoys spending time at the beach and playing sports.

Megan Young, MS, MSEd, CSCS, FRC, USAW SPC, RSCC*D, is a lifelong learner of human performance optimization, health and well-being, strategic integration of sport science, human optimization technology, data systems, and cross-functional management to support winning organizations. She is in the process of obtaining her doctoral degree from Auburn University. With over 15 years of high-performance experience, she has applied these areas of expertise in various roles, including strength coach and high-performance director in collegiate athletics and women's and men's professional soccer. Coach Young ensures her coaching leverages data-influenced decision making, contextual compassion, and tactical empathy. She has been fortunate to train elite U.S. and international athletes, Olympians, and World Cup champions. She is often sought after as a thought leader, speaker, and expert in the evolution of the global coaching paradigm. Outside of her professional commitments, she elevates and educates others in awareness of leukemia, a cancer she survived in 2015. She also invests time in any activity in an ocean or lake, hiking, pickleball, and reading articles that challenge her current perspective. She resides in Seattle with her dear pup, Kilo, and her fiancé.

ABOUT THE CONTRIBUTORS

Ryan Alexander, PhD, currently serves as the director of sport science for Atlanta United FC. He came to Atlanta in October 2016 after leaving a position at U.S. Soccer, where he worked for the men's national team as a sport scientist. Prior to his time with the men's national team, he worked in the youth national team system for U.S. Soccer. Alexander received his PhD in sport and physiology performance from East Tennessee State University.

William E. Amonette, PhD, CSCS, is an associate professor and the executive director of the Health and Human Performance Institute at the University of Houston–Clear Lake, where he leads a team of scientists, engineers, and medical practitioners striving to empower individuals, through leading-edge research and technology development, to overcome barriers that limit human performance. Amonette previously served as a strength conditioning and rehabilitation specialist for astronauts at NASA's Johnson Space Center, was a strength and conditioning coach for the Houston Rockets and China's Olympic basketball team, and supported sport science testing and screening for collegiate and professional sport organizations, including the Houston Dash.

Bob Bradley is one of the most successful American soccer coaches of all time, with over 20 years of head coaching experience in six different countries. He was appointed as Toronto FC's head coach and sporting director in November 2021. Bradley has been named MLS Coach of the Year three times and ranks third in league history, with the most regular-season wins (185). He has led teams to an MLS Cup (Chicago Fire in 1998), an MLS Supporters' Shield (Los Angeles FC in 2019), and two U.S. Open Cup titles (Chicago Fire in 1998 and 2000). In addition to his work at the club level, Bradley coached the U.S. national team (2006-2011) and the Egyptian national team (2011-2013).

MLSE

Ivi Casagrande, MEd, XPT, Mobility WOD certified, is a high-performance consultant and currently serves as a technical expert consultant for FIFA and UEFA. Casagrande started her coaching career as a performance coach for the women's soccer program at Bowling Green State University (NCAA Division I) before joining Redline Athletics as their director of sport performance and serving as a network sport scientist with U.S. youth national teams. In 2019, Casagrande was the lead strength and conditioning coach

for Orlando Pride (NWSL), and her latest role was as a sport scientist for the Brighton and Hove Albion FC women's and girls' teams.

Garga Caserta, FRCms, XPS, has been a strength and conditioning coach since 2009. His work experience includes five years as the performance manager for the Portland Thorns FC (NWSL). He was a performance specialist for EXOS at Adidas' American headquarters and has been a consultant for club and collegiate soccer programs. Caserta founded TALO in 2017 to make comprehensive performance development and return-to-play support available for youth and professional athletes outside professional sport organiza-

tions. Caserta earned a bachelor's degree in exercise physiology and physical education.

Scott Caulfield, MA, CSCS,*D, RSCC*D, directs the development and management of individual and group strength and conditioning programs for over 600 student-athletes competing on 20 Division III varsity athletic teams at the oldest private military college in the United States, Norwich University in Northfield, Vermont. Caulfield is recognized as a Certified Strength and Conditioning Specialist with Distinction (CSCS,*D) and a Registered Strength and Conditioning Specialist with Distinction

(RSCC*D) by the National Strength and Conditioning Association (NSCA), and he has USA Weightlifting's Level 2 Coach certification. He earned his bachelor's degree in physical education from Castleton University in Vermont and a master of arts in sports coaching from the University of Denver.

Jo Clubb, BSc, MSc, is a performance consultant. Her company, Global Performance Insights, works with sport teams, organizations, and individuals around the world to optimize performance. She has previously worked as an applied sport scientist for the Buffalo Bills, Buffalo Sabres, Chelsea FC, and Brighton and Hove Albion FC. She has a bachelor's degree in sport and exercise science from Lough-borough University in the United Kingdom and a master's degree in high-performance sport from Australian Catholic

University. On the Global Performance Insights website, she publishes content that discusses the best ways to implement sport science in the applied setting.

Kevin Cronin, MS, CSCS,*D, RSCC, has 12 years of experience in the field of sport performance. Cronin currently serves as the sport science data analyst with 10th Special Forces Group at Fort Carson in Colorado Springs, Colorado. Cronin previously served as head sport performance coach at University of Massachusetts–Lowell for two seasons along with a 2019 summer stint as a part-time assistant strength and conditioning coach at Mike Boyle Strength and Conditioning. Cronin served as the head strength and conditioning coach at Colorado College for seven years. Prior to that, Cronin served as assistant strength coach, performance center coordinator, and education coordinator for the National Strength and Conditioning Association (NSCA) along with stints at Western Washington University, Stanford University, and the University of Texas.

Julia Eyre, MSc, CSCS, serves as lead psychologist at TSG Wieseck youth soccer academy in Germany, where she is currently the sport scientist and athletic coach for the U19 team. She lectures on sport sciences, psychology, and neuroscience at the university level and for national sport federations. While earning her master's degree in psychology from the Deutsche Sporthochschule Köln, she led and published multiple scientific projects on the intersection of stress, pain, and elite sport. In 2017 Eyre founded White Lion Performance, where she advocates for athlete physical and mental health over everything else.

Joey Harty, CSCS, is the director of sport performance and science for Sporting Kansas City (MLS). Harty is in his sixth season at Sporting Kansas City and has nine years of industry experience in strength and conditioning and sport science. He has worked across the entire American soccer landscape at the MLS, USL Championship, MLS Development Academy, and collegiate levels as a sports performance coach and sport scientist. He attended Grand Canyon University, where he majored in exercise science. Harty currently resides in Kansas with his wife and son.

Sporting Kansas City

Matthew Howley, MS, has over 14 years of industry experience in strength and conditioning and sport science. He holds a bachelor's degree in exercise and sport science and a master's degree in exercise science (strength and conditioning). Howley is a member of the Australian Strength and Conditioning Association and holds a Level 2 certification. Howley is an Accredited High Performance Manager and Level 2 Accredited Sports Scientist, certified by Exercise & Sports Science Australia. Howley has experience in various strength and conditioning and sport science roles in both NCAA soccer (University of Notre Dame) and professional soccer (Real Salt Lake).

Ian Jeffreys, PhD, CSCS,*D, NSCA-CPT,*D, RSCC*E, FNSCA, is a professor emeritus of strength and conditioning. He is the academic director at Setanta College in Ireland and the proprietor of All-Pro Performance, based in Brecon Mid Wales. A former professional rugby player, he is a recognized world leader in speed and agility development. He has coached at the international level and has authored several books, numerous book chapters, and articles in peer-reviewed journals, and he has given keynote presenta-  tions at conferences around the world. Jeffreys is the editor of *Professional Strength and Conditioning* and is an associate editor of *Strength and Conditioning Journal.* He is a fellow of the National Strength and Conditioning Association (NSCA) and United Kingdom Strength and Conditioning Association (UKSCA) and has been on the board of directors and been vice president or vice chair for both organizations. In 2021 he was awarded a Career Achievement Award by the Strength and Conditioning Society.

Bryan Mann, PhD, CSCS, RSCC*D, has been involved in the field of strength and conditioning since 1998. At the University of Miami, Mann is an associate clinical professor of kinesiology and sport science, the program director for exercise physiology, and the director of performance science for Olympic sports. In addition, he volunteers his time in the athletic department to provide advisement regarding many of the teams' training methods and programming. He was previously a strength and conditioning coach at the  University of Missouri, Missouri State University, University of Tulsa, and Arizona State University. Mann is recognized as a Registered Strength and Conditioning Specialist with Distinction (RSCC*D) by the National Strength and Conditioning Association (NSCA).

Scott Piri, CSCS, is the performance director for Galatasaray FC in Turkey. He coaches and manages the performance, sport science, and return-to-play staff. Piri was also the performance director for Galatasaray FC from 2011 to 2013. He was the strength coach and performance lead for Athletico Paranaense FC in Brazil from 2015 to 2017. Piri was also the performance director for the Turkish national soccer team for the 2016 Euros and 2008 Euros. In addition, he was the strength coach and performance lead  for the New York Red Bulls in 2010, the Mexican national soccer team in 2008 to 2009, Everton FC (England) in 2008, and LA Galaxy in 2007.

Ernie Rimer, PhD, CSCS, is the director of sport science for University of Louisville Athletics and UofL Health. His role uses scientific principles to support athlete health, safety, and performance through research, education, and innovation. Rimer was previously the director of sport science at the University of Utah. He was also a strength and conditioning coach for the U.S. Ski & Snowboard Association and Northern Arizona University (NAU). Rimer is the cofounder of FYTT, a high-performance software company. He received his doctorate from the University of Utah and both his master of education and bachelor of science degrees from NAU.

Melissa Terry, MSEd, MBA, CSCS, is a United Kingdom–based agent at Remington Ellis Management, specializing in consultation, contract negotiation, and player management for some of the top U.S. women's national team players. Prior to this, Terry spent over a decade in the sport science and performance industry working for multiple collegiate, professional, and international soccer organizations. Terry continues to work in a freelance and consulting capacity for U.S. Soccer and other organizations as a sport science consultant.

Real Salt Lake Media

Cat Wade, MS, CSCS, USAW, FMS L2, was a four-year starting goalkeeper at University of Oklahoma (OU), where she earned a bachelor of arts degree in psychology in May 2005. A team captain for the Oklahoma Sooners in 2003 and 2004, Wade is OU's career record holder in goals against average, saves, and shutouts. After graduating, she spent two years at Syracuse University as a graduate assistant coach for women's soccer before moving to the strength and conditioning staff. Wade spent a year at the University of Houston, where she worked with swimming, track and field, and women's basketball. From there she moved on to Columbia and then to the University of Portland. In 2016 Wade's collegiate coaching came to a close, and she entered the private sector, where she currently works with individuals and teams across the country. Wade has a master's degree in exercise science from Syracuse University. She holds the Functional Range Conditioning, StrongFirst Level 2, DNS Sport, and Certified Strength and Conditioning Specialist (CSCS) certifications.